The author's profits from book royalties will be donated to VIDEA's Orphan and Vulnerable Children Education Programme. For more information on VIDEA or to make a charitable donation, please visit *www.videa.ca* or email *info@videa.ca*.

HOSTILE SEAS

A MISSION IN PIRATE WATERS

JL SAVIDGE

DUNDURN
TORONTO

Editor: Allison Hirst
Design: Jesse Hooper
Printer: Webcom

Library and Archives Canada Cataloguing in Publication

Savidge, J. L. (Jennifer L.), author
    Hostile seas : a mission in pirate waters / JL Savidge.

Includes bibliographical references.
Issued in print and electronic formats.
ISBN 978-1-4597-1937-8 (pbk.).--ISBN 978-1-4597-1938-5 (pdf).--ISBN 978-1-4597-1939-2 (epub)

    1. Savidge, J. L. (Jennifer L.). 2. Canada. Royal Canadian Navy--Officers--Biography. 3. Canada. Royal Canadian Navy--Women--Biography. 4. Canada. Royal Canadian Navy--Sea life--Anecdotes. 5. Ville de Québec (Frigate)--Anecdotes. 6. Piracy--Somalia--Prevention. 7. Hijacking of ships--Somalia--Prevention. 8. Canada--History, Naval--21st century. I. Title.

V64.C32S29 2013   359.0092   C2013-903915-5
                                            C2013-903916-3

1 2 3 4 5   17 16 15 14 13

We acknowledge the support of the **Canada Council for the Arts** and the **Ontario Arts Council** for our publishing program. We also acknowledge the financial support of the **Government of Canada** through the **Canada Book Fund** and **Livres Canada Books**, and the **Government of Ontario** through the **Ontario Book Publishing Tax Credit** and the **Ontario Media Development Corporation**.

Care has been taken to trace the ownership of copyright material used in this book. The author and the publisher welcome any information enabling them to rectify any references or credits in subsequent editions.

J. Kirk Howard, President

Printed and bound in Canada.

VISIT US AT
Dundurn.com | *@dundurnpress* | *Facebook.com/dundurnpress* | *Pinterest.com/dundurnpress*

Dundurn	Gazelle Book Services Limited	Dundurn
3 Church Street, Suite 500	White Cross Mills	2250 Military Road
Toronto, Ontario, Canada	High Town, Lancaster, England	Tonawanda, NY
M5E 1M2	L41 4XS	U.S.A. 14150

To my father, Ian Savidge,
for imparting his sense of adventure, and for his generosity and endless patience

And to my mother, Lyn Savidge,
for her warmth and practical wisdom that is always tinged with humour

In memory of Alicia Foreman White, phenomenal woman, exceptional sailor.

You remain in our hearts.

CONTENTS

PREFACE

Personal stories are subjective and memories fallible. While I attempted to relay the facts of HMCS *Ville de Québec*'s deployment accurately, my observations of my fellow crew and other characters and events in the book, including the circumstances of Amanda Lindhout's kidnapping, are only as I perceived them, through my own filters and biases, and not unwavering truth — whatever that is.

This story is a personal and anecdotal exploration of shipboard life during a naval deployment, set against a backdrop of piracy. It is not intended as a comprehensive account or analysis of Somali piracy. The events that are depicted in this book are how I remember them, or, in cases where my memory was not to be trusted, experiences I was able to re-create through discussion with friends and colleagues with a better recollection than mine. Others who shared in these events will no doubt have experienced them differently. Dialogues and interactions within the book are re-created from memory and so adhere to the spirit of the event rather than the letter. Many of the names have been changed. Any inaccuracies and errors are my own.

The story line of the Abdi character is pure fiction. It draws on available literature on the origins of piracy and life in Somalia, but has no doubt missed nuances of Somali culture and left gaps in Abdi's motivations and environment. For this I must apologize.

The views contained herein are personal ones, and do not represent the views of the Canadian Forces or the Department of National Defence.

ACKNOWLEDGEMENTS

Numerous people were instrumental in the development of this book. I must thank the captain and crew of HMCS *Ville de Québec* for their obvious part in creating such memorable experiences and a supportive environment. In addition to their friendship, Jeff, Michèle, Billy, TiFou, Kevin, and other close friends and colleagues who will remain unnamed were instrumental in helping to re-create on-board events and providing context. My husband Scott assisted immeasurably in structuring and clarifying the manuscript's narrative from the early days. My friend Roy van den Berg, drawing on his experience as a Canadian soldier on the ground in Somali in 1993, provided invaluable input into the fictional story of Abdi. Thank you to Edil Absiye for reviewing the Abdi storyline through the lens of Somali culture.

A debt of gratitude goes to my writing mentor, Stan Dragland, who was instrumental in dragging the "show" rather than the "tell" out of me and provided extensive writing and editing support during the course of writing programs in Chile and Banff. I must also thank Beth Follett for her mentorship during the Los Parronales writing program, as well as the generous support of our hosts, Susan and Gordon Siddeley. My appreciation goes as well to the talented participants in Banff's Wired Writing Studio for their encouragement, as well as to the gifted poets and writers at Los Parronales. Karen Connelly and the Humber School of Writing deserve my gratitude for helping to elevate the first drafts of the manuscript. Thank you to my longtime friend Pam Osti for advice on the publishing industry, and to Dundurn for seeing the possibilities. My gratitude is owed to Lynn

Thornton, the most dedicated, tireless and visionary champion for social justice I know, for her mentorship and example.

My first readers provided the invaluable feedback that gave me the courage to publish this book. Thank you to my father, Ian Savidge, for his skilled editorial support and constructive feedback now and over the past thirty-five years; to my mother, Lyn Savidge, for her honest and light-hearted practicality; to Jeff Murray, for his unfailingly humorous commentary; to Roy van den Berg, for his generous editorial support; to Sarah McNeill, for her skilled eye and aesthetic sense; and to Scott, for his unflinching but gentle feedback and unique ability to clarify the opaque.

Finally, my gratitude goes to my caring family, most notably Scott, my mom and dad, Chris, and Julia, as well as my dear friends — you know who you are — for putting up with five years of pirate talk and writing angst, and the tedium and distractions that go along with that.

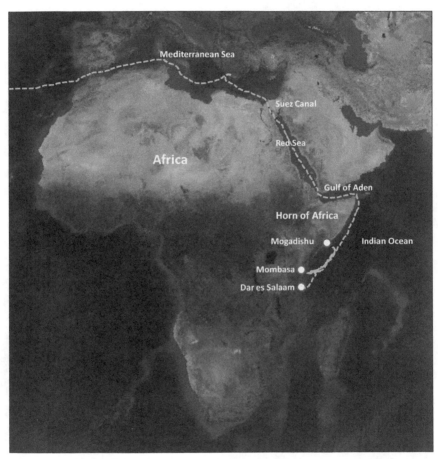

Map 1: HMCS Ville de Québec's *approximate route. Screenshot used by permission. Copyright © 2013 Esri. All rights reserved.*

CHAPTER 1

SUBMERGE

Mediterranean Sea, July 2008

It's my turn to jump.

As I peer over the edge, the rippled waters seem impossibly far below and suddenly unwelcoming. I hesitate. Then, determined not to lose face before witnesses, I bypass the primal instinct that screams at me to keep my feet firmly planted on the deck's non-slip surface. I push off and out, and then — plummet. For interminable seconds I fall through the air, more than two stories I drop, then, arms by my sides, slice through the surface and slide deep under water.

Submerged. A calm instantly envelopes me. Gone are the tense voices, the white noise, the drone of the ship's engine. It's only me down here, in my essence.

A few seconds later, when my head pops back up, I'm euphoric with the adrenaline coursing through me, at finding myself swimming in the middle of the Mediterranean. The sea, surprisingly warm, strokes my enlivened body as I drift happily beside the ship.

"This is amazing!" I call out to an unknown swimmer a short distance away, beaming at him. Rank and position, refreshingly irrelevant, have no place in these waters.

"I know! I can't believe it's so warm!" he calls back, before beginning a gentle breaststroke back to the ladders.

I pass another swimmer floating on his back with eyes shut, absorbing life beyond the constraints of shipboard living for a few precious seconds.

I want to linger too, but instead I swim to the ladders cascading down the ship's side, which a handful of sailors are now scaling.

I grab the bottom loops of a rope ladder three metres across. My nearest neighbour is climbing above me, a metre or so to my side. The deck looms high above. At first I make fast progress up the ladder, still invigorated by the spell of freedom, then slow as the rope digs painfully into my bare feet and my arms begin to ache with each upward haul. Exhausted, I grip the edge of the deck and pull myself up and over.

In front of me, in full uniform, stands Jeff, a bemused smile on his long face.

"I thought you might have forgotten about the navigation brief," he says. "It's in five minutes."

~

Mediterranean Sea, November 2008

Her coffee eyes show no expression, but it's clear that Kate is tense on her day of judgment. She stands with her back pressed against the bulkhead. Her usual flight suit has been replaced with a smartly pressed air force tunic and wool pants. A neat bun beneath her wedge cap takes the place of her regular braid.

We wait in the flats to be called into the captain's cabin. Kate stares ahead, saying nothing.

"Are you doing okay?" I ask. The formality of these trials, with the commanding officer sitting in judgment, is enough to instill fear in the most stoic of sailors.

"Yeah, I'm fine," Kate says in a neutral tone. But she keeps her eyes averted. "I'd just like to get this over with."

On cue, the door swings opens and the coxswain, Chief Richards, pokes his head out.

"March yourself in."

Inside, we halt in front of a wooden podium. Behind it stands the captain as Presiding Officer. He's grim-faced behind his glasses as Kate salutes him smartly. We remain at attention, arms thrust down at our sides.

"I bring this trial to order," says the captain, and bangs his wooden gavel on the podium. Then he adds, firmly, "I solemnly affirm that I will duly administer justice according to law, without partiality, favour, or affection."

"Stand at ease," says Chief Richards.

We step out our left legs to broaden our stance and simultaneously link our left hands with our right behind our backs.

"Remove headdress."

Kate reaches up and removes her wedge cap.

"Attention!" orders Chief Richards. Our heels click together, arms thrust to our sides.

"Coxswain, read the charges," orders the captain.

"Captain Kate Mason," reads Chief Richards from a paper in his hand, "is charged with transgressing Queen's Regulations and Order's 19.36, Disclosure of Information or Opinion, that is, publishing, without permission, in any form whatever any military information or the member's views on any military subject to unauthorized persons."

The next question is addressed to Kate and me. "Have you had enough time to fully review your case?"

"Yes, sir, we have," I reply for us both.

Baladweyne, Somalia, January 1993

Abdi lies on the straw mat, eyes wide with fear. Around him he can hear his baby sister's strangled mews of hunger, his younger siblings' restless movements as they press tightly together in the one-room hut. His mother's breathing is punctuated by agitated cries from recurrent nightmares, but fatigue from her daytime labours has left her mercifully unresponsive to the chaos outside.

Machine gun fire rings out in the night, not far away and seeming to move closer; Abdi fears — knows — it must be a hostile clan attacking his.

Abdi's thin body trembles with fear. He is twelve, but he is the man of the house. What is he to do? He should be used to this by now. His father has been dead eight months, shot in the chest by a rival clan, though he never really knew what the rivalry was about.

~

Abdi must have fallen asleep despite his responsibilities, because in the morning's early hours his mother is shaking him awake.

"Go, Abdi, go quickly!" she says, her gaunt face tense with urgency. "The soldiers are coming with food. You must be the first there!"

He doesn't question what she says; his mother has a way of knowing where to find food in Baladweyne, an instinct honed by raising children through years of famine.

His sandals pound red sand, raising clouds of dust, as he flies the short distance to the village centre. There he stops to catch his breath, his rail-thin body struggling to recover with the miniscule energy reserves it has stored.

At the centre of the village sits a white armoured vehicle. Five white soldiers stand around it. They wear faded green uniforms and are already bathed in sweat and dirt, rifles slung loosely over their broad backs. From the five-tonne truck behind them they haul sack after sack of food — unbelievable wealth — placing them on the ground beside the vehicles.

Abdi knows they are from Canada because he has seen them before and he can read the word CANADA stencilled on the sack, the one skill he picked up when he was a young boy and still went to school, before the civil war.

CHAPTER 2

MISSION CHANGE

The 190m-long bulk carrier *Stella Maris* was carting more than 40,000 tonnes of zinc concentrate and lead bullion .... Pirates took the ship hostage near the Suez Canal, off the coast of Somalia in the Gulf of Aden on Sunday and although the 21 Filipino sailors on board are safe for now, a large ransom has been demanded for their release.[1]

— *The Townsville Bulletin,* July 25, 2008

The whistle breaks into our slumber at 7:00 a.m. sharp. It starts on a low note, disruptive but bearable, before climbing gradually to a high, jarring shriek that shatters the otherwise-tranquil morning. There it hangs, before a series of stutters leads into two nosedives of penetrating noise. Then quickly down, up, down, then up and down once more before it finally ceases. Wakey wakey, piped every morning by the bridge watch — an abrupt start to the day. "I hate that whistle," I mutter to myself, head tucked firmly beneath my rack's slim pillow.

"Good morning, *Ville de Québec!*" chirps the meteorological technician-in-training in a heavy francophone accent, her voice turned metallic by the ship's piping system. "Here is today's weather report. The next twenty-four hours in the western Mediterranean will see a high of twenty-two degrees Celsius with light winds from the west at nine to twelve knots. There will be a slight chop with seas from the west at less than half a metre."

At least there will be no high seas to battle today. I pull the pillow tighter around my ears as the MetTech repeats the weather in French, but fail to block out her inevitably mangled delivery of the daily joke.

"Two dog owners are arguing about which dog is smarter," she says in a stilted voice, occasionally stumbling over the words. "The first dog owner says, 'my dog is so smart, every morning he waits for the paper boy to come around and then he takes the newspaper and brings it to me.' 'I know,' the second dog owner says. 'How?' asks the first dog owner. 'My dog told me.'" [2]

Coordinated groans emanate from the bodies stowed above and across from my bottom rack, first stirrings in the still-darkened room. If solidarity is the object of these early morning jokes submitted by the crew, then that much has been achieved for those of us in the cabin's six triple-stacked racks.

Next is the operation room officer's bilingual recitation of the "flex," or Fleet Exercise Schedule — the constantly changing program for the day ahead. To this I feel obliged to listen carefully, lest I miss briefings in which I have to speak.

By the time I roll out of my rack it's seven-fifteen, and I no longer have to compete with my five mess mates for access to the two sinks in the heads. I wander down the flats in my bathrobe, eyes bleary, hair wild. At the male heads immediately adjacent to the ones I'm aiming for, a petty officer I know vaguely nods as we pass. He wears only a towel around his waist, a hairy beer gut protruding above it. I'm struck, as always, by the contrast between the tightly controlled front we present to each other at work and the flash of intimacy we share in these flats.

After washing up, I dress in the semi-darkness of my mess. Aside from the two women recently returned to their racks after a long night on watch, my mess mates have already left for breakfast. From the hooks on my locker I pull on black pants made of thick fire-retardant material and an equally durable blue collared shirt. I leave off the uniform belt, blousing out my shirt to hide the place where navy regulations dictate it must be — a small rebellion that reminds me I'm not just an automaton in the military system. I throw my curly hair up in a messy ponytail and head to the wardroom for breakfast.

The whir of the treadmill in the lobby outside the mess draws my attention. There, the captain is running up a sweat in shorts and T-shirt.

In his early forties, the commanding officer is a tall man with brown hair that spills over his forehead. I've learned during my daily briefs to him that he's a highly astute and capable mariner who combines a rare degree of perception and intellect. As CO, he's a man apart. His personal routine is usually kept private by virtue of his separate living quarters, where he also takes his meals — served by his dedicated steward. My observation of him now, bare of the three commander's bars that ordinarily adorn his shoulders, smacks of transgression.

"Good morning, Captain," I call out deferentially as I pass, but he's too absorbed in his run to notice.

Most officers have cleared out of the wardroom by the time I arrive. A few are sunk into the plush pseudo-leather couches that monopolize the centre of the room, sipping on cups of coffee underneath the neglected flat screen television mounted on the wood-panelled wall. A varnished bar takes up the corner of the room closest to the door, with spirits, wine and beer glasses hanging securely above it and a cappuccino machine tucked beside the wall at its far end. Everything movable is always secured for sea in anticipation of rough weather that may hit at short notice.

At the opposite end of the room, adjacent to a serving window connecting to the officers' pantry, is a long dining table that comfortably seats thirteen. Only a few chairs are currently occupied. I grab a cloth napkin from the wooden holder on the wall before choosing a seat at the far end.

"Hey, Kevin. Hey, Kate."

Blond head tilted toward his plate of scrambled eggs, Kevin sits across the table. He's an American exchange pilot with the twenty-five-person Helicopter Air Detachment that came on board for the mission. Across an empty seat sits Kate, a raven-haired pilot in her late twenties. She is the aircraft captain; Kevin is her co-pilot.

Kevin pauses in his task, glancing up at me with blue eyes intensified by his tanned skin.

"Hey, what's up, Jen?" he asks in his Chicago twang.

"Not much. How about you?"

"Just following the US election campaign. It'll be bad news if Obama gets into office," he says, shaking his head.

I stare at Kevin in wonderment. "How can you be twenty-nine years old and a die-hard Republican?"

I wonder that all the time!" Kate laughs, meeting my eyes. I grin at her. Though I don't know her well, I sense a kindred spirit.

"I believe in Republican fiscal policy, not necessarily their social one," Kevin replies, then smiles cheekily. "Besides, I thought you weren't supposed to talk politics in the Canadian military. On another note, I *am* looking forward to the port visit in Italy next week — I'm ready to skip right over this patrolling business."

"Kevin, we've only been at sea two weeks!" I shake my head. Then I relent. "But I could use a nice long port visit too."

~

For the crew of Her Majesty's Canadian Ship (HMCS) *Ville de Québec*, a naval frigate based in Halifax, the road to high readiness has been a long haul — eighteen months to prepare the ship for the North Atlantic Treaty Organization (NATO) mission that we're currently operating on in the Mediterranean. I came on board only a month ago so can claim credit for none of the preparation.

As a thirty-three-year-old naval reservist on hiatus from my civilian work, I was at short notice parachuted in to the job of ship's intelligence officer. For years I'd alternated between civilian and military employment, permitted to do so by the grace of an understanding civilian boss and a military system that, in a rare show of flexibility, allows reservists to determine when and for how long they will be available for full-time work. It's this flexibility that keeps me in the military, since love of change — or perhaps fear of constancy — inhibits my willingness to commit for the long term.

I was offered the deployed Intelligence position in April but delayed accepting the contract. In March I had just returned from seven months spent working for a non-governmental organization in Zambia, a southern African country blessed with relative peace but cursed with the burdens of poverty, an astronomical AIDS rate, and low levels of education. The Canadian-based organization with whom I had worked for five years collaborated with Zambian organizations in an effort to help rural communities pull themselves out of poverty. As a project manager, I coordinated internship placements and acted as on-the-ground liaison with our partner organizations. The work was rewarding, but after five years the constant struggle for resources eventually eroded my energy and motivation. I returned from Zambia done with under-resourced work that was and is important but which burned me out from the inside.

It's said that a change is as good as a rest. The prospect of visits to European ports was appealing, even though my travels there during my twenties had always struck me as too easy. I had grown up with a family mythology, only one and two generations removed, of brave missionaries and colonial adventurers who challenged themselves in exotic lands. Alone among my two siblings, I had trapped myself within it, coming to equate life success and achievement with the conquering of similar challenges. Europe's pleasures seemed entirely too attainable. I had a mental block about them.

My idealized Africa had fit smoothly into my vision of exotic challenge, so it was no small admission that I'd had enough of the oppressive heat and poverty and unpredictability of the Africa that I had experienced. I had few qualms about embarking on a mission on which I imagined myself sipping cappuccinos on terraces, stroked by the balmy Mediterranean breeze, exploring labyrinths of cobblestone streets lined with museums and bakeries. My younger self would have balked at the ease of surrendering to the allure of European civilization, but my current self celebrated the shedding of naive idealism — much delayed — that had led me to romanticize Africa, or any place in which it is hard to be comfortable.

The European mission wouldn't all be roses. This I knew. Two years spent on board ships had educated me about the trials of life at sea. But those stints had involved limited time at sea and were, for the most part, closer to home. My youthful determination to embrace new experiences had transformed me into an enthusiastic sailor, even if I disliked much of the day-to-day routine. Though the experience was no longer novel, I did the hard sell anyway, convincing myself that the port visits would make the at-sea portions endurable, if not worthwhile. Besides, I'm an officer now, and I think I enjoy my job.

The frigate had left Halifax mid-July to join five other NATO vessels participating in Operation Active Endeavour, part of NATO's response to 9/11. Our warship was detailed to patrol a NATO-assigned sector of the western Mediterranean, monitoring shipping in an effort to detect and deter terrorist-related activities.

The first week at sea, as we crossed the Atlantic, left the crew exhausted. To prepare for the mission, we were drilled at all hours by Sea Training, a team of naval trainers intent on discovering and exploiting our weaknesses as a seagoing unit, whose blessing we required to undertake our operation. A simulated helicopter would crash on deck and tragedy would be averted only by the quick reactions of firefighters and their skilled removal of "casualties." Sea Trainers crept around the ship, throwing smoke bombs in corners and dummies overboard at ungodly hours. These disruptions required rapid interventions of the crew to save ship, life, and limb. Tired sailors wore their uniforms to bed, even their heavy boots, anticipating the *bong bong* of alarms followed by hell breaking loose. Sightings of the Sea Trainers' trademark red ball caps in the flats, the signal that we would soon need to force our exhausted bodies into action once again, evoked tired groans from the crew. Like all crews, ours cursed those Red Hats, considering them a breed apart — transformed from hard-working sailors to merciless examiners the instant they joined that elite club. The exercises are all for the good, of course, ensuring as they do the preparation of the crew for challenges that might lie ahead — fires or floods or small boat attacks while at sea.

As that endless week drew to a close, we exited the temperamental Atlantic, sailing through the Strait of Gibraltar, the narrow gap that separates Europe from Africa and links two seas, and into the calm of the Mediterranean. This, together with the isolated Black Sea, far to the east, was to be our domain for the next five months.

The work of patrol is draining. Workdays on board a deployed ship can seem interminable, permitting only limited amounts of sleep. So we anticipate the itinerary of regular port visits throughout the Mediterranean and Black Seas to break the monotony and offer a welcome reprieve from the hard work that is an integral part of any mission.

I'm working in the communications control room when the captain's voice breaks through the buzz of equipment that is the ship's constant soundtrack. Announcements made over the ship's piping system are not intended to be impersonal. They are a practical means for the captain to reach 250 crew members at once. If he fails to do so, partial information circulates and inevitably feeds rumour — dangerous on board a ship. In cramped living conditions, good crew morale is a prize to be fought for, and even a hint of negativity is contagious.

"D'ya hear there. This is the captain speaking. I have some important information to relay." The seriousness of his tone makes all activity cease. The five of us in the communications control room space go stock still and strain to hear his words.

"As some of you may know, there is a significant problem of piracy off the coast of Somalia. At the same time, the United Nations World Food Programme is shipping food aid to the country to address a shortage of food due to drought and civil war. The piracy problem threatens the safe delivery of these food shipments to millions of Somalis in need. The World Food Programme has appealed for naval escort for these vessels carrying food aid."

Here he pauses, aware of the effect that his next words will have. "The government of Canada is strongly considering re-tasking *Ville de Québec* to escort cargo ships carrying World Food Programme food aid to Somalia. If approved, we would detach from NATO for the duration of the escort mission to operate in the Indian Ocean."

I maintain my composure, displaying a calm, intent expression, but I feel my heart sink. The other faces around the room, illuminated by the glare of fluorescent lights, also appear unemotional as they focus on the disembodied voice.

"If this tasking is approved, I'm confident that you will all rise to this new challenge and put forth your best efforts for this very important mission." There is now a hint of appeal in the captain's voice. "The government will make the final decision by next week. In the meantime, you are not authorized to tell your friends or families anything about the potential re-tasking until the decision is finalized. I'm telling you this now on trust. Once the decision is made, you will have time to tell your families before it's announced to the media."

The captain's voice reflects a careful balance of assurance and empathy, but he clearly expects no complaints. *Max flex* is one of the navy's unofficial mottos, for good reason. When he's finished speaking, the bare bones of the message remaining with us are these: our ship is very likely going to Somalia, and the mission is a worthy one. The unspoken fallout is that any plans the crew has made to ease the burden of a five-month deployment away from loved ones — visits to European ports or leave to visit partners and children — are in jeopardy.

CHAPTER 3

NEW HORIZONS

We have been appealing ... for anyone to step forward to protect
ships carrying WFP food into Somalia, especially now because in
the coming months we need to double the tonnages that we bring
into Somalia because the needs have gone up. Basically, we aim to
feed 2.4 million people by December.

Last year, pirates attacked three ships chartered by the UN
agency to carry food into Somalia, Mr. Smerdon said. While none of
the World Food Programme vessels have been taken over this year,
he said, shipping companies are reluctant to send large vessels into
the area without protection.[1]

— Courtesy of The Halifax Herald Limited, August 6, 2008

I've read a little about the piracy taking place in waters off Somalia, but most
of my scant knowledge is derived from superficial media reports. The news
of piracy — proof of its existence in the modern world, in the waters off
Indonesia, Nigeria, Somalia — has fascinated me. The reality of modern-day
piracy contradicts the entrenched association with swashbucklers of old,
such notorious historical figures as Captain Kidd and Blackbeard, or their
fictional counterparts, Captain Hook, Long John Silver, even Jack Sparrow,
Hollywood's most recent incarnation of the pirate.

Beyond an initial fascination with piracy, most consumers of news
pay only fleeting attention to the reports, easily dismissing them on
account of distance and dislocation: acts of piracy happening on the

other side of the world don't affect us, we tell ourselves, so active engagement in the matter isn't required. But piracy has suddenly become central to the lives of our crew, and will be for the next several months. Until now, the extent of my knowledge has been that Somali pirates sometimes hijack merchant ships in the waters near Somalia. Now a second factor has vaulted into the spotlight: piracy is threatening the delivery of ship-borne food aid to Somalia in a time of famine. The short timeline for deepening my knowledge of piracy will be no excuse for ignorance, if I know military commanders.

As I tackle the first of numerous reports on Somali piracy, the myths gradually fall away. Instead of pirate ships, there are speedboats with outboard motors. Instead of bearded swashbucklers, there are young Somali men, mostly uneducated teenagers with seagoing experience. Instead of treasure for booty, there are innocent crewmen and vessels ripe for ransom. Instead of swords and cannon, there are rocket-propelled grenades and AK-47s. Instead of romantic adventure, there is struggle for survival and fear of dying — on all sides. Despite all these differences, though, the driving force of piracy across the ages remains the same: poverty, opportunity, and greed. It's more complicated than that off Somalia's coast, given the lawlessness and violence ashore, but what's happening there is no exception. Unlike pirate lore, though, there is nothing fun or romantic about this enterprise.

Less than a week later, we're patrolling with the NATO task force in the central Mediterranean when the captain makes it official: the Canadian government has approved the re-tasking of *Ville de Québec* to the World Food Programme escort mission off Somalia's coast. Our NATO group is tagged as a quick-reaction force designated to respond at short notice to natural and man-made emergencies in the region, so we have known that mission change is a possibility.

"I guess I won't be seeing my wife any time soon!" declares Master Seaman Davis, supervisor for the previous watch, retrieving something from his desk in the communications control room when the pipe is made. He rounds off his outburst with a forced chuckle, his voice boisterous in its attempt to dispel the sombre quiet that has fallen over the room. Two of the communicators turn back to their work, taking cover behind computer screens while they absorb the news.

"It sucks that we're going to miss out on so many great ports now," a young naval communicator declares to anyone who will listen.

His sentiments are understandable, but the watch supervisor, Petty Officer, 2nd Class Marcotte, knows enough to nip this one in the bud.

"Yeah, but we have to think of the bigger picture. This mission is important. We'll still get some good port visits."

She imparts this gently, aware the junior sailor's outburst is his way of dealing with his disappointment. PO Marcotte is a consummate professional; any personal reaction she has about the change is held firmly in check.

The professionalism of the entire crew in response to this news is, in fact, impressive. For the past week, we have all speculated on what a change of mission would mean to each of us. Reactions have been mixed. There were emotional outbursts from those who would likely be forced to put off plans to see families or partners. Beyond the disappointment is fear that partners won't wait or that toddlers won't remember parents when they finally come home. I've been in the naval reserve for sixteen years, long enough to know the stress that deployments — unpredictable by their very nature — can create for families and relationships. Others reacted differently: seasoned sailors loudly declare that it doesn't matter to them or to their equally seasoned spouses which ocean they sail. Away is away, part of the deal they signed up for and for which they are reasonably well-paid. Naval experience teaches us to roll with change. We will all be experts at change by the time this mission is done.

Jeff, the combat officer, is perched at the computer across from me in the communications control room when the announcement is made. A tall, slender man in his mid-thirties, the fine features of his long, thin face lend him a dignified, reassuring air. Although I report to the captain on Intelligence issues, Jeff is my direct supervisor. By the nature of his position as chief planner for operations he has a role in nearly every ship evolution, every meeting, every decision made on board. The Intelligence function is meant to support operations, so it's imperative that he and I work well together and integrate our efforts. As he raises his eyes to meet mine, I realize that he has known about this re-tasking before the rest of us.

"I guess I have a little planning to do, Int," he says, his face deadpan. His tone is serious, but the deliberate understatement and the spark in his brown eyes reveal the humour underlying much of what he says, complemented by undeniable competence and stoicism.

"Had you been planning to take leave to see your family while we were in Europe?" I ask. Photos of Jeff's six-month-old twin baby boys adorn the otherwise spartan walls of his cabin below.

"I was probably not going to see them anyways." His voice is flat now. His eyes are glued to the monitor. "My wife and I decided that it would be harder for all of us if I went home for a few weeks and then had to leave again. It's just easier to stay away for the five months."

My baby niece Sofia is almost the same age as Jeff's sons. Imagining my sister or her husband having to leave her for an extended period of time, when she's so little, is nearly impossible. It's done all the time in the military, one parent or the other absent for six-month periods, but suddenly this requirement strikes me as an unworkable condition of employment. Jeff would never complain, though. His own father was a naval officer; the lifestyle is no surprise.

"What about you, Int? Did you have plans?"

"Vague ones," I say. "Scott and I were going to try to coordinate something in Europe, but with him being deployed as well, timing might have been difficult." Scott, my long-term partner, is a naval officer currently working in Israel.

The next morning, the Department of National Defence will announce the change in mission to the media. But word spreads quickly in the military community. Most of the crew are anxious to ensure that their families hear about the change first-hand. Already this week hints of an impending escort mission have circulated in the Halifax-based media, and astute readers will have put two and two together. Anxious communications will clog shipboard phone and Internet lines this evening.

I'm in no hurry to notify friends and family about the new mission. No young children depend on me. Scott has been deployed to the Middle East for over a year. While this will likely force the cancellation of our tentative plans to spend time together in Europe, not seeing each other has, regrettably, become our status quo. But I miss him just the same. My parents and two siblings live busy, independent lives, so informing them is more for interest's sake than for any real impact the change will have on them. I'll send them a quick email. The alteration to our plans won't shock them; my adult life has been characterized by changing scenery. But the irony of my heading back to Africa won't be lost on them, just as it's not lost on me.

Still, the moment Jeff exits the communications control room, a sudden and surprising anxiety grips me. Lurking underneath it is excitement, the superficial rush I've come to associate with the promise of change. My heart pounds in my chest and my face flushes as I stare blankly at my computer screen. A thousand thoughts scramble through my mind, but I can make no real sense of any of them. I'm bursting to express, to rant, to talk through the jumble in my head.

But I say nothing to the five on-watch naval communicators who share this space with me. I'm silenced here by the code of conduct that discourages any discourse that might have a negative impact on the work or attitude of those junior to me. This is challenging at times, and I sometimes fail, but trying to lead by example is imperative. Right now, because there's no telling what might escape from it, I keep my mouth shut.

It's near midnight when I wrap up the day's work. I'm a day worker, my watch lasting from early morning until the work is done or until I'm too tired to be productive. The mission change means a steep learning curve. My days will be long as I learn about an entirely different area of operations than the Mediterranean for which I'd prepared.

I leave the communicators, standing in a one-in-two rotation, to the last hour of their watch. Like most of the crew, they're on for seven hours, off for five, on for five, off for another seven. Then the cycle begins again. Amidst the noise associated with shared accommodation and opposite watches, no one gets enough sleep at sea.

As I head toward the exit, a few of the communicators are munching on licorice that Master Seaman Davis received in a care package from home.

"Would you like some licorice, ma'am?" he asks, extending a bag toward me.

"No thanks, I'm just heading to bed."

"Have a good night!" he calls out cheerfully as I slip out the door.

In the foyer outside, I let my eyes adjust to the red-tinged darkness. Each evening as the sun sets, the crew darkens the ship by extinguishing white lights and switching red ones on in the flats and operational spaces, to allow those working on the bridge to maintain night vision as they navigate the dark waters. After a few seconds, I make my way through the commanding officer's flats. This large lobby, located near the front of the ship and replete with firefighting gear, is an intersection of sorts. One steep ladder leads up to the bridge while two other ladders connect it with the main deck below. One is for ascent, the other for descent. The separation of up and down ladders is crucial. When the crew rushes about during emergency stations, we can't afford the hazard of an inadvertent kick in the head or a slow-down in response time because of a traffic jam. The commanding officer's cabin is located on the starboard side, a few steps from where I exit the communications control room. A door on the port side leads to the upper decks and fresh sea air, at least once one is clear of the sheltered and well-frequented smoking area where rumours tend to find their most fertile ground.

I descend the ladder the quick way, facing away from it while holding on to the railings behind me. Wearing clunky boots, I always half expect to tumble down, imagining myself lying at the bottom of the ladder. In this daydream I'm conflicted about returning home from the mission early as a result of my injuries. Today, as usual, my boots make secure contact with the deck below.

After snaking through another series of darkened flats, I'm back in the wardroom, snug in the private domain of officers. As I sit back on one of the plush couches under low lights, I reflect on what a welcome refuge this is for the thirty-five officers, a place of freedom from the eyes and ears of subordinates. Even so, my guard remains up. I haven't yet reconciled myself to life back on board a navy ship, much less to the prospect of heading back to Africa.

Eric, the navigating officer, and Tom, a bridgewatch keeper, are seated on the couches, immersed in a video hockey game with impressively realistic graphics. Helmz, an engineering officer, sits at the table eating peanut butter and crackers and staring off into space. Dan, the anti-submarine warfare officer, takes a bag of chips from behind the bar, then dutifully records it on his personal tab.

While only officers are allowed here, the room is still no forum for free self-expression. I am new on board, an unknown quantity. Experience has taught me that complainers in the military are not well-liked. I don't need to be liked as an end in itself, but having others willing to cooperate in an environment based on teamwork will make my life easier over the next five months. I already have three factors with the potential to work against me: I'm a reservist among regular force sailors, a female in a vastly male majority, and the sole intelligence officer among sailors with much better established seagoing trades. A misstep and I could easily lose credibility.

Prior to coming on board, I had also expected to be one of the few anglophones. The ship is designated as the only French-speaking vessel in the fleet, and an effort is made to populate it with francophone sailors. I speak decent French, but it was with some relief and a little disappointment that I discovered at least half of the crew to be native anglophones, though most would count themselves as bilingual. The international language of operations is English, so English has become the default language on board. But all other communication tends to alternate between English and French, often in mid-conversation. I'm by no means alone as an anglophone, but I still need to bridge this cultural divide.

Leaning back on the settee with a cup of herbal tea in hand, I feel increasingly edgy and blame it on the noisy distraction of the video game. I don't know where else to go to absorb the news, so head for my rack. As I make my way through the dark flats connecting the wardroom to my sleeping mess, I'm guided by the dark shapes of emergency equipment attached fast to the bulkhead, and the occasional light peeping out of a cabin.

"*Bonsoir,*" I say softly to the few sailors I pass, although most are strangers to me. I quietly open the door to my mess deck so as not to disturb the other sleepers. It's not until I have crawled into my narrow rack and slowly drawn the curtain across it that I can relax.

I'm neatly tucked into bed, the cheap grey wool of the military issue blanket scratchy against my cheek. I consider myself lucky to have a bottom rack because it's easy to crawl into, and I won't fall far if I roll out in rough seas. I'm also fortunate to be fairly short, five foot four, and so have more than a foot of thin mattress-length, and some width, to spare. A big man of generous girth would have more reason to complain. I use the extra space at my feet wisely, storing extra blankets for when I feel particularly cold and clean sheets in case I miss the weekly linen exchange. At my head is a metal alcove housing two shelves, allowing easy access to an alarm clock, headlamp, a rarely opened novel, miniature Kit Kat bars, socks for my perpetually cold feet, and a gas mask. Along with toiletries and uniforms hanging from the hooks on the front of the locker, these are the only items to which I have ready access. My locker is poorly situated — immediately beside the racks — and I am doing my best to avoid a scolding for opening it while someone is sleeping. Given the twenty-four-hour watch system, this is almost always. Eventually, I will find a quick opportunity at lunchtime, during the turnover of watches when no one is in their racks. Sneaking back to remove items I need for the day ahead will become part of my daily routine.

Sleep eludes me. I toss and turn in the narrow bed, unable to sit up due to the closeness of the rack above me. I'm often restless — physically, mentally, emotionally — but tonight's anxiety is epic. My head is filled with worries: How will I perform in a new area of threat that I know nothing about? How will I ensure the health of my long-distance relationship with Scott? How well will I survive the ship's confines for another five months? And even though I know that the eastern portion is vastly different from the southern, what about heading back to Africa? These concerns drive a growing self-doubt.

I'm finally drifting off when the gentle nudge of a foot breaks the sanctity of my curtained refuge and startles me awake: someone stepping up to reach the middle bunk. Sometime in the night I expect another intrusive nudge by someone heading for the top rack. I hope by then to be too fast asleep to notice.

Baladweyne, August 1988

Abdi sits at his bench, dark eyes affixed to the blackboard at the front of the classroom. He's pressed up against the other students but he doesn't mind. His cousin Mohammed and his friend Abdullah sit beside him.

At the front of the room, his teacher, Mr. Sadiq, is speaking of their Victorious Leader, Guulwaadde, General Siad Barre. He's the reason Abdi and his classmates are now learning written Somali, Mr. Sadiq tells them, which didn't exist before General Barre united the clans, and the country.

Abdi knows that there are still clans, that Mohammed and Abdullah and he come from the same one, the Hawiye, although while he and Mohammed come from the same sub-clan, the Habagedir, Abdullah comes from the Hawadle sub-clan. But they are not supposed to talk about it.

Abdi has gotten quite good at writing since he first started learning. He might even like to be a writer someday. A teacher has too many children to look after, and, as a storekeeper, his father seems busy all the time. But as a writer, he could just wander around and follow his curiosity, talk to all of the interesting people in the dusty streets of Baladweyne.

At the end of the day Abdi hurries out of the cinder-block compound of the school with Mohammed and Abdullah, and they run through the town's streets, through the throngs of donkey carts and market vendors selling bananas and lemons, red packets of Sportsman cigarettes with a horse on the front, and individual cigarettas. They pass tables where women wearing hijab sell bundles of khat, the leaves that his fathers' friends often chew, a few stray stalks fallen to the ground. The boys are covered in fine red dust by the time they reach his father's shop on the town's main thoroughfare.

FARMACY is stencilled in large letters on the whitewashed adobe storefront. Inside, beans, rice, grains, cigarettes, *uomo* — laundry soap in small pouches — and Italian pasta line the narrow shelves. The boys eagerly eye a large glass-and-metal box, placed carefully on a wooden table underneath a single hanging light bulb, unlit against the bright day. Inside lies a mound of crushed ice, above it a container of sweet, sticky syrup. Behind it a small generator hums.

"See something you want?" says his father, a tall, wiry man, smiling as he emerges from the store's dim interior and lights a cigarette.

Abdi smiles back at his father. "*Assalam Alaikum, Abo.* We were wondering if we might have an ice treat…" he says tentatively, nodding his head toward the machine.

His father laughs again, then places his large hand on Abdi's shoulder. "Do you boys deserve it?"

All three nod vigorously.

"Okay then. But Abdi, only if you go help Hoyo with your brothers and sisters."

Abdi smiles at his father, happy. "Thank you, Abo, I will."

The call to prayer issues from the loudspeaker adjacent to the nearby mosque. Without a word Abdi's father pulls closed the shutters to his shop and, prayer mat in hand, disappears into the street.

Vessels held by Somali pirates: *Rockall, Stella Maris*

CHAPTER 4

LIFE AT SEA

A Canadian naval frigate will provide protection from pirate attacks for ships carrying food and other supplies through the waters off Somalia. Defence Minister Peter MacKay said the federal government is sending HMCS *Ville de Québec* at the request of the UN World Food Program.[1]

— *CBC News*, August 6, 2008

At breakfast, I choose a seat at the dining room table's near-deserted far end, across from Kevin. The other end, where most of the officers are seated, is the de facto "business" side of the table, presided over at its head by Lieutenant-Commander Sands, the industrious executive officer (XO). A tall woman in her thirties with short, practically cut blond hair, the XO is second-in-command of this warship. In keeping with tradition, to the left of the XO's position is the seat reserved for the logistics officer, Jean, and to the right is that reserved for the engineering officer, Mike. This allows the three to confer on work matters during meals, as they do now, the two men's dark heads turned away from me toward the XO. No other officer is permitted to sit at their places until they have come and gone at mealtimes. I do my best to avoid that whole end of the table, having no interest in work talk during meals unless it's absolutely required, and particularly at breakfast when I prefer not to speak at all. But in such constant company, it is difficult to maintain one's personal preferences.

"So, Jen, happy to be going back down south?" Kevin chortles as I slide into my seat, his grin showcasing brilliant teeth. I've used him as a confidant enough times in the past two weeks that he knows my history. Before I can reply, he launches into his own saga, the story of how he ended up on this mission.

"I can't believe the squadron would send me here. This exchange is supposed to be my *shore* posting — and they send me to sea! Who does that? And now we're going to Somalia. Great. I'll probably be sent to Iraq as soon as I get back to the US, too. Real great shore posting."

"Are you flying today?" I ask, in an attempt to distract him from the subject of the mission.

"Yeah, but not until this afternoon. I think I'll do some time travel before hitting the gym."

Time travel is the air crew's slang for sleeping, a means of making the time on board pass more quickly. Because air force regulations mandate a minimum amount of uninterrupted sleep for air crew when they're on notice to fly, they spend significantly more time in their racks than most others. Even out of uniform, goes a bitter joke on board, air crew are immediately identifiable by their big muscles, since they have time to spend in the ship's small gym. With muscular arms and a beefy torso on his compact frame, Kevin fits this image to a T.

"Madame?" One of the five wardroom stewards is awaiting my order with an air of resignation. He often appears disgruntled, as now, his face an expressionless mask.

"*Bonjour. Je prends de pain doré, s'il vous plaît.*" I smile appreciatively, and watch to see if that will lighten his dour mood. It doesn't. He nods curtly and stomps soundlessly back to the serving window to place the order with the stewards in the pantry.

Only officers are served their meals by stewards, a privilege new to me. When I last worked on board ship I was a master seaman — a junior rank — used to cafeteria-style meals and cleaning up after myself. For my first meal at sea on this mission I waited awkwardly at the serving window to collect my lunch, not understanding that wardroom etiquette dictated service at my seat.

Initially, I felt that service by stewards was a misplaced relic of our British naval roots. Nevertheless, I settled easily enough into the comfortable routine of it, appeasing my egalitarian sentiments with the thought that our navy is not as thoroughly class-based as the Royal Navy of old. Here, serving officers is just a job for which the stewards are well-compensated.

At five to eight, the wardroom fills up for "morning prayers," military slang for the regular morning meeting. Usually just heads of department attend morning prayers, but on Fridays, and when there is significant news to relay, all officers not on watch are expected to be present. With more than twenty-five of us on board, there are more people than seats. People crowd the sofas and dining chairs, where Kate has squeezed in, eyes bright with genuine interest. Most of the air crew ensconce themselves behind the bar. The XO sits in one corner of the sofa scribbling notes, her fair head down and seemingly oblivious to the activity around her. She has likely been up half the night with Jeff and the captain, planning for the arduous weeks ahead. Her eyes are underscored by dark circles that weren't there when we left Halifax. Once the heads of department confirm the presence of their subordinate officers, she opens the meeting.

"Good morning, everyone. After last night's announcement, we obviously have a lot of information to relay," she says in clipped tones, her distinct French-Canadian accent suffusing her fluent English. "There's an enormous amount of work to be done over the next few weeks, and we need to ensure that we are planning ahead as much as possible so that the transition to the new mission goes smoothly." Her role as principal administrator and disciplinarian will keep her particularly busy over the next long while.

"Here is the program as it stands now," she continues. "We will plan to transit the Suez Canal in four days time. The ship will proceed alongside at the NATO base in Crete tomorrow, where we will store ship, fuel, and allow the ship's company time ashore before we transit toward Suez. There are lots of things that need to be done before then, but that's the basic outline. Now let's go around the room. We'll start with Combat."

Jeff, seated beside the XO, is all seriousness now. He looks at each of us in turn.

"The XO has given you our general timing for getting to Suez," he says in a calm, efficient voice.

"NavO," he says, addressing Eric, the ship's navigating officer. "I need you to verify with the port authority the exact timing to pick up the pilot in Souda Bay, and then calculate the speed required to arrive on time.

Also do the calculations this morning to figure out what time we need to depart Souda Bay to arrive at the entrance to Suez on time."

He looks at me next. "Int, I need you to request threat assessments on Souda Bay and the Suez Canal immediately."

I look up at him. "Understood."

"I'm assuming that you've already started researching the new area of operations?"

"Yes, I have."

After Jeff finishes, it's the supply officer's turn to speak. Jean is a lanky francophone in his late twenties. A strong Québecois cadence dominates his English, which creates the erroneous impression that he speaks it poorly.

"The fuelling trucks will be there when we go alongside tomorrow," he says intently. "Stores will be on the jetty soon after that, so we should be able to store ship right away."

We finish the round, and the XO nods her head to dismiss us.

Under the harsh lighting of the communications control room, I'm struck by the sensation that I've never left the place, that the deployment thus far has been one long day broken into near-identical parts. The feeling is reinforced by the lack of windows in this space, and in all rooms of this ship except for the bridge. In fact, there are no indicators of day or night in here at all. The communications equipment lining the bulkheads hums twenty-four hours a day. Because the watch has just turned over, even the naval communicators are the same ones who were here when I last left. Master Seaman Davis munches on candy just where I left him, caramels this time. I make a mental note to visit the upper decks more regularly for a gulp of fresh sea air and a dose of Vitamin D.

"Hi, ma'am," Master Seaman Davis calls out as I pass, his round face beaming. "Any grand plans for Souda Bay?"

"I can't even think that far ahead, I have so much to do," I say, half-apologetically, making my way toward my desk at the far side of the room. "I should probably study up on piracy before I think about getting off the ship," I conclude with a laugh. I'm conscious that the busy pace of my job has so far prevented me from getting to know the communicators with whom I share this space.

Compared to others on the ship I have little to complain about. Space is a precious commodity on board. Unlike many of the more junior personnel, I have a desk of my own and a computer for my dedicated use. Communication equipment is precious and, for a crew this size, in short supply. In fact, the senior naval communicator, Petty Officer, 1st Class Tracey, graciously gave up his desk so that I would have the computer systems I need. He relegated himself to a corner behind my desk space, buried by an equipment rack. Through the slats of shelves and dangling wires, I glimpse his dark head there now, tapping away at his keyboard. Thanks to his accommodating personality, I have obtained prime real estate.

I spend all day hunched over my desk, researching piracy and the complexities of Somalia's political and humanitarian situation. The captain expects to be briefed daily on events in the region that could impact our mission. I'm daunted by the amount of information I have to absorb quickly. A substantial stack of reports sits untouched on my desk, at once a flag of my ignorance and a beacon of the knowledge I hope to obtain. At least the sea is calm as our ship slices through the central Mediterranean toward Crete. I can keep my eyes fixed on the screen for long hours, without suffering the light-headedness that inevitably results from prolonged swells.

As I read about Somalia's history of conflict and famine over the past two decades, the lack of central government to impose structure on a now-fragmented society, any mystery around piracy's ability to flourish dissipates. In 1991, Somalia's long-standing military dictatorship, led by Major General Mohamed Siad Barre, was toppled by a coalition of opposition groups. These clan-based groups, most notably those led by General Mohamed Farah Aidid and Ali Mahdi Mohamed, clashed over control of the capital, Mogadishu, in the ensuing power vacuum, leading to the country's descent into civil war and lawlessness, in which countless civilians were killed by the ensuing violence and starvation resulting from years of drought. Amid warring factions in 1992, Canadian Airborne soldiers deployed on an American-led mission called Operation Restore Hope, which, alongside a concurrent UN mission, sought to ensure security for the delivery of humanitarian aid. The Canadians completed their mandate in 1993, while the Americans withdrew in 1994 and all UN forces in 1995 after incurring significant casualties. In the absence of central government, ongoing conflict among clan-based, and later, Islamist militias fighting for supremacy, led hundreds of thousands of refugees to flee the violence to safer havens and refugee camps both within and beyond Somalia's borders; this, combined with long-term drought, flooding, high food prices, and and the collapse of the Somali currency has led to extreme food insecurity and humanitarian crisis on a grand scale, particularly in the country's south.

The World Food Programme (WFP), the United Nations organization fighting world hunger, has been providing food aid to Somalia for years. According to the World Food Programme Somalia website, it's estimated that more than three million Somalis are in need of food assistance as of this month. This is a 77 percent increase since the beginning of this year; as it stands now, the troubled nation's food situation is at one of its lowest levels in seventeen years.[2] Somalia is also considered one of the world's most dangerous places, with increasing frequency of attacks on aid workers threatening the very viability of humanitarian operations within the country. Only days before, a World Food Programme staff member working in the south was abducted and killed, bringing to an alarming twenty-three the number of aid workers murdered within Somalia this year — with another eleven currently held captive.[3]

Photo by Roy van den Berg

Unloading World Food Programme aid, Somalia, 1993.

The World Food Programme's goal, according to their Somalia website, is to deliver 150,000 metric tonnes of food by the end of this year, enough to feed a million and a half people for a six-month period. Ninety percent of their food aid is delivered by sea to Mogadishu and Somalia's four other ports. This is where we come in. Amid the lawlessness that has perpetuated the humanitarian crisis, piracy has flourished. Somali pirates hijack vulnerable vessels, including those carrying food aid, undermining the World Food Programme's ability to ensure continued delivery of food critical to the survival of thousands of their starving countrymen. In an unlikely extension of the 1993 Canadian role in Somalia, ours is a humanitarian mission to safeguard those shipments and ensure that food aid continues to be delivered ashore. As such, I assume that this operation is uncontroversial for the Canadian government, a reassuring win-win no-casualty mission at a time when that in Afghanistan is perceived as anything but.

Still, there must be some nervousness associated with it, representing as it does Canada's first military engagement in Somalia since our withdrawal from that country after the debacle of the early nineties. Members of the Canadian Airborne Regiment were indicted for the torture and murder of a Somali teenager, Shidane Arone. The report of the Somalia Commission of Inquiry found that the response to this and other violent incidents, in which soldiers transgressed their rules of engagement and their moral code, pointed to systemic failure caused by unaccountable leadership and the breakdown of organizational discipline at all levels.[4] It was one of the lowest moments in Canadian military history. The scandal disgraced the Canadian military and led to the disbandment of the Canadian Airborne. This precedent leaves no room for error on our part as we prepare to re-engage in Somalia, albeit in a maritime setting.

More than twenty thousand commercial vessels pass through the Gulf of Aden each year, on a key trade route between Europe and Asia, unavoidable for vessels travelling to or from the Suez Canal. In the first seven months of this year alone, Somali pirates in small speedboats have successfully hijacked *thirteen* vessels and their crews in the Gulf of Aden and the Indian Ocean. These waters are now considered the most dangerous in the world. Shipping companies are increasingly reluctant to send their vessels through unprotected, but few other options are open to them. Insurance rates for vessels passing through these waters have already increased tenfold in response to the upsurge in piracy.

The alternative is routing their vessels all the way around South Africa, adding an average of twelve days to a typical voyage from Europe to the Gulf, which could potentially increase freight rates by at least 25 percent, time being money in this industry. Through higher prices in goods, the increase in shipping costs is ultimately passed on to the consumer.[5] In the global economy, then, young Somali men in small speedboats *do* affect the comfortable lives of people like us who live half a world away.

~

Kevin and I linger over lunch the next day in the wardroom. I quietly sip my third cup of coffee and try to clear my head, still heavy from a late night spent researching. Kevin is bent over his plate, demolishing a second plate of pasta. Beyond the table, Kate and two other officers from the Air Det, Billy and Marcus, lounge on the sofas reading news synopses downloaded from the Internet.

"Good morning, *Ville de Québec*," booms the captain's voice, unexpectedly, over the pipe. The officers on the settees look up from their reading, while Kevin, undeterred, continues the attack on his pasta.

"This is your captain speaking," he continues in an upbeat tone. "At thirteen hundred we'll be having a Swim Ex off the starboard boat deck. I encourage as many of you as possible to participate, as your watches allow. That is all."

The other officers resume reading, their faces impassive.

"This will be fun!" My head has instantly cleared in my excitement. "Kevin, you'll come, right?"

Warships occasionally hold swim exercises in warm waters when schedules allow, permitting the crew to launch themselves into the sea right off the boat deck. This Ex is probably an attempt to bolster crew morale that may be still dragging after the Somalia announcement.

"I might come," Kevin says in a mock-intense voice that gives way to a deep chuckle, "But I warn you, I'll be wearing my American flag Speedos."

Sailors spill into the flats in their swimsuits after lunch. I emerge onto the starboard boat deck in shorts and T-shirt, squinting into blinding sunlight and inhaling warm sea air — a welcome reminder that August is the height of summer in the Mediterranean, a fact easily forgotten while working in the windowless spaces below decks. A line of sailors is already snaking along the dark grey deck, beginning just forward of the helicopter hangar and extending crookedly past the five-and a-half-metre inflatable resting in its steel cradle. The line culminates at an open space in the chain railing, from which sailors are already leaping, one by one, into the sapphire blue waters.

I wait my turn in line and gaze around. The odd officer or petty officer waits to jump, but the majority of those lining up are junior ranks, the men clad in shorts and the few women wearing shorts and sporty bikini tops. Kevin is nowhere to be seen. A young man in a T-shirt covering a substantial gut stares unabashedly at the smooth, tanned midriff of a fit brunette. He's oblivious to the overtness of his attentions. I can't blame him, nor the few others staring openly at women whose outfits are only revealing when compared to the mannish uniforms we wear every day. After three weeks, the men's limited contact with the opposite sex is starting to show.

At the midway point in the line the coxswain, Chief Richards, collects military identification cards as an easy method of accounting for everyone at the end of the Swim Ex. A tall balding man in his forties, he's the senior non-commissioned officer on board and is responsible for managing discipline and personnel matters. His amiability is in constant competition with his overpowering confidence.

"Thanks, ma'am," he says, unleashing on me the full power of his grin. His blue eyes hold my own for an extra beat as I relinquish my ID card. I'm not certain of the intent of his prolonged gaze and conspiratorial smile, but I'm gripped by a twinge of embarrassment for participating in the Swim Ex with the junior sailors. I force myself to dismiss the thought. Rare opportunities like this one make going to sea worthwhile.

The girl ahead of me barely hesitates before leaping into the cloudless blue sky to plunge nearly eight metres into the waters below. Cheers of encouragement issue from the line and from the bridge wing above, where the captain and XO are smiling encouragement.

I'm certain there's a shark shooter hidden behind them, a designated sailor watching with a loaded semi-automatic rifle for the hint of a fin or dark shape to appear. Dozens of shark species inhabit the Mediterranean.

While it's unlikely, the chance of an attack during a Swim Ex is taken seriously. A common joke is that the shooter's actual job is to put the swimmer — an easier target than a fast-moving predator — out of his misery once a shark has had a chomp.

It's my turn to jump. I push off and out, and then — plummet.

~

Back in my mess and nearly late for the navigation brief, I hurriedly tuck in my shirt and throw on my boots, then half-run through the flats to the communications control room to grab my notes. I arrive out of breath in the crowded wardroom and plant myself in front of the bar beside Jeff.

"Int, you're a mess," he says benignly, glancing at the watermarks darkening my blue combat shirt from a dripping ponytail.

"At least I made it on time," I counter hopefully. Jeff raises his eyebrows, his skepticism driving home what I already know: in the military, unless you're five minutes early for a meeting, you're late.

All of the key players are present for the navigation briefing, the formal presentation held before entering or leaving any port or restricted waterway: the Command Triad, comprised of the captain, XO, and coxswain, the heads of department and their chiefs, the bridge watch that will take the ship in, and the sailors responsible for handling lines as the ship goes alongside the jetty. The wardroom settees, now filled to capacity, have been rearranged in three neat rows to allow for viewing of the flat screen television that displays the navigating officer's presentation. The coxswain and the XO sit at the front, reserving the space between them for the captain. Still more people are packed into the space around the dining table at the back of the room. I see Kate, a voluntary spectator, near the rear of the pack.

"Room!" Jeff calls out sharply, causing the conversation to immediately cease. We snap soundlessly to attention, driving our arms to our sides and clamping our legs tightly together.

The captain walks through the door, his long face expressionless, and walks to the front of the room in long, heavy strides. "Good day, everyone," he says in his slow drawl as he takes up his seat. "Please relax."

We release our postures, and then Eric launches the briefing from his position at the front of the room.

"Good afternoon, sir," he states confidently. "This is the navigation brief for the entrance to Souda Bay. We'll begin with the intelligence update."

"Good afternoon, sir," I start, in a dismally thin voice. My heart is pounding in my chest and my mouth is suddenly bone-dry. Years of public speaking have failed to conquer my shyness.

"Louder!" interrupts an anonymous voice from the rear of the room.

"Sir," I say stridently, staring directly at the captain. "The latest threat assessment for Souda Bay doesn't include anything that's especially notable for us, given that we'll be secured alongside the NATO base and there for only a short duration."

Peering at my notes, I mention some potential hazards to the crew found in most foreign ports — health considerations, criminal activity — but I keep my summary short.

Eric briefs the navigational aspects of the alongside: the pickup time and place for the pilot who will help us to navigate local waters, marine traffic patterns, the use of tugs, how we will approach the jetty and put our lines across. Then Jeff speaks about force protection — the security posture the ship will adopt in this port.

At the conclusion of the brief, the captain stands to face us, his solid frame towering over us. The room is silent as all attention focuses on him.

"I know that everybody has been working hard this past week to ensure that we're operationally ready to go through the Suez Canal in a few days," he says, eyes behind his glasses scanning the room. "I want to ensure that we maintain that operational focus as we go into Souda Bay, do everything we need to keep departure timings tight. However, I also want the crew, all of you, to get some time ashore to decompress and to take care of personal business before we head through the canal. It could be a long while before we next go into port." *Thank God*, I think to myself. *I need off this ship — at least for a little while.* Only a few weeks into the deployment, cabin fever has already infected me. As the captain turns toward the exit, we snap to attention once more, relaxing only once he is clear of the wardroom.

Baladweyne, January 1993

As the soldiers have directed him and the others, Abdi watches, from a safe distance, the unloading of food. The adults, the men in their *ma'awis* and women in their faded *direh,* and the children in their filthy, holey shorts and hand-me-down Western T-shirts stand back in small clusters divided into gender and clan. The clearing is fraught with tension. Abdi does not completely understand the root of the hostility he feels all around him, but he knows that his father's death and the nightly gunfire is associated with it. Abdi stands close to the cluster associated with his clan, the Habagedir, turning away from the familiar faces in the Hawadle and Jajeleh groupings.

Once the soldiers have finished unloading the sacks of rice and beans, a few stand watch over the food, rifles affixed with bayonets held at the ready. One olive-skinned soldier, dark hair sweaty underneath his soft field hat and rifle slung over his back, picks up a large sack of rice and walks it to the doorway of a nearby hut. There, he takes a knife from his pocket and slices the bag open, slitting it diagonally from end to end. Abdi has seen this before. He knows this practice makes it impossible for the food to be carried off by would-be thieves. He watches as he and the other soldiers move from hut to hut delivering food. When he sees the soldier move in the direction of his hut, on the far side of this makeshift village on the edge of Baladweyne, he finds the courage to join him.

"Ka-na-da," says Abdi to the strong, rice-carrying soldier as he falls into step beside him.

"Yes," says the soldier, smiling at him, his kind green eyes growing friendlier as they leave the tense gathering behind them. "We are from Canada."

"Ka-na-da nice," says Abdi, though all he knows of it is the maple leaf affixed to the soldier's shoulder. He smiles, happy for a moment to hold his attention.

As they approach his hut, Abdi's mother emerges. *"Subax wanaagsan,"* she greets the soldier. *"Is ka warran?"*

The soldier heaves the bag of rice from his shoulder onto the hard ground beside the doorway, then slits it with his knife. *"Waan fiicanahay,"* he replies in greeting, his humble smile respectful.

Abdi's mother laughs, her haggard face transforming into delighted surprise as she expresses her thanks. *"Mahadsanid."*

"*Adigaa mudan*," replies the soldier. With a clasp of Abdi's shoulder, he hurries back to the unloading point to deliver the rest of the food.

That night from his family's hut, Abdi can hear the sound of gunfire. Past the silhouettes of his sleeping siblings, not hungry for the moment, of his exhausted mother, he can see the slight shape of the AK in the back of the room, hidden beneath a mat — his father's legacy passed down to him, the man of the house, for his family's protection. His father had been man of another house, their comfortable compound near the river, a lovely area where majestic animals had once fed, and which had once been so green. After he died, and with the famine, they were forced to flee to the outskirts of town, to this makeshift home with none of the security he used to associate with that word.

The next morning, Abdi follows a short distance behind a group of clansmen to another part of town. They carry the shrouded corpse of a victim — perpetrator? — of last night's violence. The graveyard, a parched expanse of land, is dotted with recently dead bodies — violence, famine, disease — reluctantly covered over only with rocks, the sole means to bury them in the sun-hardened dirt. The stench of decaying flesh mingles with that of the hundreds of cattle carcasses strewn nearby, dead where they fell, and across to the now-defunct airfield where the Canadian soldiers have set up their camp.

Downtown Baladweyne, Somalia, 1993.

Abdi peers across the barbed wire boundary, not even waist high, and into the camp. He's not the only one: children and adults alike cluster outside and stare inside at the show. Soldiers, several shirtless in the heat, mill around. Their base is modest, too, holes dug into the red dirt and tarps for shelter. But despite the camp's humility, he knows there is promise there.

Vessels held by Somali pirates: *Rockall, Stella Maris*

CHAPTER 5

ASHORE

A Nigerian ship has joined a long list of vessels hijacked by pirates off
the coast of Somalia when a new ship bound for Nigeria, the *Yenagoa
Ocean* was, last week seized by Somali pirates.
— *Nigeria Daily News*, August 10, 2008[1]

By late morning the ship is tied alongside the NATO naval base in Souda
Bay, Crete. Colourful graffiti from sailors off ships previously docked
here animates the near-empty jetty, lending it a jaunty air in contrast
with the stark white concrete of the naval establishment. Just beyond
the base, dry hills dotted with whitewashed houses remind us that we
are in Greece.

A long chain of bodies clad in heavy black combats now snakes from
the produce truck on the jetty, across the ship's brow, over the upper
decks, down ladders, through flats, and into the fridges and storage
spaces below deck. Everyone who can be spared, regardless of rank,
is helping to store ship, and all are sweltering under the glare of the
Mediterranean sun.

A half-dozen of us stand on the flight deck, legs planted wide to
balance the weight of the boxes we are swinging to the next set of arms.
My black ship's ball cap draws the heat. Sweat dribbles down my face.
Already my combat shirt, sleeves rolled up as high as they can go, is
darkened with sweat.

To my left stands Billy, an air navigation officer for one of the air
detachment's two crews. With his dimpled grin, he is as laid-back as his

east coast roots would suggest. I have yet to hear him complain on this deployment.

I flash him a smile. "Lucky you in your flight suit," I say, looking enviously at his tan one-piece as I drop a bag of potatoes into his waiting arms. "It looks cooler than this outfit I've got going on."

As if for show, Billy peels off the top portion of the flight suit and ties it around his waist, so that only a tan T-shirt covers his torso.

"You could always join the air force," he replies, fixing me with his baby blues.

I'm about to retort that I'd settle for flight suits, when Marcus's voice chimes in from my right.

"Unless, for some bizarre reason, you *want* to stay a fishhead," he says, a grin animating his tanned face as he passes me a box of plums. Marcus is one of four helicopter pilots who came on board with the air crew. Though I've only known him for three weeks, it's clear that the fishhead comment — his slang for navy sailors — is a joke.

From what I know of them so far, Marcus seems to be Billy's polar opposite. What he lacks of Billy's easy-going nature, he makes up for with a passion that matches his dark good looks. Marcus, with rare conviction, hates going to sea. But he loves flying with equal fervour.

A sweet, raw smell precedes a large box of strawberries coming down the line, making me nostalgic for summer. We've been out here for what seems like hours, storing enough to feed 250 people for a month, and I'm suddenly aware of my stomach growling. A cook standing beside Billy grabs some strawberries as the box passes and pops them into his mouth. I follow his lead, as do others, and soon we're all munching on summer fruit as we work, making just a tiny dent in the long stream of food flowing past us and into the holds below.

Once the storing and fuelling are complete, it will still be some time before the crew is free to go ashore. A few of them are already pacing the flats in civilian clothes, antsy. Still in uniform, I kill time in the wardroom, flipping through a report on the Suez Canal, seeing words on the page but absorbing nothing.

Finally, the pipe we've been waiting for: "Secure. The brow is now open for Ship's Company not required for duty. Leave expires at zero six three zero, ninth August."

Dozens of crew burst out of their messes and into the flats, up the ladder and onto the upper decks in pursuit of the fading day. Walking through the flats, I'm struck by the transformation of crew members in their civilian clothes.

"Hi, ma'am. Going ashore?" asks PO Marcotte in her molasses drawl as we pass outside our mess. Her long brown hair is unleashed from its high ponytail and cascades down her back in a smooth, shining mass. Her makeup is subtle, expertly applied. In her sleeveless dress and delicate sandals, she looks quite different from the professional sailor I usually bunk with.

"I hope so. You look great!" I tell her, now feeling frumpy in my baggy combats.

For the first time in weeks, the lights in our mess are burning brightly. Becky, the junior logistics officer, stands in capris and a T-shirt applying mascara in the small lobby mirror. Petty Officer, 1st Class Adams buttons up a pretty blouse, her fit body showing to advantage in stylish blue jeans.

"It's *so* nice to see people in civvies again!" I call out cheerfully as I open my locker.

HMCS Ville de Québec *alongside NATO base Souda Bay, Crete, July 2008.*

I fish around in the drawers of my locker, grateful that, for once, I'm not searching blind under cover of darkness. I settle on a pair of jeans, a fitted T-shirt, and some sandals. In the heads, I take a pusser shower, the only kind allowed, owing to limitations in the supply of fresh water aboard the ship. Water on, get wet. Water off, lather up. Water on, rinse off. The rule is to use no more than two minutes worth of running water. Accomplishing this while washing a head of long, tangled hair is an art form. Today I steal an extra thirty seconds, scrubbing hard to drive the feel and smell of the ship from my skin. Hemp body lotion, smoothed luxuriously over my body, finishes the job.

After dressing, I apply light makeup, then let my brown curly hair flow loose over my shoulders. I remove my staid, uniform-appropriate stud earrings and replace them with dangly silver ones. I apply pink nail polish to my toes, then clear polish to my closely clipped fingernails.

Not one to indulge in self-pampering, the extent to which I relish applying these feminine touches now surprises me. Looking in the mirror I feel renewed, fresh in body and spirit, but what shocks me is the realization that I've accomplished more than that. The mere act of choosing what to wear, of applying makeup and doing my hair in this rigid shipboard environment, feels absurdly like creative expression.

Many of the officers are gathering in the wardroom for a drink before going ashore. When I step across the room's threshold, stripped of the anonymity of my uniform, I feel like a new girl entering a party alone. A dozen officers surround the bar with beers in hand, Becky the only female among them. Their gaze shifts toward me en masse.

"Jen! Hey, you look like a girl!" Eric, in a blue polo shirt, calls out from behind the bar.

"Thanks for noticing. You look like a boy," I reply, with sarcastic tone intended to hide my embarrassment. I lay my forearms on the gleaming wood of the bar. "Would you mind grabbing me a beer?"

I lean back on the bar and survey the room. Clumps of officers, now indistinguishable from civilians in their jeans and T-shirts, are talking in small groups. They range in age from mid-twenties to early forties, but the majority fall somewhere in between. From the snippets of conversation overheard in recent weeks, I know that all but a handful of them are married or engaged, and several have young children.

Already social groups are forming. The male officers of the air det — Kevin, Billy, Marcus, and their air det commander, the Maj, also known as Tifou — are the most clearly defined set, standing slightly apart from the others. Like me, they aren't part of the ship's core crew, but, unlike me, they came on board as an already-formed unit so they have an instant group of friends. Absent from today's festivities is Nathalie, an air navigator, who does not drink and rarely socializes. Kate, an outspoken and obviously astute young woman, often stands removed from the others, both literally and figuratively, as she does now. Across the room, we exchange smiles.

Other clusters are more fluid. Most of the francophone officers have congregated at one end of the bar, while a group of sub-lieutenants — the most junior officers on board — inhabits the other. But a few individuals like Helmz, a stocky, perfectly bilingual engineering officer, flow effortlessly between. He mingles now with the air det circle, his dark head tilted back in easy laughter.

I could join any one of these groups and be welcomed, at least on the surface, yet I have rarely felt so alone. I get along well with most people, I'm a decent conversationalist, but large groups are not my thing. Forging close connections with a select few better suits my introverted nature. The shipboard lifestyle, with personal space to retreat to in short supply, runs fundamentally against my grain.

But most individuals can suspend their personal needs without suffering much damage — for a time. Basic military training at seventeen taught me that. For seven weeks on the Nova Scotia coast, I spent every waking moment with other equally bewildered recruits. Our platoon's disoriented, shorn-headed young men teamed with me and other dazed young women, all of us newly androgynous in faded green combats, to wax floors, polish boots, iron uniforms, shovel down food, tackle obstacle courses, and endure verbal abuse. Like me, many were mystified as to how we had ended up there. A summer away from home was all I'd wanted. The recruiting officer, a balding lieutenant seated comfortably in his Toronto lakeshore office, had promised gentle adventure and afternoons sailing under a wind-cooled Atlantic sun. Still in high school, and knowing nothing about the military, I signed up.

Basic training was nothing like the recruiting officer had promised. I suffered for a while that summer, as we all did, crying quietly to our families on the rare occasions when calls were permitted from the payphone in the barracks stairwell. But quitting was never an option. The training was highly effective: our military masters broke us down, and when they built us back up, loyalty, camaraderie, and obedience — qualities critical to ensuring an effective military response in times of conflict — were what drove us. Brainwashing, some would call it, but the term lends the process a sinister cast it doesn't deserve. By the end of training, our tears were for the surrogate families — our squad, our platoon — from which we were wrenched away when we returned home.

I could stomach it then; I could subordinate my personality for the sake of group dynamics. But I was a kid then, and malleable. During basic officer training, more than ten years later, I was less inclined to participate in the games whose ends were by then transparent. Now, at thirty-three, I am less malleable still. Life experience has bolstered my confidence, perhaps made me less flexible in some ways, and I'm now less willing to subjugate my preferences to the will of others.

So, as my eyes scan the dimly lit space, I relieve myself of the responsibility of conforming to this wardroom. Personal rigidity, though, will not help me in this already unyielding shipboard environment. And I need to connect.

I work my way over to Kate, still in her flight uniform, on the far side of the room.

"Hi, Kate," I say, smiling at her. "You're not going ashore tonight?"

"I'd love to, but I'm on duty," she replies. "It's no big deal — I'll go ashore tomorrow. Try to get a bit of alone time."

"Fair enough. It's been an intense few weeks since we left Halifax. And who knows when we'll get ashore again," I say. "Speaking of going ashore, I'm going to see what the other guys are up to."

"Hey, KGB, how's it going?" asks the Maj as I breach the air det circle, inserting myself between Kevin and Marcus, who exudes an air of European sophistication even when dressed down in T-shirt and jeans.

"Good, but I'll be better once I step off this ship," I say good-naturedly, eliciting what I now recognize as the Maj's characteristic cackle.

A francophone in his mid-thirties, the Maj reportedly lives up to his nickhame. TiFou, or "Little Crazy," has been known to lose his cool in defence of his close-knit team. With his mature countenance, he seems older than his years — a perception reinforced by his role as leader of the air det and by his imminent retirement plans, though belied by his wiry climber's frame. TiFou has been in the military close to twenty years already, having known early on that he wanted to be a pilot. Now he plans to retire at thirty-seven, with a generous pension, and sail around the world with his wife.

"I don't know about you guys, but once I finish this beer I'm going ashore — and not coming back tonight," says Kevin. He's looking pointedly at Marcus and Billy, cobalt eyes narrowed in an I-wait-for-no-man glare. His short blond hair is coiffed into stylish, spiky messiness in direct affront to military conformity.

I breathe in deeply, then force myself to say it.

"Do you mind if I tag along?" I cringe inwardly at my earnest tone.

This isn't a given. Hanging out together on the ship is one thing, but transcending the ship/shore friend boundary is another matter. The air det guys and I have only a casual acquaintance. They come from the West Coast, like me, but they take their posse entirely for granted. I don't need a posse, but neither do I want to be alone on my runs ashore over the next five months. Besides, I like these guys. The air force culture they're drawn from is more laid-back, more based on teamwork, than that of the Maritime Surface and Subsurface (MARS) officers who drive and command warships and dominate our wardroom.

MARS officers are notorious for the competitive drive and obsession with work that seems to be a prerequisite for success within the trade. There is logic in creating a perfectionist culture: although the commanding officer is ultimately responsible for the safety of the ship and the lives of the crew, a MARS officer, standing as officer of the watch on the bridge, has practical responsibility. Still, few MARS trainees are prepared for the intensity of the training and the high failure rate. The ship's bridge is the MARS officer's high-stakes stage, and they need to perform consistently on it. Mistakes, immediately evident, are publicly humiliating and judged harshly by their MARS officer peers.

As I view the military spectrum, the army is the most boot-camp, living-in-the-dirt stereotypical military, followed by the navy with its unique brand of Brit-inspired old-school-hierarchy traditionalism. The air force, more modern than the other two services, leans toward a civilized, pleasure-affirming reasonableness that suits its taskings and differentiates it from the other two elements. To me, the air det represents an alternative military culture that is as close as it gets to civilian on board the *Ville de Québec*. So I can almost pretend that Kevin, Marcus, and Billy are straddling that military-civilian divide right along with me.

As I await the response to my plea for company ashore, a warm body brushes against my elbow.

"We'll come along too," announces Becky, who has inserted herself into the circle and appropriated the space to my right. The confident expression that plays across her wide, freckled face reveals no qualms about inviting herself along. Jean, face relaxed, slouches his tall frame beside her.

Kevin's body visibly tenses, and he looks away, clearly annoyed. "Fine," he says resignedly. "But we're leaving *now*."

We hurriedly pack overnight bags and scramble up the ladder to the now-dim flight deck and across the ship's brow, but we've missed the bus that Jean, in his capacity as logistics officer, has chartered to take crew to Chania, the closest town of decent size.

Kevin, legs pumping in his designer jeans, is already halfway to the security gate at the base entrance. He's a man on a mission: to get as far away from the ship as possible, and as soon as possible. By the time we reach him, he has already had the security guard call two taxis.

The first hotel we check in Chania can take us. As we mount the carpeted stairs to our single rooms, a dozen of the ship's company, including Master Seaman Davis, are already socializing in the balconied lounge area on the second floor. Davis throws us a polite wave as we pass, then turns back to his conversation.

"Fantastic, more fishheads," grumbles Marcus beside me.

But one glance at the tanned, relaxed lines of his face, curving into a smile, tells me he doesn't really care. By this point, even Kevin is too relieved at having found a bed ashore to maintain his dour mood. A temporary reprieve from the fishbowl of the ship is all we need to make us happy.

~

Street lamps softly illuminate the warmth of the summer evening. Bronzed Greeks and pasty-faced European tourists on their August break pack

Chania's winding, cobblestoned streets, lined with small shops selling everything from colourful leather purses to flamboyant beach wear to pricey jewellery. The narrow streets open up to reveal the bustling port. A spacious square leads to wide café-lined promenades fronted by waters lapping at stone-and-concrete seawalls.

Our group settles into a long table at an outdoor patio and orders cocktails. I suck back a pina colada through a straw, the sugar wave jolting me awake and instantly buoying my sagging spirits.

"It's so amazing to be here. This is perfect!" I exclaim, beaming around the table.

The others are suddenly animated too. Rest, drink, and huge, heaping platters of shish kebab, rice, and olive-laden salads chase away the last vestiges of discontent.

Out of my purse I pull a Greek mobile phone that Jean's supply department is renting for those on call.

"I'm going to call the brow to give them our contact details for tonight, before I forget," I tell the rest of the table. "Tell me your room numbers if you want me to report in for you."

Crew members sleeping ashore are required to call in with hotel details by midnight. I'm in my mid-thirties; reporting in makes me feel like a kid asking my parents' permission for a sleepover. But the alternative is being declared AWOL — absent without leave — a chargeable offence under Canada's military justice system.

I dial the local number for the ship's brow. The leading seaman who answers sounds indifferent as I recite our contact details. He's part of the ship's duty watch, the rotating skeleton crew required to man the ship twenty-four hours while alongside in foreign port, to keep the ship minimally operational and responsive to emergencies. I picture him now, leaning against the varnished wood podium at the ship's gangway that leads ashore, now in the fourth hour of his brow watch and bored with the infrequent and mostly uneventful comings and goings of the crew. If he's lucky, a sailor too inebriated to be allowed to cross the brow and go ashore might create a diversion from his mind-numbing duty.

"Hey, isn't that Manny over there?" says Kevin, pointing at a group of people staggering toward a nearby nightclub, its indecipherable name spelled out in pink neon letters.

Billy cranes his head around and peers across the lit square. "Uh huh," he says disinterestedly. He turns back around and draws on his drink.

I recognize Manny, a young officer with classic good looks and an eager-to-please demeanour. From this distance, he seems to be propelling a group of junior sailors toward the nightclub.

Marcus snorts derisively. "Leave it to Egghead to be already fraternizing."

"What's he thinking?" I ask. Discouraged as a practice, Manny's public fraternizing with junior ranks is a lapse in judgment.

"I know. At least when I fraternize I'm smart enough not to get caught," says Kevin, taking a long swallow of his cocktail.

I shoot him a quizzical look. He chuckles and grins cheekily. "The ladies on board ship always love me."

And from docile Billy, "Who cares what anyone else does anyway?" From his resolute expression, it's clear that he plans to waste no time thinking about Manny or other people's private lives. None of us really want to know.

The captain has a rule, tucked into the Ship's Standing Orders, that every crew member is meant to read. It's derived from higher policy and common to naval units: no fraternization. No romantic relationships between officers and junior ranks and senior non-commissioned members serving together on board ship. Romance even within messes is generally not permitted, and definitely not encouraged. If romantic relationships develop, as they inevitably do when people live and work in such close quarters, they are to be declared to supervisors. Then the decision will be made as to whether both individuals may remain on the ship. This is possible only if the pair can remain professional and the relationship does not interfere with performance or otherwise degrade crew morale. Otherwise, one or both will be relocated — inevitable if they are in the same chain of command.

Even non-romantic fraternization between messes, like going out drinking together, is frowned upon on board ship. The logic of separation between ranks is solid: adherence to orders passed from superiors to subordinates down the chain of command must be immediate and unquestioned to ensure effective action in times of conflict. Familiarity *can* breed contempt. Have a few drinks, get cozy with your boss, let the lines of authority grow fuzzy, realize his limitations, lose respect for him, and, finally, lose respect for his orders. Rules can't be relaxed just because it's peacetime. And there is potential for real conflict in the theatre of operations we're entering.

But while separation between messes may be necessary to maintain military discipline, its class-system feel — so at odds with assumptions of contemporary Canadian society — can lead to feelings of alienation. It's the innocent and human need for connection that drives fraternization on board ship. What is shocking is the guilt we feel, ensnared in a tangled web of military regulations and human imperative, for transgressing the sensible but anti-intuitive rules of conduct that constrain us.

～

The next morning, I'm having breakfast with Becky and the guys at a waterside café when Jeff wanders by.

"Jeff! Hey! You got off the ship!" I call out, surprised by his escape. I had forgotten all about his burial beneath a mountain of work.

"Hey Jen, hey guys," he says, pausing in front of our table. "Yup, I managed to get ashore." Jeff's skin is alabaster white, his brown eyes hidden behind dark glasses. By the look of it he hasn't seen the sun in weeks.

"Why don't you join us?" I offer, shuffling my belongings off the seat beside me.

"Thanks, but I've only got a few hours before I need to get back. I'd like to pick up a few things. I'll see you later." And he's off with a light wave.

We head to the beach after breakfast. The smooth white sand slides into turquoise water, ruffled by waves that break timidly six metres from shore. The sea's cool is irresistible in the sun's glare and heat at its edge, where we dig our toes into warm sand. Poor planning: none of us have brought swimsuits. Kevin and TiFou strip off their T-shirts and walk straight in wearing their shorts, then quickly submerge themselves in the welcoming blue. I hesitate a moment, looking down at the indigo sundress I so carefully chose to wear this morning. *Ah, to hell with it.* I wade in fully clothed.

"My dress is quick-dry, an active wear brand designed to be versatile," I call back to Marcus, half-fibbing. He is reclined in a lounger tanning his already-brown torso. He raises his sunglasses an inch and shoots me a skeptical look.

The sea is bath-water warm, but its still-cool edge provides relief from the baking air above. When the water reaches my thighs I dive in and slide under. Emerging, I float on my back a few yards from Kevin, pre-break swells lifting and lowering me in easy rhythm.

On the beach later, we sprawl on sun-soaked loungers like lizards on a hot rock. Marcus looks pointedly at the massive wet splotches that have made a patchwork of my dress. "I see that your Amish swimsuit isn't so quick-dry after all," he says.

"Maybe not," I say, "but it was worth it." And I lean back contentedly in my recliner.

In the post-midnight quiet outside our hotel, the day's intense heat still bounces off the pavement. The guys have chosen a last night of refuge at the hotel before an early morning return, so only Becky and I board the last chartered coach back to the ship.

The bus is only half full. A few of the crew are obviously drunk. Their voices rise to a near-shout as they regale one another with stories of their night out. I insert the purple bud earphones connected to my iPod and crank up the volume. I gaze out the window at dark, abandoned streets as the bus rumbles toward the undulating route that winds through dry hills toward Souda Bay.

A chief in his mid-forties sits across the aisle. When his loud, drunken voice penetrates my reverie, I glance over in irritation, catching his eye. Then there's no stopping him.

"Hi, ma'am!" he says enthusiastically. "You know, believe it or not, the briefs that you give are sometimes interesting."

"Oh, thank you," I say, noncommittal. I lean back toward the window.

"No, I mean it. Seriously," he continues loudly, as if I had contested his half-compliment. Now he's slurring his words. "Most of the ops room brief is really boring. But occasionally, yours are interesting."

"Thank you," I repeat. "There's a lot of interesting material to brief."

He pauses, narrowing his eyes, then delivers the great equalizer. "That's when I can hear you. Usually I can't even hear what you're saying."

I nod politely and jack up the volume on my iPod again, in no mood to engage with drunken colleagues.

As I curl up in my seat and shut out the surrounding racket, I reflect on the intricacies of inter-mess dynamics. There is an easier separation between messes on a frigate like ours because of the size of the vessel and crew. Officers have the opportunity to make thirty-five new friends in the wardroom alone. Still, it surprises me how few of the crew I've gotten to know. I've been so focused on my work, so immersed in trying to keep up with the demand for informed briefs that I've invested little time in getting to know those around me. I've been telling myself that there's lots of time, that friendship will occur naturally during our six-month confinement. At the moment, I'm not so sure.

June 1998 — Baladweyne

The white broken-down truck trundles down the potholed road from the airfield toward town. Abdi, in his *wa'ala* and pouncing tiger T-shirt, balances atop mounds of khat piled in the open back, its leaves separated into small bunches beneath him. He holds his AK — the one requirement for this job — by the wooden stock in his right hand. His eyes scan the road ahead.

His job is to protect the daily delivery of the mild narcotic, a precious cargo under constant threat of banditry, to the market for a local distributor after it is flown in from Kenya each day. His father would not have been proud, expecting more from his son, but Abdi knows he's lucky to have a job at all. Everywhere in town idle legions of young men like him, full of restless energy. If they are lucky they have a weapon, the only means of wielding any control at all, even over oneself, in this weapon-addled town. The ones that can afford it chew khat. Their cheeks bulge as they while away hours under the shade of the acacia trees. That's not how he spends the little money he has. As it is he barely earns enough to ensure that his mother and his brothers and sisters have enough to eat; there's certainly not enough to send the little ones to school.

The truck halts at the market on the town's busy main street. Abdi hops off, his sandals making solid contact with hard-packed earth. Direh-clad women surge toward the truck and collect their bundles of khat from the truck bed, the driver managing the exchange, and display their prized merchandise on trolleys, besides stands selling Chiclets and cigarettes and tiny pouches of laundry detergent. Men, young and old, descend on the tables from out of nowhere; then, drug in hand, they begin their chew.

"Abdi, come here," says Hassan, the truck driver. Holding tight to his rifle, Abdi moves toward him. The older man leans in. His head is only inches from Abdi's own. "You are a good boy, but there is no money to pay you. You will have to find different work."

Abdi looks up at him, meeting his eyes before quickly shifting his gaze downward. "Okay." What else can he say? He turns away from Hassan before his eyes can reveal his panic.

Abdi walks toward the river, his gait slow. He spends time there most days, passing the time with Mohammed and other friends before he heads back to his modest home on the outskirts of town. They laughingly beg him to bring them khat, but he doesn't have the money for that, nor the inclination. Today he slows his approach. He is not ready to admit, even to his friends, that he no longer has work.

"Abdi, finally you are here," says Mohammed, jumping up from where he reclines on the dry riverbank and shaking Abdi's hand. "Where have you been?"

"I need work, Mohammed," says Abdi, his worry spilling over. "Hassan told me there is no money to pay me."

Mohammed gives him a steady look. "Is that what he told you? There is money, lots of it, with all that khat he brings in."

Abdi looks at him, perplexed. "What then? I was a good worker."

"Abdi, you are so trusting. I heard at the market that Hassan has a cousin he needs to give work to. We will see him working the delivery tomorrow, I promise you — at twice the pay."

Abdi scuffs the ground with his sandal. "I cannot tell Hoyo that there will be no more money. I need to find work." He manages a grin for his friend. "I can't be idle like you."

"I won't be for long," counters Mohammed with uncharacteristic eagerness. "Our uncle in Harardheere has invited me to the coast, to earn money fishing on his boat. There are enormous tuna and sharks in the seas there, and they earn good money in the market." He pauses. "Why don't you come with me? Our uncle was close to your Abo. He would be happy to help you."

Abdi looks at his friend, the first glimmer of hope in his eyes. "But how could I leave my family? They need me here."

"They need you to have money," says Mohammed. "You can send money back to them, visit sometimes. You have no work to keep you here."

Abdi cannot dispute his logic. Maybe he will make more money there, enough even to send his brothers and sisters to school. His mother will be able to manage if he can send her money.

That afternoon, at his tumbledown home, he tells his mother the news. His siblings line the walls of the one-room hut, the youngest only five, and the eldest, Fatima, still only a girl at twelve. They stare at him with wide eyes.

It is hardest to look at his hoyo. Her hollowed-out cheeks and mournful eyes age her twenty years, though she was little more than a girl when she married his abo, and is not yet thirty-seven. Her indoor direh is brighter than the one she wears in public, but even its once-vibrant turquoise is fading toward a neutral grey. She averts her gaze before speaking.

"Abdi, you must do what you have to. I don't want you to go — the coast seems so far away. But what are we to do if you don't have work? I have no skills to get paid work. All that I can manage is finding food and water, raising these children and keeping them safe."

Abdi knows she has no choice but to agree. He will send money back and they will be all right, he tells himself.

Vessels held by Somali pirates: *Rockall, Stella Maris*

CHAPTER 6

SUEZ

The Suez Canal is one of the pillars of Egyptian economy; it contributes around four percent of national income and 10 percent of foreign currency. The Canal is the gateway to the Arabian Sea and links Asia to Europe. Notably, the Suez Canal is often used by oil shipment vessels. It's argued that the increasing rate of piracy would lead ships to opt for the old, longer route via the Cape of Good Hope.[1]

— *Daily News Egypt*, October 17, 2008

Early the next afternoon we depart Souda Bay. Sailors making up the watch required to take the ship safely out of harbour are standing or sitting throughout the bridge. Eric is the officer of the watch and directs the casting off of lines that hold the ship fast to the jetty. Once the crew accomplishes that, he orders the helmsman to alter the ship's course and speed.

"Port fifteen," he calls out. "Steer course two seven zero!"

"Port fifteen, steer course two seven zero!" acknowledges the helmsman in a voice that resonates throughout the bridge. His hands nudge the helm — two independent joysticks a generation removed from the giant wooden wheel on which I learned to helm — in the ordered direction.

From the elevated captain's chair affixed to the bridge's port side, the commanding officer presides, surveying the scene on the water through a broad expanse of wraparound windows.

I wander onto the starboard bridge wing, empty but for the lookout scanning boat-speckled waters with hefty binoculars. I lean my bare forearms on the wooden railing. It's slippery-shiny, a rich, appealing ochre against the dull ship-grey paint of the wall beneath it. Beyond it, the white concrete of the naval base grows smaller, dwarfed now by its cradle of thirsty yellow hills.

I'm not sure how I feel about leaving this port. The safe haven represents what the Mediterranean pitstops of our planned deployment would have been like: lazy days spent beachside, sipping summery cocktails, browsing in local markets, drinking fine wine. Part of me is reluctant to let this all go. But the adventurous part is eager to transit the Suez Canal, the barrier that so clearly distinguishes our new mission from our last as well as separating two vastly different worlds, and get this mission underway.

I close my eyes and tilt my head back into the sun, mellowed by the breeze blowing over the water. I remain for a moment like this, quietly content, my usually chaotic mind wonderfully still. Without warning, the wind lifts the rim of my ball cap, flicks it off my head and almost overboard before I manage to grab it. My reverie disrupted, I'm reminded that the sunless zone below decks awaits me.

~

The crew is markedly more relaxed after the port visit. A companionable air now connects the five communicators scattered at work stations around the communications control room. An opened cardboard box sits on one of the desks. On it leans a clear plastic bag of candy.

"I see your wife sent another care package," I say, smiling over at Master Seaman Davis.

His round face lights up. "Yeah, she's a good one for that. I left some candy on your desk."

Sure enough, there is a small pile of chocolate caramels on my desk atop a scrawled note: *From your favourite watch!* The gratitude I feel is almost overwhelming. In the moment I open a caramel and pop it into my mouth, I become more at home on the ship.

While the port visit allowed most of the crew to decompress, those with the heaviest responsibility for preparing the ship to transit the Suez have had little time ashore: the CO, with overall accountability to headquarters in Ottawa for operational readiness; the XO, with the lead on the overwhelming amounts of requisite administration; Jeff, in charge of operational planning, including the timing of the World Food Programme escorts; and the coxswain, handling ever-present personnel issues. Jeff had a few short hours ashore; the others likely had less. The ship's leaders are focused only on the mission.

We are figuring out much of the mission preparation as we go. While it's occasionally stressful, the challenge of tackling a problem head-on, in the absence of set procedure, is also rewarding. It's no simple task to conduct an escort mission in an area of high piracy and high terrorist threat complicated by prolonged civil war. The French and Dutch navies have carried out similar escort missions off Somalia's coast this past year, but ours is the first Canadian ship to escort World Food Programme vessels, and we have much to learn.

When our ship enters the Suez Canal in less than forty-eight hours, we will officially leave NATO command. Three Canadian naval ships are already patrolling in the Arabian Gulf, carrying out surveillance and monitoring shipping to detect and deter terrorist activity. They constitute the Canadian Task Force Arabian Sea, of which we will become the fourth unit. The three ships are also part of the multinational Combined Task Force 150. Comprised of ten warships and supply vessels from Germany, Pakistan, France, Canada, and the United States, the task force is currently led by one of the Canadian ships, HMCS *Iroquois*. Despite the difference in our mandate from that of the other three Canadian ships, our participation in the World Food Programme escort mission is a national tasking, arranged directly between the Canadian government and the United Nations. Once we chop from NATO, we will report directly to the flagship, HMCS *Iroquois*.

I was originally slated to join *Iroquois*, but the ship left Halifax in April. That was too soon after my return from Zambia to sign up for such an intense mission, so I switched places with Michèle, a fellow reservist and close friend from Vancouver Island. She joined *Iroquois*, while I joined *Ville de Québec*.

The *Iroquois* mission in the Gulf will be more interesting, she told me before she left, tucking shiny dark tresses behind her ears. She was in the midst of mad last-minute preparations to leave her home for the next six months, but in her trademark friend-prioritizing fashion she'd found time to meet at a café in our shared seaside neighbourhood. "But you'll get better port visits," she said with her usual easy laugh. "It seems a fair trade."

It was. Now, even if only via satellite email between ships, I'm looking forward to working with her over the next few months. Having the detached but sympathetic support of a friend who understands the pressures of the job will be welcome.

But while *Iroquois* and the other Canadian ships patrol the waters of the Arabian Gulf, including the high piracy area of the Gulf of Aden, they are not tasked with a specific anti-piracy mandate. Nor will they sail as far south as the Indian Ocean off Somalia's coast, where we will be operating. For the most part, we'll be on our own.

I sink happily into my chair, its rough grey fabric lined with pillows to ease the long hours at my desk. For the first time, I realize that my time ashore has rejuvenated me. I may not be post-three-weeks-vacation rejuvenated, but having time off has made me interested in my job again. I'm lucky to be here. For the first time since the captain's fateful pipe, excitement about the new mission has overtaken the feeling of being overwhelmed. I pluck a recent report on the Suez Canal from the pile of reports on my desk, and begin to read.

~

Luc, a MARS officer in his mid-twenties, leads his first workout on the flight deck that evening. He faces us, skinny white legs planted wide apart on the grey non-slip surface, bracing his body against the gentle rolling of the sea beneath us. Ten officers clad in an eclectic assortment of gym gear are lined up behind a row of mats set at the centre of the deck. I'm near the end, beside Billy and Kate. TiFou and Marcus are here, too. Annette, the shipboard air controller who has obtained official sanction to date Luc, stands at the far end.

It's fast becoming imperative for me to find an hour to work out once the busiest part of the day is past. Most days I head to the well-used cardio machines that are scattered throughout the ship — the treadmill in the flats outside my mess, the stationary bike in the ops room flats, or the stair-master in the hangar — but after a workday cloistered with my computer in the corner of the communications control room, the social aspect of group workouts is appealing.

Better yet, they're held outside, at the time of day that is the essence of summer dusk perfection. Beyond Luc, the sun hangs large and low over the horizon and casts a comforting fire-glow on the few scattered clouds. The steady wind blowing across the water is warm against my bare legs and has already dissipated the worst of the day's heat, while the ship slowly rocks over tiny swells. Even the drone of the ship's engines fails to detract from this setting.

"Okay, today we're going to work on abs and upper body, with some cardio thrown in," shouts Luc in rapid, French-accented English, breaking into my reverie.

I expect a gentle start for the first session. But immediately Luc has us on our backs, driving our legs toward the darkening sky in long sets of abdominal thrusts. And then we shift into prolonged sets of pushups that eventually, to my shame, have me on my knees and finally flat on my stomach, unable to raise my leaden torso even one more time.

"Come on, people! Drive your bodies!" Luc is yelling at us now, serious, his usual toothy smile in hiding as he issues commands. I laugh out loud, almost a guffaw; his ardour surprises me so. In between sets, Kate and I exchange amused glances.

And it keeps me going. I gradually float sideways across the deck as I speed-skip above the easy swell, connecting solidly with the surface with each descent. Then we immediately roll into gut-wrenching crunches, and finally launch ourselves, in succession, onto the steel ladder that rises up the outside of the hangar and serves as a makeshift chin-up bar. Marcus, waiting his turn behind me, spots me as I struggle to pull myself up.

By the time the sun is sinking into the sea, the group of us are splayed flat out on our darkening mats, rapid breaths slowing but now drained of the will to move. At least I am. Billy, a sedate starfish to my right, glances over at my silhouette.

"High-five?" he offers, stretching his hand feebly toward me.

"Sorry, I can't move. I'm all done."

When we peel ourselves off the mat a quarter-hour later, I recognize that, despite the physical exhaustion, I feel amazing; my body is vital, my mind clear — and I haven't thought about work for forty-five minutes.

The metal latch of the heavy watertight door, greasy in my palm, slides stiffly to the open position. I push the door open and latch it behind me before descending the ladder into the darkness, illuminated by an occasional red light, of the ship below.

"I think we should keep women off the bridge during the canal transit," says Jeff. "Just to avoid potential problems." The heads and chiefs of department, and a few additions like me, are facing one another on the settees that encircle the lounge portion of the wardroom. Jeff sits next to the XO, who is directing this meeting on the conduct of our canal transit.

"We're not going to change society here," he continues in a low voice. "I'm not comfortable putting our female sailors in the position of possibly being harassed, just for doing their job."

He's talking about dealing with the pilots who work for the Egyptian Suez Canal Authority and who, one at a time, will be on the ship for the entire transit. It's well-known that in Egyptian society, as in most countries of the Middle East, women do not enjoy equal opportunity with men. Women are certainly not found on the bridge of an Egyptian warship. But the XO cuts Jeff off without missing a beat. "No, we're not doing that," she asserts in clipped tones, her weary eyes pinning him. "We are a sovereign Canadian ship, and this is how we do things. We're not going to make our female sailors second-rate just because things are done differently here."

She eagle-eyes us around the room now. "This is an opportunity to introduce them to Canadian culture," she says. "If they don't like women on the bridge, too bad. We'll just make sure the women who are up there understand the context we're working in." I keep my eyes fixed on the XO's blond head, notebook-clutching hands motionless in my lap. In this moment she is my hero. Jeff is nodding now too, clearly converted by the XO's passionate stand.

"Right," says the XO. Then turning to Jean on her other side, she asks, "Do we have enough cartons of cigarettes to give to the pilots?"

~

It's late the next night when we arrive at the anchorage area where ships await entrance to the Suez Canal. Before heading to my rack I slip through

the dark ship and onto the darker bridge, my night vision ruined by working under the communications control room's fluorescent lights. There's a
full bridge watch on, but their black silhouettes are barely distinguishable
from those of the box-like equipment modules spread over the bridge.
A VHF radio, tuned to emergency Channel 16, crackles to life amidst the
silence, and a guttural-voiced man utters words in a foreign tongue before
static obliterates him. Sneaking behind the helmsman's station, I emerge
onto the bridge wing to be met by refreshingly cool wind.

The lights of Port Said, the Egyptian community that marks the
northern entrance to the canal, twinkle in the distance. Several other
ships display navigation lights that reveal their proximity to us in the
anchorage area. Like us, they are awaiting the formation of the next
day's first southbound convoy through the canal in the early hours of
the morning. Otherwise, I see only black night.

I squint into it anyway, hands light on the railing. I'm trying to reconcile where we are with the imagery — always vague enough to retain
its romantic charm — that my mind unfailingly conjures of Egypt and
of the canal itself. I want to anchor the ship in time and space so as
to gain a full appreciation for where we are: in the Mediterranean Sea
just north of Egypt at the entrance to one of the world's most famous
manmade waterways. We are at the setting of the Suez Crisis, the 1956
war that pitted Britain, France, and Israel against Egypt and resulted in
the formation of the United Nations Emergency Force, the brainchild
of Canadian politician Lester B. Pearson, that paved the way for future
UN peacekeeping.

I don't emerge often enough into the outside world. It's so easy to
become immersed below decks, nearly forgetting that the progress we
follow on radar and charts down there is a mere reflection of the open-
air reality that our ship is sailing through at that moment. Even though
all I have to go on now is distant lights in a dark night, I want to inhabit
that reality. Nearly 10 percent of world sea trade passes through this
waterway connecting Europe with Asia. More than eighteen thousand
ships passed through it last year. I want to capture this moment, but
already it's sliding away.

And continuing with this time-and-space game: not far to the northeast, in Israel, is Scott. I gaze into inky blackness in that direction and

exhale deeply. That he is so close is more difficult to fathom than the reality of the Suez Canal. Given the little contact we have on our respective deployments, we might as well still be half a world apart.

I consider staying up all night to witness our entrance to the canal itself. I did that once before, when my former ship transited the Panama Canal overnight. All that remains of that decade-old memory now is a blurry image of dark local men working the lines on the ship's deck underneath harsh yellow light as we passed through the different locks. My youthful curiosity now diluted by age, I hit my rack in pursuit of a clear head for the next day's canal transit.

~

"Ah, Int. I see you've decided to join us," Jeff deadpans as I emerge, squinting, onto the bridge the next morning. In stark contrast to the night before, the bridge is an affront of disorienting, glaring-white brightness whose source I can't immediately discern.

"Good morning to you, too," I retort grumpily. I'm only now shedding my grogginess as I gulp back a silver travel mug of bad coffee. And then, stupidly, I ask, "Why's it so bright?"

"Oh, I'm sorry. I thought you were in intelligence or something. Because we're in the desert!" He's a little giddy, playing with me. I peer at him more closely. His eyes are glazed, underlined by swollen pockets.

"You've been up all night, haven't you?"

"Jennifer, an officer's job is never done."

It's rare to get a straight answer from Jeff about the amount of work he does. As combat officer, he's responsible for ensuring that operations unfold, wherever possible, as planned — or for coming up with plan B when the first plan fails. Some degree of sleep deprivation is standard for MARS officers. They typically stand watch at odd hours or are overloaded with work, or both. They're expected to perform just the same.

The CO sits in the elevated captain's chair port side forward. From the rear, I monitor the movements of his gold-encrusted black ball cap as he alternates scanning through the windows and then zooming in on objects of interest with the high-powered camera, its display mounted in front of him. I know without asking that he too has been here all night.

People are everywhere on the bridge — standing at windows with binoculars glued to their faces, leaning against radar consoles with bored expressions, sitting at the helm, the communications desk, on top of the box storing helmets and flak jackets for the bridge watch. Some are just interested onlookers, but, in addition to the usual bridge watch of seven, extra crew are providing the increased surveillance required for transit through narrow or hazardous waterways.

The Suez Canal is definitely that. A mere three hundred metres wide at its narrowest point, the canal allows only a single lane for most of its 192-kilometre length. This means that ships passing through are constrained in the speed of their transit and their ability to manoeuvre, making them easier targets for terrorists than they would be in less confined waterways.

Ship security measures here have been especially stringent since 2000, when Al Qaeda successfully carried out a suicide attack on the naval destroyer USS *Cole* while it was anchored in the Yemeni port of Aden. A small craft laden with explosives approached the ship and detonated, killing seventeen sailors. The incident highlighted the capacity of Al Qaeda and other groups to carry out acts of maritime terrorism and the heightened requirement for ships to protect themselves.

I venture onto the starboard bridge wing and a wall of uncompromising heat slams into me, almost driving me back into the bridge. Until now the baby's breath–gentle breeze rolling off the Mediterranean has kept us cool while at sea. It's as if we've crossed an invisible climate-change boundary. Suddenly the heat of the densely still air is stark, untempered by wind, and the sun is blindingly white as it reflects off the long sandy banks stretching on either side of us. Mere hours have passed since we entered the canal, but everything is already changed. A giant WELCOME TO EGYPT sign in enormous green letters sprawls hospitably along one gleaming bank before a backdrop of straggly palm trees. Ugly squat buildings — security and military installations offering Egyptian security, beefed up in light of the terrorism threat — slide by us at staggered intervals on both sides. Khaki-uniformed personnel, miniatures from this distance, patrol with stick rifles.

Petty Officer, 1st Class Tremblay, the ship's information management director, leans his tall, slim figure against the railing as he stares out at the western bank.

"Hey, PO," I say, holding a hand in front of my face against sun's rays penetrating my ball cap. "Ready to turn over?"

"Good morning, ma'am," he replies in a lilting French accent. He turns his handsome silver head toward me and reveals a delightful ivory smile under a salt-and-pepper moustache. His movements, all grace and elegance, are often complemented by an authentic belly laugh.

"We can turn over if you want," he says, shrugging.

As the sole information management director on board, he's used to being a one-man show, often standing eighteen-hour shifts in the ops room. But for the Suez transit we will share watches, recording details of any incidents that occur and information on the canal transit that hasn't already been captured in military documentation.

"There's not much to turn over," he says. "This is where we are." He points to a spot on the map he holds, about a third of the way through the canal. He removes a small digital camera from around his neck and hands it to me. "It's all yours." He gives me one of his prized smiles, then vanishes into the bridge.

I settle myself against the railing and glance around. Farther forward on the bridge wing stands the Egyptian pilot. He's recognizable by his uniform, its stark whiteness rivalling in dramatic effect the brilliance of the ubiquitous sand. His crisp white shirt is tucked into white walking shorts, leaving a few inches of dark skin peeking out above white socks that extend from spotless white shoes and reach just below the knees. It's white overload reminiscent of the unpopular naval whites, formal version of summer naval dress often likened to a vanilla ice cream cone. But while we're the ones sweltering in dark, heavy uniforms clearly not intended for this climate, the pilot maintains an effortless cool.

The Egyptian Suez Canal Authority requires that all ships transiting the canal carry a local pilot to assist in navigating the waters. At the requisite eight knots, a canal transit typically takes between eleven and sixteen hours and requires four pilots for different stages of the journey. The first pilot boarded during the night to supervise the movement of our southbound convoy from the anchorage area to the entrance of the canal at Port Said.

This pilot is the second to have embarked. A short man in his late forties, he's engaged in conversation with a female leading seaman, an attractive brunette posted on the bridge as an extra lookout. He smiles at her warmly as I watch his lips move in silent monologue. From the repeated shifts of her gaze from the water and back to the pilot, it's clear that she's struggling to balance her attention so as not to offend him while remaining focused on her job.

According to wardroom gossip, this pilot has paid close attention to all the women he's encountered on board. Female presence on ships passing through the canal would be a relative novelty for him, the overwhelming majority of crew on both military and merchant vessels, from all nations, being men. Many navies do not employ women on board ship at all.

But the man is doing his job, helping to identify the assortment of small boats that approach our ship: police boats, boats with vendors selling cigarettes and Egyptian souvenirs, and fishing vessels that, on occasion, approach slightly too close for comfort. Near the shoreline, narrow wooden boats provide small-scale transport for people and goods from point to point along the canal. At several places on our route children splash and play in shallow waters close to shore. A train on the west bank emerges from the sand, chugging southbound with sluggish determination. The canal is not merely a sanitized conduit of international commerce, but also a local stomping ground where people live, play, and earn a living by whatever means they can.

A small fishing skiff, nets folded on deck, approaches close enough to draw the attention of the bridge watch, then, as if realizing their mistake, quickly draws away.

Watching the skiff and its five occupants, I'm reminded of the presumed origins of Somali piracy in the protection of local fishing grounds. Illegal fishing proliferated off the country's coast in the 1990s in the wake of the overthrow of Siad Barre, Somalia's long-serving military dictator. In the absence of a functioning government with the capability of patrolling the Exclusive Economic Zone in Somalia's territorial waters, foreign fishing trawlers illegally fished those waters, depleting stocks, dumping waste, and earning the wrath of Somalis who earned their livelihood from fishing. Some Somali fishermen took it upon themselves to drive off these foreign trawlers in self-defence, organizing into groups like the "Somali Marines" out of Harardheere, a town along Somalia's central coast. The fishermen would threaten the foreign trawlers with rocket-propelled grenades and AK-47s, then demand a ransom for the vessels and crew. Eventually, the fishermen-turned-pirates realized that it was less dangerous and more lucrative to target the unarmed commercial ships that regularly passed near their fishing grounds. From there, piracy escalated into what it is today.[2]

By the time I refocus my gaze on the scene around us we are well past the fishing vessel. Glancing into the bridge, shady and cool in contrast to the scorching bridge wing, I make out a white-clad figure beside the officer of the watch — a new pilot, this one taller and lankier than the last. Later I'll learn that this new pilot spoke inappropriately, in a condescending and aggressive manner, to the women working on the bridge. There's little the team can do beyond holding their ground and keeping women on the bridge, but Jeff's point in the first briefing was obviously well taken.

Late in the morning we sail into Great Bitter Lake. In this enormous body of salt water, along with the other ships of the southbound convoy, we anchor in our assigned spot well clear of the transit area. This will allow the northbound convoy of vessels that entered the canal from the Red Sea side to bypass us and enter the narrow section we have just exited.

A container ship twice our length is anchored a fair distance to our south. The decks are piled six high with truck-size containers in various hues of red and green. She looks impossibly top-heavy, as if she could topple with the weight of the containers rising almost the height of the bridge that caps the white superstructure. I know she's stable, engineered to withstand most seas fully laden, but an underlying vulnerability to her belies the ship's sheer enormity. Like us, she is preparing to transit the Red Sea, then run the gauntlet of the Gulf of Aden.

After only a few hours in Great Bitter Lake, we weigh anchor and continue our voyage, distantly trailing the ship ahead of us in the convoy. By mid-afternoon we exit the canal. The waters around us widen into the Gulf of Suez and a warm wind breaks the back of the searing canal heat that we leave in our wake. Sailing south, we're sandwiched between kilometres of sand on either side: the Sinai Desert, lying hot and flat to our left, and the Eastern Desert, with its undulating hills rising into scorched, barren mountains to our right.

Somali Coast, June 1999

Mohammed and Abdi haul the *houri*, their uncle's tiny fishing boat, and its weighty catch ashore. It's been a long series of days at sea, the young men returning salt-speckled at the end of each day, their skin parched from the sun's glare.

Their uncle Asad is a hard taskmaster. Early each morning, after prayers, as the sun is rising, Abdi and Mohammed and Asad's two sons rise in Asad's modest tin-roofed house and hurriedly drink the tea and *canjeero* prepared by Asad's wife, Fatima. Then they carry their nets and their daily rations and water down to Asad's two dilapidated houris that await them just offshore. Abdi and Mohammed cast nets and lines, and haul in tuna or mackerel, depending on the season, for long hours. They are never too far offshore, always able to see the reassuring stretch of sand that beckons them back at the end of each day. Back at that safe haven, they gut, salt, and dry their catch before carrying it to the market. His pay, when it comes, is small, based on what he and Mohammed have managed to catch and only after the heftier portion of the market price is diverted to Asad.

Abdi knows better than to complain though. He's learned a new trade, a new livelihood — something he didn't have before. His muscles ache at the end of each long day, and fishing is nearly all he has the energy for, but he is able to send money to his mother. His pay is not enough to cover the children's school fees, which seem always beyond reach, but at least they have food, are not malnourished as they were during the worst part of the war. And it's an honest living. His rifle is hidden securely beside his sleeping mat in Asad's house.

Occasionally, he and Mohammed spend time at the tea shops, lounging about with the other young men as they drink sweet tea and exchange stories. Most of them fish, too, so they often tell boastful stories about the size of the catch they brought in, competing loudly for the glory of hauling in the single biggest fish. There is also talk of the foreign fishing trawlers that have become more frequent around their waters in recent years, sophisticated vessels that dwarf their houris and skiffs. Some of the boys are certain that the catch is less abundant now. Then the talk, in respectful undertones now, will inevitably move on to a different subject, the young women who tend the market stalls a short distance away.

One in particular has caught Abdi's eye. On the few occasions he has glimpsed her selling fruit at her mother's stall, he cannot fail to notice the lovely oval of her face beneath her hijab, the warmth of her brown eyes, which she quickly averts, her elegant nose. She is a cousin of his friend Garaad, so he knows her name is Amal. But he knows better than to approach her. He's of marrying age, of course, but he has no money to take a wife or start a family. Still, after seeing her only a few times, it surprises him how often he thinks of Amal.

Vessels held by Somali pirates: *Yenegoa Ocean, Stella Maris*

CHAPTER 7

THE GULF OF ADEN

NAIROBI, Kenya (CNN) — Pirates have hijacked a Thai cargo
ship in the Gulf of Aden off the Somali coast, the Kenya Seafarers
Association said Thursday.[1]

— CNN, August 14, 2008

The ship slices through the Gulf of Suez, tropical waters that soon broaden
into the long, continental divide of the Red Sea. Bordering us on one side
is the russet, sand-blown escarpment that marks the edge of the Arabian
Peninsula and the beginning of Asia, beyond visual range from our position in the well-trafficked shipping lanes. On the sea's western side lie the
arid lands of Africa. Sudan, Eritrea, Djibouti. Western perceptions elicited
by these exotic names simplify, from this safe distance, the colourful
shades of local life that reside here, just over the horizon.

Commercial vessels conveying their goods between Europe and Asia
populate the Red Sea shipping lanes. Most of these Goliaths repeat their
routes, lingering in ports only for the brief time required to discharge or
take on cargo before moving on to the next. With little time for crew runs
ashore in this dirty, expensive business, the circuit has all the glamour of
a long-distance bus route. Fishing vessels of various origins and sizes and
states of disrepair are interspersed with cargo ships, passing through the
lanes to the fertile fishing grounds that abound in this area.

As our ship crosses the Red Sea, I bury myself in the windowless
communications control room, reading and preparing briefs under the
fluorescent lights that blaze eternal and meld day with night.

PO Tracey disappears down below for lunch, and I steal into his corner behind the equipment racks and log on to our shared computer. A group email from UK Maritime Trade Operations Centre (UKMTO) sits in my inbox. The Dubai-based organization acts as an interface between merchant shipping and military operations and keeps both updated about recent piracy activity. The centre is also the first point of contact for ships in the region reporting acts of piracy. I click on the email and my chest tightens.

"Shit."

I note down the details and hurry across to the captain's cabin. The outer door is hinged open, but a heavy fuchsia curtain obscures the interior from view. I reach a hand through the curtain and knock three times on the metal door.

"Captain, sir, Int!" I call out in a voice deliberately shrill, then step inside the truncated, weakly lit corridor. On one side is a tiny pantry. I peek inside and the captain's personal steward, a dark-haired boy in his early twenties, glances up from the tray of food he is preparing. He nods and inclines his head in the direction of the cabin.

"He's in there."

I thrust my hand through a second fuschia curtain at the end of the corridor and knock on an interior door.

"Sir?"

"Yes, come in," comes the brusque voice.

I step through the door, hovering halfway between doorway and dining table where the captain sits before an untouched plate of lasagne. Behind him, a framed photograph of a blond preteen girl who I presume to be his daughter sits atop a dark wood cabinet. Just beyond is a small sitting area with a leather loveseat and matching armchair where he occasionally invites me to brief. Jeff is usually in attendance on those occasions, when the captain muses over the larger significance of the events I report and seems to relish the company. I sometimes think he must be lonely in his spacious cabin, which also serves as his solitary dining room. Today, though, he stares straight ahead, barely acknowledging my presence. It must have been a stressful or tiring one. Or perhaps, like the rest of us, things in his life outside of work are impacting his mood. Finally he looks up, unsmiling eyes weary behind his wire rims. I take a deep breath.

"Sir, another vessel, MV *Thor Star*, has just been hijacked in the Gulf of Aden, about a hundred miles off the Yemeni coast."

The captain stares at me blankly. Almost imperceptibly, he begins a slow shake of his head.

"*Thor Star* was transiting from Southeast Asia carrying timber when she came under heavy fire by pirates," I continue, glancing down at a few scrawled notes. "The vessel transmitted a distress signal before the pirates boarded and took the ship hostage, along with her twenty-eight Thai crew. The pirates are likely taking the ship to Eyl, off the east coast, like the others."[2]

I glance up. The captain gazes straight ahead, lips pressed tightly together.

"Those are all the details we have so far, sir."

"Thank you," he says curtly, his eyes seeming worried about more than just the piracy.

I take my cue and exit his cabin. Being captain of a warship and able to do nothing must grate. But even if it was within our mandate to go chasing pirates, there would be nothing we could do for *Thor Star*, now that her crew's lives are in the hands of pirates.

∽

The ship is approaching the Strait of Bab el Mandeb, Arabic for "Gate of Tears" — so named for the precarious navigation through the narrow chokepoint.[3] Only thirty-two kilometres wide and divided into two channels by a small Yemeni island, the strait connects the Red Sea to the now-notorious Gulf of Aden.

Extra watch personnel, required for the hazardous passage, fill the bridge and drive me onto the starboard bridge wing for the last section of the pass. As the lookout before me scans the horizon with chunky binoculars, we pass through the wider western channel, sandwiched between the sunburned rocklands of Djibouti and Yemen's Perim Island. Then we are through, and into pirate territory.

I lean against the railing and into the vigorous wind that blows off the gulf. My hand shades my eyes against a late-afternoon sun only now beginning to soften, and I squint into the distance. Around us, as far as the eye can see, is only rippled dark sea, unblemished by tiny fishing skiffs or supertankers. High seas drama in these benign-looking waters is difficult to imagine.

"Officer of the watch, sir!" calls the lookout, taking one step into the open bridge door, the leading seaman's face half-obscured by aviator sunglasses.

"Officer of the watch!" says a figure in the centre of the bridge, only a dark silhouette against the glare outside.

"Oil tanker bearing green four-five on the horizon, moving left to right."

"Got it. Thank you."

God, he has good eyes. I haven't seen a thing. But then the lookout has binoculars, and plenty of practise scanning the waters. On windy days like today, when small boats could easily disappear from view as they dip into troughs of the swells, good lookouts more than earn their keep.

On average, sixty ships cross the Gulf of Aden, nicknamed "Pirate Alley," each day. This waterway is vital for shipping, particularly for the export of the Persian Gulf oil that is transported in tankers to regional refineries or through the Suez Canal to the European market. So far this year, pirates have commandeered thirteen vessels passing through the Gulf of Aden on Somalia's east coast. Most were eventually released after ransoms were paid. But pirates still hold at least three ships and a few dozen crew near their strongholds off Somalia's north and east coasts.

Recent reports of both successful and failed attacks provide insight into deceptively simple pirate tactics. The pirates typically travel in groups of two or more skiffs. Powerful outboard motors fitted to these small boats allow them to chase commercial vessels targeted for capture. Slow-moving vessels and those with low freeboard — the distance between the deck and the water-line — are the most vulnerable targets, the easiest for these agile young men to scramble aboard. They usually approach the vessels at high speed from one or both sides, then often fire at the bridge with AK-47 machine guns or even rocket-propelled grenades (RPGs) to intimidate the crew into halting the vessel. Impressive boat-handling skills enable pirates to manoeuvre their boat alongside or astern of the ship, then use grappling hooks or ladders to clamber up the side and board even as the ship travels at high speed.

Somali pirates have been especially active this year, attacking vessels not only in the Gulf of Aden but also off Somalia's east coast, most notably near Mogadishu, where we'll be operating.

Piracy doesn't pose a significant danger to us as we sail through the Gulf of Aden. It's one thing for pirates to attack unarmed commercial vessels, and it's quite another — unusual and unwise — to attack a heavily armed warship. Likely of greater concern to the captain is ensuring that we are as prepared as possible to carry out our high-profile World Food Programme escort mission.

With this in mind we have arranged to rendezvous with our sister ship, HMCS *Calgary*, in the Gulf of Aden. *Calgary* is en route to the Red Sea to continue patrols as part of a multinational task force. It will be useful to connect with my counterpart on board, but I find myself wishing we were meeting HMCS *Iroquois*, still hundreds of kilometres away in the Arabian Gulf, instead. The warm presence and professional advice of Michèle, my friend from home, would be reassuring.

From my desk, I email her to see how she has been in the few months since we last met. Her instantaneous, emotional reply paralyzes me in my seat. It's about the death only a few weeks ago of her mother, who was only in her late fifties but had been chronically ill. My heart clenches. Michèle was very close to her, and had been granted compassionate leave from the ship when her mother was in hospital. They spent a few weeks together. Her mother's health had seemed to improve, but on Michèle's long trip back to the Arabian Gulf, to rejoin the ship, she passed away. The ship's padre met Michèle in Dubai and broke the devastating news. At the same time, he informed her that the commodore had already decided that she would not be permitted to return home for the funeral, to grieve with her family. The padre had fought for her, but had lost. Operational requirements. The ship apparently could not do without her.

When I finish reading Michèle's email, I continue to stare dumbly at the words on the screen. My sadness has turned to anger, an expanding, broiling mass in my stomach that rises to my chest as I absorb the full impact of what she has told me.

How could they not let her go to the funeral? How could they deny her the time to grieve her mother, the closest person in the world to her? What could they possibly gain by keeping her there?

Jeff wanders into the communications control room, his eyes taking in my incensed expression as I glare at the screen.

"God, what's wrong with you?"

For a moment I am unable to speak. My words, when I finally allow them to escape, are furious.

"My friend Michèle's mother passed away," comes my spluttering response, "and *Iroquois* wouldn't let her return home for the funeral. Can you believe that? I am *so* angry."

"I can tell," comes his measured response. His eyes hold my own, willing me to be calm. "I'm not sure what their reasoning would be. Prioritizing the mission, I'm assuming."

On our ship, several crew members have already been flown home for compassionate reasons, most less serious than the death of a parent. I don't know how Michèle can even function on board in the immediate aftermath of such a loss. From her email, it seems that she's keeping it together. Barely. She must be stronger than I am. I think of my own mother, of her practical wisdom and support on which I depend. In Michèle's situation, I might have gone AWOL, sunk into a deep depression, been unable to work. Michèle does none of these things. She continues to carry out her tasks, to reach out to the people around her — mere strangers a few months ago — for support when she needs it. Still. I know that hot anger has piled on top of her grief, and will long continue its slow burn.

I wish I could see her. But while we are finally in the same region of the world, Michèle and I remain hundreds of kilometres apart, stranded on our respective islands. The military system, to which she has given so much, will never be able to compensate for the way it has let her down.

~

HMCS *Calgary* has been sailing in the Arabian Gulf since July. Because this is the first time the Canadian Navy has conducted an escort mission in this particular threat environment, the tactical details of how it will be carried out are still under development, their effectiveness untested.

When we meet up with *Calgary*, the practice scenario is simple:[4] *Calgary* plays the role of a World Food Programme–contracted vessel carrying food aid that *Ville de Québec* is escorting. Our rigid-hulled inflatable boat (RHIB) loads the eight-person *Ville de Québec* security team that will provide security for the escorted vessel on board *Calgary*. Then the two ships steam through the lanes in escort formation, *Ville de Québec* abeam of *Calgary*, two RHIBs acting as unidentified small boats — presumed to be pirates in this scenario — closing fast on the two ships.

"Bearing two-seven-zero, range four thousand yards, two small visual contacts closing, sir,"[5] the officer of the watch reports to the captain on the bridge. The captain orders him to issue verbal warnings to the boats over a loudspeaker, which he does, but they continue to close in. The simulated warnings escalate while *Ville de Québec* and *Calgary* manoeuvre erratically, in zigzag patterns — evasive action intended to prevent the small boats from approaching too closely or boarding the vessels. Throughout these events, *Ville de Québec*'s bridge is in constant contact with the security team leader on board *Calgary* via handheld VHF radios. He, in turn, provides direction to the master and crew of the simulated commercial vessel we are escorting.

During the three-hour window in which we are in close proximity to *Calgary*, we leverage the other crew's regional maritime expertise, based on their past three months operating in this region, to improve our situational awareness of these waters. Their Ops team is familiar with fishing and shipping patterns and the surprising frequency of people-smuggling operations across the Gulf of Aden, in which thousands of Somalis and Ethiopians risk their lives each year in dilapidated boats to reach Yemen, itself a very poor country, in hopes of finding a better life.

A small number of crew from *Ville de Québec* and *Calgary* are chosen to "cross-deck" via helicopter to the other vessel. A crew member from *Calgary* who has come over on their helo later finds me in the communications control room and hands me a package. It's from Derek, their intelligence officer whom I know vaguely from the West Coast. The slim stack of CDs I pull out are loaded with useful information about the region. The package reminds me that I'm part of a larger team outside of the ship. As we continue our cruise through Pirate Alley's deceptively calm waters, I'm grateful for it.

Somali Coast, September 2000

Things are looking up for his Uncle Asad. With years of fishing proceeds and profit from selling his two houris, the enterprising man has managed to purchase a single skiff, twice as long as his traditional fishing boats and, with an outboard motor on its stern, countless times as fast. Now, it is the five of them — Asad, his two sons, Mohammed, and Abdi — who crew the speedy boat, which enables them to expand their fishing grounds and double their catch. But while Asad profits, Abdi's pay remains dismally low.

There have been other changes in the village, too. Some of the fishing skiffs like theirs, with powerful outboard motors, are going out armed with rifles. This is not a surprise in itself — weapons are everywhere here. But now the skiffs sometimes return at the end of the day with not only a good catch but also with additional money for the fishermen to spend in the village market and food stalls, purchasing extra khat from the vendors. On the main street can be heard quiet references to foreign fishing vessels from as far afield as Korea and Spain, of unofficial fines levied against them by local fishermen for illegally fishing Somali waters. Why shouldn't fishermen take curtailing this activity into their own hands, Abdi has heard queried, when there are no Somali authorities to do it? Somebody has to protect their fishing grounds; these trawlers are depleting their fish stock by the day. Soon there will be none left for them.

Abdi understands this reasoning. How can he not? He himself has seen the big boats out there, hauling in huge quantities of catch that should be theirs. What gives them the right to fish in Somali waters? Still, it doesn't seem right to demand compensation at the point of a rifle. That reminds him too much of the worst days of the war in Baladweyne, when he was still a child. Mohammed and he argue about this at times, as his practical friend sees nothing wrong with retaking what he claims is theirs in the first place. But Abdi wants no part in it. His pay is small, but it supports his family. And it's honest.

Vessels held by Somali pirates: *Yenegoa Ocean, Stella Maris, Thor Star*

CHAPTER 8

ROUGH SEAS

The sailors were abducted with their yacht on 28th June 2008 while on their way through the Gulf of Aden and later were carried off into remote hideouts within the Cal Madow mountains in Northern Somalia. They were freed only on 9th August 2008 after a lengthy ordeal, during which they had to experience mock executions and other torture, and after a substantial ransom payment.[1]

— *Sail-World*, October 19, 2009

The seas become steadily rougher as we complete our eastward voyage through the Gulf of Aden. When our ship alters course to sail south around the Horn of Africa, the peninsula that juts into the Arabian Sea, there is still no reprieve from the growing swells. We've been lucky on this deployment: except for a day of stormy Atlantic seas, the weather has been fair since leaving Halifax. But this morning's weather report, warning of high winds and waves, has sent sailors hurrying to sick bay to collect their dose of Bonamine, the favoured motion sickness medication.

Inclement weather is typical of the summer monsoon that stretches from the Indian Ocean's southern reaches north to the waters around the Horn. With summer's end approaching, the monsoon season will soon be over but, for now, strong westerlies whip up waves that our ship meets head-on at regular intervals, forcing us to climb up, up, up walls of towering water before gliding down the other side. Harder to bear is the erratic pounding of swells that strike us sideways at awkward angles, causing the ship's steel hull to shudder violently. Inside, we are thrown against bulkheads if caught unprepared, fumbling for reliable handholds as we stumble through narrow passages and down ladders, vigilant to a sudden strike that might vault us through the air. The bridge watch-keepers avoid these sideways seas when they can by altering our heading, but at times our course leaves them little choice.

Such is the sea we're stuck with today. I'm sunk into my chair that is secured by a rope to the desk, itself bolted fast to the deck with large steel screws. I stare at my computer screen, willing myself to lock onto the words playing erratically across it. I make little progress in preparing my evening brief. A deep throbbing begins at the back of my skull and creeps forward until my whole head pounds in its search for equilibrium amidst the ship's constant movement.

The high seas affect others the same way: the naval communicators on watch move sluggishly or not at all, listless as zombies at their stations. They do the bare essentials of their jobs. The usual chatter is absent. Premium Plus cracker packets are strewn throughout the space within ready reach, displacing Master Seaman Davis's ubiquitous candy. Only PO Tracey, lodged in his makeshift cubicle behind the equipment racks and seemingly immune to seasickness, is cheerful and talkative.

"Hey, ma'am, not feeling too well? You gotta love this — it's what it's all about!" His voice brims with unfeigned enthusiasm. He laughs good-naturedly as the ship shudders from another hard-hitting breaker.

"It's great," I mutter and lay my head heavily on my desk.

The rest of the communications control room was neatly secured for sea well before it got rough, equipment strapped down to fixed surfaces or stuffed into drawers. But organization isn't my strong suit; papers and supplies now sprawl in tumbled heaps across my desk and spill onto the floor.

"Goddamn it!" I growl as a swell flips my lidded coffee mug to the floor, spilling the contents. I'm setting a bad, un-officer-like example, but I feel too sick to care. I heave myself to my feet and grab a handful of tissues from Master Seaman Davis's desk to sop up the cold coffee.

I stumble toward the exit as another wave strikes, unbalancing me. I fight the leaden door to get into the flats — the door fights back — and then vault down the ladder with both hands gripping the railing, my feet hovering in mid-air for most of the descent. I fail to coordinate my progress through the flats with the sea's undulations and make hard, unanticipated contact with the bulkhead.

I finally stagger into the wardroom. The faces of the few officers present are drawn. Slumped into the settees, they gaze absently at nothing. The constant struggle against the movement of the ship has worn everyone down.

Everyone, that is, except Manny, who holds court with an audience of two. Haggard with fatigue, they appear decidedly uninterested in what he's saying, so he targets me as I flop down on one of the couches as it begins a slow slide across the room.

"Hey, Jen, how's it going? Are you seasick?" He guffaws. "You're not looking too good."

He spots the crackers in my hand, the only food I'm sure I can keep down.

"Ah, I see you're onto the Premium Plus. Don't have much of an appetite?" His gleaming grin trumpets how fantastic he feels. I narrow my eyes.

At that moment Marcus walks in. His usual purposeful stride is unaffected by the ship's rocking, but his tanned face is rigid and he's as unsmiling as the rest of us. He gets a glass of water from the dispenser in the far corner and then comes to sit beside me.

"This is so lame," he says in his low drawl, his soft brown eyes flicking over my white face. "Why would anyone choose to go to sea? How can anyone enjoy this crap?"

It's hard to disagree. I don't dislike being at sea the way he does, but bobbing virtually imprisoned in a tin can in the middle of the ocean does strike me as an absurd way to live — if we forget why we're here.

"Where's Kevin?" I ask. "I haven't seen him all morning."

"He's in his rack, sleeping."

"Right. I guess you can't fly in these conditions. Lucky Kevin." I'm envious. "Why aren't you in your rack?"

"I would be if I could. But I have some administration to do." He pauses. "I wouldn't be able to sleep in this anyways. I'd fall out of my rack — and it's a long way down from the top one."

Just then Kate enters the wardroom. She moves more slowly than usual, and when she sits down beside me I can see that her brown eyes look weary, their shine diminished.

I manage a wan smile in her direction. "How are you feeling, Kate? Faring better than the rest of us?"

She smiles back. "I'm doing okay. It wouldn't feel like going to sea if we didn't have at least a few days like this!"

Hands-to-dinner is piped and the first round of officers sits down to eat. Those going on watch eat first, and quickly, to make room for the rest. I wait until a seat is vacated before sitting down. Bland food seems like a safe bet. Big swells slide our chairs together in cacophonic crashes. Despite the rubber mats designed to hold our dinnerware in place, the dangerous tilt of the table dumps food off plates. The faces around the table are clearly annoyed. Only Billy, placidly eating a full dinner across from me, appears unperturbed.

Whatever the state of the sea or the health of the crew, the standing of watches continues. So too does the evening operations brief. Heads of department brief the CO daily on facets of operational planning. The critical elements — supply of food, material, and personnel; status of engineering equipment and combat systems; training readiness — enable the ship to function smoothly and operations to continue as projected. Planning for the escorts is the central component of this evening's brief.

The operations room is crowded when I arrive, as it is for most evening briefs. Luminescent computer and radar screens cram the perpetually dark space. Small lamps placed strategically around the room illuminate only the essentials: a ship recognition book, a keyboard connecting us through online chats with Ottawa, and a daily situation report from the other ships of Task Force Arabian Sea.

"*Excusez-moi, excusez-moi,*" I mutter, squeezing past the shadowy bodies crowding the narrow passage between the equipment. About a third of the people here are on watch, monitoring the computer and equipment terminals lining the perimeter of the room. The senior watch-keepers sit at a central island of terminals. Some, like Serge, the operations room officer in charge of the watch, monitor multiple computer screens.

Another third of the attendees are there voluntarily, eager for the latest update on mission planning. They fill the standing room within hearing range of the speakers.

The last third are those with speaking parts. I line up with the other briefers, behind Jeff's tall figure.

"Got something interesting for us today, Int?" asks Jeff, watching me expectantly. A slight smile plays across his face.

"The usual. Just going over some recent hijackings and attacks," I reply nonchalantly. Then I'm struck by the absurdity of what I've said. It appears suddenly obscene that acts of piracy now seem almost commonplace in my mind.

The low hum of voices steadily rises as we await the captain's arrival. An angry voice to my right pierces the din.

"Keep the noise down!" barks Master Seaman Barton, the ops room supervisor, his moustached mouth red and menacing. "This is an operations room, not a singles bar!"

A few people titter at this, but his aggression douses the chatter like water on hot coals. Maintaining discipline and decorum in the ops room is his job, and there is deliberate jest in his harshness. Still, this evening his yelling is like fingernails on a chalkboard.

Seconds later, the captain enters.

"*Ville de Québec!*" hollers the coxswain from his perch by the door, snapping us to attention.

"*Bonsoir tout le monde. Reposez, s'il vous plaît.* Relax please." The CO strides smoothly across the room — a task in these seas — and takes his seat next to the XO and coxswain.

For the next fifteen minutes, the slides flick past and the briefers drone on, their words indistinguishable to me as I focus solely on keeping the contents of my stomach down. Beside me, Jeff seems impervious to the ship's constant roll. Occasionally he glances over at my pale face and nudges my foot with his boot, and I smile wanly back at him.

It's Jeff's turn.

"Sir, after consultation with our World Food Programme contact, we have a preliminary escort schedule," he states in a confident monotone. "Our first escort is scheduled for August 19. We will rendezvous with MV *Abdul Rahman* in Mombasa and escort them to Mogadishu.

"We will then return to Mombasa and escort MV *Zang Za San Chong Nyon Ho,*" — he mangles the Korean name and offers a self-deprecating smile — "hereafter known as *Zang Za*, to Mogadishu."

I'm up next. I take my place in front of the captain, legs braced wide apart.

"Good evening, sir," I begin, my body swaying with each roll of the ship. Behind me, a visual representation of the waters around Somalia, marked with the most recent pirate incidents, flashes up on the screen of my PowerPoint presentation. "I'd like to give a brief account of recent hijackings and attacks, to get everyone up to speed."

"A few weeks ago, on July 25, the Japanese-owned bulk carrier MV *Stella Maris*, en route to the Suez Canal, was hijacked by heavily armed pirates north of the port of Caluula, at Somalia's northeastern tip." I use a laser pointer to indicate the position. "Officers on the ship's bridge alerted UKMTO Dubai via satellite communications that pirates were on board, repeating the alert '*Stella Maris* pirates on board' three times before the line went dead.[2]

"The ship, with its crew of twenty-one Filipinos, was forced to steer south down the east coast of Somalia and anchor near Eyl, the coastal town that serves as the main pirate stronghold in Puntland. The ransom demanded by the pirates, negotiations for which are ongoing, is reported to be in the millions of dollars.

"Last week, pirates hijacked Nigerian tug MT *Yenegoa Ocean* along with her ten-person Nigerian crew in the Gulf of Aden. They're demanding a ransom. Now they've added MV *Thor Star* to their growing portfolio."

I glance at the captain before continuing, as his intelligent eyes study the chart of attacks.

"Of course, sir, the majority of attacks are unsuccessful. For example, the bulk carrier *Gem of Kilakarai* was attacked a week ago but the RPG fired by the pirates failed to detonate. Helicopters conveyed by USS *Peleliu* were then able to drive the pirate boats off.[3] Another fast-moving container ship was attacked a few weeks ago, but the vessel prepared fire hoses and moved erratically and were able to repel the pirates."

A comment comes from an anonymous voice in the back row: "In this sea state there shouldn't be any more pirate attacks for now."

Given the extent to which we're rolling in these seas, the assumption seems a fair one. Ours is a decent-sized ship, at just over 134 metres in length and weighing five thousand tonnes, and these swells toss us about as if we were a toy. The skiffs used by pirates are open boats measuring between six and eighteen metres. Pirates would take a much worse beating than us in rough seas. It's hard to believe they could operate in such conditions.

Still, the attacks of the past few weeks occurred during the summer monsoon season, when wind speed and wave height were consistent and considerable. Pirate attacks during the monsoon remain frighteningly regular and, as the crew of the three ships currently held would confirm, enjoy an alarming rate of success. Tackling stormy seas in their tiny boats, Somali pirates have proven themselves resilient and enterprising.

~

That night, as *Ville de Québec* continues her great rocky ride, I strap myself into bed using the belt attached to my rack — insurance against ending up on the floor tonight. I close my eyes and try to ignore the shudders and the jolting. At that moment, a heavy wave strikes us abeam and the ship begins a slow roll to starboard which continues until we are leaning far over, tilted at an unnatural angle. I grip my rack, my blood running cold, and hold my breath. *This is what capsizing feels like.* My imagination running wild, I envision the ship going right over, the chaos and terror that would ensue on a dark, rough night like this one. These ships are designed to take worse rolls than this, but I can't quite suppress the fear — *what the hell am I doing here anyway?* — that one of these rolls will be too much, and will take us too far over for the ship to recover.

Finally the ship rights herself and I exhale a long, slow breath.

On my way to fitful sleep, I think of the pirates, most of them young men. I imagine them in their small, open boats being tossed about on this same sea, under cover of darkness, far from home. I imagine their fear, as they drift and lie in wait for the next passing merchant ship that makes a viable target, fear of the sea and the anticipated attack as well. Something could go wrong, they might not see their families again, their children, their wives.

Do they take such risks because they think they have no choice but to do what they do? Is piracy the only way they can survive in a country of such limited opportunity? Maybe it is. Or maybe it's just plain greed that drives them, greed fuelled by the false courage supplied by khat, the narcotic so many of them chew.

I wonder if they think about the merchantmen who must sail those waters to earn *their* livelihood, many from poverty-stricken countries where work is also hard to come by. Those crewmen sail through here in full knowledge of the threat of pirate attack, hostage-taking, even death.

My musings about the pirates are only fantasy; we are a world apart. From the safe haven of Canada, or even this ship, I'm in no position to judge. I know so little about them. But I want to learn more, I want to understand.

Somali Coast, January 2003

His little village — Abdi's adopted home now — is changing. The changes began slowly, but within the past year they have become impossible to ignore. The fishing skiffs are still plentiful, anchored in the shallow waters just off their beautiful white beach or pulled up and turned over on the sand. And the crews of many of them still fish their clear waters. But there are more and more skiffs that carry not only their fishing gear out with them when they head out, but their rifles and multiple containers of fuel and water, remaining at sea sometimes for days. Often they return empty-handed, their skiffs empty even of catch. But sometimes they'll return steering a foreign fishing trawler back toward shore, their two skiffs towed at the stern.

No longer are these former fishermen content to levy fines on the foreign trawlers. From the beach, Abdi can see a trawler now, secured a half-mile out by an invisible line sinking into the seabed. A few skiffs are tied alongside the weathered hull. He knows there are crewmen on board, has seen associates of the vessel's captors order quantities of food in the local market and deliver it to the stolen vessel over the few weeks it has been anchored. He knows they expect a payoff in exchange for the vessel, but he can't imagine anyone possessing the amount of money they are requesting.

Mohammed, having left their Uncle Asad's service to work with another cousin, is part of the crew that holds the vessel. "Abdi, we are only taking back what is ours," Mohammed had told him. "And think of what we can do with the money. Our lives will be better. You should join us!" And Abdi can see that Mohammed's life is changed, now that he has shared in the payoff from his first captured vessel a month before. He spends money in the market now. On khat, always in evidence in his bulging cheek, on clothes — Western pants and fancy shoes — which catches the attention of the young women in town.

Abdi misses his family back in Baladweyne, to whom he still sends nearly all his pay. The children are growing up — he'd been to visit a few months ago, and they are older and stronger now and help tend the family's few livestock and crops. He has even managed to send enough money for school fees for the two youngest. They both want to go on to secondary school, but he can only afford to send his brother. His sister must make do with the education she has.

The month before, Amal, that sweet-looking girl from the market, had married a well-off colleague of Mohammed's. Abdi glimpses her lovely face at her market stand now, and his heart aches. He quickly averts his gaze. A wave of loneliness washes over him. A thought strikes him, a factor he has never truly considered: what does he have to lose anyway? He supports his family, barely, but he has nothing for himself. Why can't he expect more? As he contemplates this idea, he feels a lifting in his chest.

Hopeful of change for the first time in a long while, he spies Mohammed, chewing his narcotic leaf on the other side of the market, and walks toward him.

Vessels held by Somali pirates: *Yenegoa Ocean, Stella Maris, Thor Star*

CHAPTER 9

THE INDIAN OCEAN

The crew of a Halifax-based frigate got a glimpse of piracy as it sailed around the Horn of Africa en route to its mission escorting food shipments into Somalia. Within the past five days, HMCS *Ville de Québec* came within about 25 kilometres of two small bulk carriers that had been seized by Somalian pirates … [1]
— Courtesy of the Halifax Herald Limited, August 20, 2008

Maritime traffic is scant as we sail southbound, parallel to Somalia's coast. The ship crosses paths with the odd fishing vessel, two from as far away as Korea, but the threat of piracy has all but cleared these waters of commercial traffic. If merchant vessels cannot reasonably avoid passing through here, most keep a wide berth of Somalia's coast, beyond the range of pirates and our current course.

The trouble is that Somali pirates continue to expand their operating area. As commercial vessels move farther offshore, pirates build on their seafaring capabilities so they can motor out farther and remain at sea longer. Now, ships can be hijacked more than 250 nautical miles off the coast. There are reports of pirates using motherships — larger vessels, some of them pirated ships — on which smaller pirate boats can hitch a ride and refuel in order to extend their range.

I step into the gloom of the ops room to check in with Denis, the on-watch ops room operator. A small group of operators huddles around the radar screen beside him.

"Denis, is something going on?" I ask. Our radar had picked up almost nothing significant until a few hours earlier, when it detected a contact hugging the Somali coastline. It could only be MV *Stella Maris*, one of the vessels recently taken captive in the Gulf of Aden. Her captors drove her south down the coast and into Somali territorial waters, toward the coastal town of Eyl, and ransom negotiations ensued.

Denis seems to be doing three things at once, his hands and bespectacled eyes alternating between multiple computer screens and keyboards. His ability to multitask without getting flustered is impressive, as is his ability to remain kind and soft-spoken — not a prerequisite for his position — in tense situations. But then, as an ops room operator, he's trained to react to all manner of emergencies. Today's low-key routine is nothing special.

Denis points to a blip on the radar screen beside him. "We're about thirteen miles away from that vessel adjacent to the land there — it's MV *Thor Star*."

Another of the captive ships.

For God's sake — the ship is this close and we can do nothing about it. Denis and I exchange a glance, but quickly avert our eyes. We know that our ship is under orders to steer clear of already hijacked vessels. A recent UN Security Council Resolution gives permission for states cooperating with Somalia's transitional government to enter Somali territorial waters for the purpose of repressing acts of piracy,[2] but intervention is much easier when pirates are still in pursuit of their target. This is why *prevention* is so important. Once pirates have boarded a vessel, it's extremely difficult for a warship to take effective action without endangering the lives of hostages. Approaching ships are seen as a threat, which risks the lives of the hostages while ransom negotiations are underway between pirates and the shipping company.

There is reason to be skittish around approaching military craft. In April, pirates hijacked the French-flagged luxury yacht *Le Ponant* and its thirty crew as it crossed the Gulf of Aden. Negotiations between the French government and the pirates led to the eventual payment of a ransom and the release of the hostages. Once the hostages were out of danger, though, French Special Forces tracked the pirates ashore in Puntland, Somalia's breakaway region and host to many of the pirate groups, and attacked them from a helicopter on a desert road. Three of the pirates were killed and six were captured, and a fraction of the ransom money was recovered.[3]

Our own mandate is to escort vessels carrying UN food aid to Somalia, deterring pirate attacks, and not to rescue already hijacked ships. Still, it's maddening to pass so close to these ships-in-crisis — an ongoing crime scene — and do nothing to help their crew. Nor will there be help from local law enforcement officials. As I watch the radar blip, so close to the Somali coast, the reality of Somalia's lawlessness strikes me anew: no government or agency in the country has the authority or means to clamp down on piracy. The captors on board those vessels will carry out ransom negotiations in relative peace. No wonder piracy is flourishing when the benefits pirates derive from it so outweigh the consequences.

～

"For the information of the ship's company, we are now crossing the equator," crackles the staid voice of the officer of the watch across the piping system. We are traversing the calm waters off Kenya, settling down to another wardroom lunch.

Across the table from me, Kevin is chuckling.

"Guess we're not having a Crossing the Line Ceremony!" He shakes his fair head as if to say, *What kind of a navy ship is this anyways?*

"I didn't really take you for a die-hard traditionalist," I say, shooting him a perplexed look.

"I'm not, but this is kind of a big one." His trademark chortle lightens his words.

According to custom shared by most Western navies, "Crossing the Line," as it's called, is an important milestone for sailors — especially for first-timers. But our escort schedule allows no time now for the two-day initiation ceremony. It will have to wait. The decision to delay the ceremony is reasonable, but my disappointment, like a kid whose birthday party is cancelled, still takes me aback. I haven't been initiated.

"What do you care anyways?" I ask Kevin. "You've already had your ceremony."

"That's right," he says mockingly, "I'm a Trusty Shellback. Better not forget it, Pollywog." The nicknames, used for the initiate and the non-initiate, denote the "status" of sailors in the context of the ceremony.

I'm no traditionalist either, but the camaraderie associated with such a ritual is satisfying on a level that I have yet to fully acknowledge, even to myself. It's this camaraderie, based on common traditions and shared experience, that has kept me in the military for so many years. And yet these same traditions are the yoke that, at times, I feel the desperate need to shake off. I dispel the thought, for now, and smile back at Kevin.

"No big deal. We'll do it eventually," I say.

"Speaking of non-traditionalists," says Kevin, nodding his head knowingly toward Kate, who is sitting alone reading on one of the couches. "Did you hear about Kate's blog?"

I look at him questioningly. "No, I didn't."

He laughs. "I don't know the details, but apparently she's been writing an online blog, not always flattering, about the mission, and now it's been reined in by Ottawa. Not sure what's going to happen."

I take a closer look at Kate. She appears more subdued than usual, her eyes downcast, seemingly immersed in her book.

"Interesting," I say, considering Kate. This is personal business, not something to be widely discussed, so I hide the extent to which my interest has been piqued. "Interesting girl."

Before this mission is through, the ship will have crossed the line twenty times as we shuttle cargo vessels between Mombasa, Kenya's largest port, and Mogadishu. For now, absent of ceremony, we sail over the equator and onward toward Mombasa.

~

Back to Africa. From the bridge wing, the distant land is barely discernable, the edge of the moon peeking from the sea. From a week spent in Tanzania only five short months ago, I know that East Africa differs sharply from the south, where I was working so recently. Still, it's strange to be back to this continent, even more so aboard a warship.

For years now, the polarized spheres of my life have been clearly delineated: my civilian work in international development, an environment in which I was sometimes labelled right-wing for my affiliation with the military, and my work with the military, where I was sometimes considered a tree-hugger and bleeding heart for my NGO affiliations. In truth, I was neither. I wasn't in development work because I was altruistic, and I wasn't in the military because I was patriotic. What I was seeking in both was a sense of meaning, adventure, life purpose. That was the common element to both careers, but the two worlds hadn't edged toward each other. Until now.

Our ship lingers beyond the port of Mombasa, awaiting our first escort duty to Mogadishu. The World Food Programme has chartered cargo vessel *Abdul Rahman* to ferry food shipments to Mogadishu's port. Our planning schedule has us beginning the escort in short order, but *Abdul Rahman* — currently loading five thousand tonnes of food cargo in Mombasa by hand — will not be ready to leave for a few days yet. Schedules, often off by several days, are mere guides when it comes to loading cargo here. Typically in commercial shipping, time is money. The arrival and departure of commercial vessels in North American and European ports are precisely planned, berths and equipment and personnel required for the loading and unloading of cargo are arranged well in advance. Delays create serious cost management problems. Here, though, things operate at a more leisurely pace. Nowhere is the concept of time more fluid than in Africa. Combined with limited and unreliable port facilities and services, it challenges all our logistics planning.

Jeff finds me in the communications control room.

"Jen, have you been in touch with the team doing the Mombasa security assessment?"

I look up from the report I'm reading. It's been years since a Canadian naval ship was last in this port, so, for the crew's safety, the security assessment is considered imperative before anyone is let loose on the town.

"Yeah, I have."

"Okay, the captain would like to see you in his cabin."

I give Jeff a quizzical look. "Okay."

I find him sitting in his plush leather chair.

"Captain, sir, Combat said you wanted to see me?"

"Yes, come in, have a seat," he says, beckoning to the loveseat opposite him.

"The security assessment team," he says as I seat myself, "when are they expected to have the report done?"

"They expect to be on the ground in Mombasa in a few days, and should have the report to us a few days after that."

His brow furrows. "*Abdul Rahman*'s not ready to leave, so we're going alongside in Mombasa shortly until she's loaded her cargo." He pauses, looking concerned. "But I can't allow the crew ashore until the security assessment is done. Is there any way they can get the assessment done earlier?"

"I'll call the team and ask, sir," I reply, "but I doubt they will be able to get here any earlier, seeing as that's only a few days away."

The captain's usually impassive face falls, heavy with concern. He knows this will trample morale. The crew has had only a single day ashore in the past three weeks. Sailors rarely complain openly, knowing that our schedule depends on those of the food-aid ships that we'll be escorting, and is beyond our control. But everyone is restless. Nobody knows when there will be another opportunity to go ashore.

"I'd rather stay out at sea than go alongside and not be able to go ashore," I overhear one of the naval communicators saying once the situation is announced to the crew. His frustration is understandable. The captain has decided that, for simplicity's sake, the crew will remain in sea watches for the short time that we're in port.

As the ship sails in, the deckhands prepare the lines for going alongside, laying them neatly on the upper deck. Then they fall in smartly. From my vantage point on the bridge, the dozen sailors cut an elegant line down the focsle, facing to port with legs braced wide and arms clasped behind them. Our sharp naval etiquette would be painting a picture of a well-disciplined and tidy crew — if anyone were looking — as we cruise past grimy container ships at anchor and warehouse-and crane-lined berths. The familiarity of this routine, juxtaposed with the foreignness of the port, jolts me anew: *How bizarre to be in Kenya with this floating piece of Canada, with these all-Canadian sailors.*

The port visits that motivate so many sailors to join the navy are part of an altogether different brand of travel than I'm used to. That it is less individualistic is obvious. The crew has a mob of fellow tourists to explore with, and while they may spend a night or two ashore, they always return to the refuge of the ship. Travel in large groups keeps one a safe, boring distance from the local culture, but for the first time I wonder if there's benefit to being mired in the familiar while exploring the exotic; perhaps it's okay to be a tourist rather than a traveller at times. It's certainly better than seeing nothing at all. In any case, I no longer have the energy for true travel, to be as open as I would need to be. Not now, not after my burnout from Zambia. And not here, while I'm dealing with culture shock of the military variety.

"There's *Abdul Rahman*," the captain announces. "She's being loaded as we speak." He peers through binoculars from his chair. Standing beside him, I see two rusted cargo ships through the bridge window, tied together as if for protection, alongside a jetty. They are smallish, paint-peeled, vulnerable: MV *Abdul Rahman* and her sister ship, MV *Golina*.

And then we are past, gliding toward our berth at the opposite end of the port, directly behind the grey hull of Indian Naval Ship (INS) *Godavari*.

Vessels held by Somali pirates: *Stella Maris, Yenegoa Ocean, Thor Star*

Alongside the Port of Mombasa, Kenya, August 2008.

CHAPTER 10

MOMBASA

A Malaysian palm oil tanker has been hijacked off the coast of
Somalia, the fourth piracy attack in a month. An international task
force was alerted to the attack and a vessel was on its way to the Gulf
of Aden to intercept the ship before it entered Somali waters.[1]
— *Sky News,* August 20, 2008

Once the ship's lines are secure, the boatswains erect the gangway that
connects the upper decks to the jetty, with its long warehouse and containers stacked two high as a security barrier — all we can see of the port.
Absent is the usual air of excitement that accompanies going alongside;
nobody will be travelling far. The command team must work fast, since it
has just been announced that the wardroom will be hosting the captain
and officers from INS *Godavari* for a buffet dinner this evening.

In the wardroom, one of the junior officers waves a sheet of paper.
"We need ten volunteers from the wardroom for tonight's reception,"
he calls out to the officers scattered throughout the room.

"I'll go," I tell him, and he scrawls my name on his paper with a half-
dozen others. I usually avoid work cocktail parties when I can. After three
straight weeks at sea, though, any change from the shipboard routine
is welcome.

~

Word travels fast in Mombasa. Before the ship is even alongside, just
beyond the security perimeter separating the ship from the world outside,

dozens of local vendors have set up flattened-cardboard stalls selling wooden carvings, artwork, and jewellery. Despite the attempt to keep the ship's movements confidential for security reasons, the vendors have obviously had advance notice, probably before most of the crew, of the influx of potential customers.

The crew is permitted onto the jetty only to peruse the makeshift market. In small groups of two and three, they straggle back up the gangway with wooden carvings of all shapes and sizes under their arms, carvings that will soon make their way into the ship's crevices, the gaps behind lockers and above racks that serve as informal storage space. Tall wooden giraffes are a real hit today. Before this mission is done, Mombasa will have bestowed upon us dozens of them — some destined to serve as coat racks, others welcoming crew into various workspaces. The ship will be transformed into an ark of wooden giraffes, and they will stare us down for the next four months.

In preparation for the reception this evening I change into my salt and peppers, the short-sleeve white shirt and black wool skirt that are a version of the navy's professional dress. The Indian officers, sharp in their white dress shirts, are already sipping drinks in the Wardroom when I arrive. A good representation of our ship's officers have shown up, more than the required ten, and are now spread out in small groups, chatting politely with the Indian officers. In the far corner of the room I spot Kate, smiling broadly as she converses with three of them. Beside me, the captain is paying dedicated attention to the Kenyan Admiral who has also come aboard for the event.

I join TiFou and *Godavari*'s communications officer, a neat man with small, discrete features.

"What's your ship doing in Mombasa?" I ask with genuine interest.

"We are on a goodwill tour of the region for a few months, also doing some training," he replies in excellent English. "We are sailing with two other Indian ships."

The nature of their mission is no surprise. The Indian Ocean region is of strategic importance to India, situated as it is roughly 4,000 kilometres to the northeast. We exchange details of our two ships — number of crew and officers, the different trades represented on board, the amount of time spent away from home. Our common naval heritage, derived from the British model, allows us to speak the same language. Naval culture connects us more than divergent ethnic backgrounds divide us.

But at least one diversion from tradition is not shared — or at least not yet fully integrated into the Indian navy. From the sidelong looks I am picking up from some of the Indian officers around us, I get the distinct impression that women on board ship are a novelty for them, unlike in the Canadian Navy, where women have worked in seagoing trades since 1989. Certainly no women sail in *Godavari*.

I turn to the communications officer. "Are there women in the Indian navy?"

He smiles gently. "Yes. But only in support trades, relatively few at that, and not on board ship."

Out of the corner of my eye I observe Kate. As a female helicopter pilot, she must be a figure of fascination for the Indian officers she's speaking with. She's more animated than I've ever seen her. Her olive complexion glows, and for the first time I'm struck by her natural, dark-haired beauty. She is part South Asian herself, and visits the region often, a connection that undoubtedly helps her to relate to these officers. More than that, though, I can tell that she is genuinely interested in other cultures and people beyond the narrow world of the Canadian military. She's in her element. I'm drawn to her. I was that way myself, before I flamed out.

Just as they are leaving the wardroom to head back to *Godavari*, one of the Indian officers turns to us.

"Would you all like a tour of our ship?"

My heart sinks a little when I hear this. I've been daydreaming of crawling into my rack for an early night, for a few good hours with my book, not yet even cracked on this deployment. But it's a unique opportunity to become acquainted with a foreign ship, and I can't say no. TiFou tells him he'd like to check out their Sea King helicopter, the same type of helo that we have on board, so I tag along.

It's early evening but already dark when I and ten members of the air det file off *Ville de Québec*'s gangway, now sloped at a steep angle due to the tides. Too late I realize how impractical for climbing ship's ladders are a wool skirt and pumps.

But all that ceases to matter the moment my foot hits the concrete jetty. When I take my first steps on land in weeks, two things strike me:

how the heat, undiffused by the sea breeze we've become accustomed to, slams into us like a wall, and how these initial strides feel like pure freedom, even though we're permitted to walk no further than the adjacent ship. *Godavari* is berthed next to us, but the security barriers are blocking the direct path, so it's a ten-minute walk through the port to reach the Indian ship. We move in small groups, talking, laughing, adjusting happily to the heat, content just to be ashore. The farther from the ship, the louder our talking and laughing. With each step I stretch my legs out as far as my skirt will allow, spontaneously filled with boundless energy. Walking has never felt so good. I love this night air, I love the romance of this port that is really not romantic at all. I say anything that pops into my head, heady with freedom, and nobody finds it strange, because they feel it too.

"It feels so incredible to be walking on dry land!" I laugh, feeling joyful. Because I don't dislike being at sea, the power of going ashore has taken me by surprise.

At home it would still be light at this time of year. We would be revelling in the long summer nights, lounging on patios in the gentle warmth of the evening sun. Near the equator, though, it's dark well before seven and the sky above is pitch black. Without all these people chattering beside me, a walk through the poorly lit port would feel dangerous. The dark shapes of warehouses rise on one side of us, while on the other rows of containers stacked three high close us in. A few men silently flit in and out of the shadows. Besides being industrial, cold, and filthy, ports are creepy places at night, and this one is no exception. My simultaneous dislike of and fascination with ports mirrors my ambiguous relationship with the military.

We each salute as we cross *Godavari*'s brow, where we are greeted by a junior officer. He is friendly, but clearly a little nervous to be speaking to such a large group in what must be his second, third, or fourth language. The commander of *Godavari*'s air detachment, however, is a different story. In his mid-thirties, he has a round, handsome face lit up by a big smile, and he speaks English with a posh British accent. By any standard, he's quite cosmopolitan.

As he leads the pilots off on a tour of their Sea King helicopter, which is considerably newer than ours, and the other members of our air det are led off by their counterparts, I find myself alone with the junior officer.

"Would it be possible to get a tour of the ship?" I inquire politely, giving him what I intend to be a disarming smile.

He looks away, not meeting my eyes, before replying shyly in his halting English.

"Yes, of course. Please wait here and someone will come for you." He disappears inside the ship.

I stand waiting on the flight deck, with three junior officers watching me from a distance. They smile and laugh, stealing glances my way. As a female on board ship I am a novelty. I smile warmly at them. After twenty minutes of waiting I approach the group, none of them older than twenty-five.

"Do you think I would be able to get a tour of the ship?" I ask in a soft voice. "The junior officer who was here went off to get someone to give me a tour but hasn't come back."

One of them giggles a little and averts his eyes. "Yes, that is no problem," he says. He too disappears inside. I wait another fifteen minutes, with no sign of either junior officer who has promised me a tour. Finally, it dawns on me that I won't be getting one. I'm surprised it has taken me so long to clue in: these officers aren't comfortable giving me a tour, but cultural norms — about which I know a little about from having visited India — mean they don't want to tell me no. Avoiding the situation altogether is a way to save face.

Their reluctance to take me around the ship likely has to do with my gender. The boundaries between men and women in India are more rigid than they are in Canada. Perhaps it would not be appropriate to lead a woman through an all-male ship, the accommodation spaces here being the private domain of men, especially as I would be on my own, not accompanied by a group or by Canadian men. I need to vacate the awkward standing-and-waiting posture I have adopted on their flight deck, so, spotting some of our air det members, I tag onto the end of their Sea King tour.

Later, when some male members of the air det report on the thorough ship tour they were given, my suspicions are confirmed. I feel a pang of self-recrimination for having created an awkward situation for the Indian officers.

~

While we're alongside in Mombasa, pirates hijack another vessel. Malaysian oil tanker *Bunga Melati Dua* had left Sumatra fully laden with Rotterdam-destined palm oil before pirates attacked her in the Gulf of Aden. The ship's mayday was transmitted on VHF Channel 16, the international distress frequency monitored by ships.

Later, I listen to recordings of the stricken vessel's transmissions: "Pirate boat is trying to board us. They have, they have guns," — the male voice climbs at this last word — "trying to board us, but they have not yet boarded, they have not yet boarded, they are attempting to board us, and we are trying evasive manoeuvres." The voice must be that of one of the officers on the bridge, his strong accent clearly indicating that he is no native English speaker. "Any naval, any navy that can give assistance to us to drive away the pirates, please come, our position 12 degrees 45 decimal 15 minutes north 047 degrees 58 decimal 0 minutes east. This is *Bunga Melati Dua* standing by Channel 16." The speaker remains focused, his urgent tone approaches panic.

Bunga Melati Dua conducts evasive manoeuvres, one of the tactics they have been instructed to adopt in the event of a pirate attack. The wake and swell caused by erratic zigzagging and other unpredictable ship movements will make it difficult for pirates to pull their small boat alongside for long enough to throw up ladders or grappling hooks. But *Bunga Melati Dua* is not a fast ship, and carrying out manoeuvres that create enough wake to deter a boarding is a challenge. To make matters worse, under her full cargo of palm oil, she sits low in the water, making it that much easier for pirates to board.

A few minutes later comes the final, gut-wrenching transmission from the stricken vessel, the voice steadily escalating: "Mayday, mayday, mayday, mayday, this is *Bunga Melati Dua, Bunga Melati Dua* ... pirates are already on board, pirates have already boarded us. There are two boats now, there are two boats. They are trying to board the vessel now. They have machine guns, they have machine guns! They are boarding the vessel. Over."

I picture the man the voice belongs to — perhaps the vessel master — looking out the bridge window as he makes his mayday call, eyes widening with panic as he watches the pirates board his ship, as he spots their machine guns.

Nearby merchant ships pick up the distress call and relay it on their own radios, reaching out to any coalition naval vessel nearby. HMCS *Calgary* is the closest when the attack occurs. On *Calgary*'s bridge, the officer of the watch hears the distress call relayed over VHF radio, but the ship is still a long distance away. At top speed it will take *Calgary* more than five hours to reach the distressed vessel's position. Now that the pirates have boarded, it is inevitable that the ship will be taken. Merchant sailors are civilians, pure and simple; they have no paramilitary training nor do they generally carry weapons. They can occasionally barricade themselves in locked spaces once pirates have boarded, but eventually they will need to come out for food and water.

The *Calgary* heads for their position anyway, but with the attack now a hostage situation, there is little her crew can do.

Later we learn that a Filipino crewman was killed by gunfire as the pirates boarded the vessel. A crew death during a Somali pirate hijacking is rare and usually occurs inadvertently, as in this case. But a man is dead. The remaining Malaysian and Filipino crew members are now held captive as pirates direct MV *Bunga Melati Dua* into Somalia's coastal waters. There she will likely join MVs *Stella Maris* and *Thor Star* at anchor near Eyl or Garacad, another pirate stronghold.

Somali pirates now hold four ships for ransom — the most they have ever held concurrently.

Vessels held by Somali pirates: *Stella Maris, Yenegoa Ocean, Thor Star, Bunga Melati Dua*

CHAPTER 11

ESCORT

The dangers of goods exported from China entered a whole new
realm on Aug. 21 when Somali pirates captured the Iranian ship,
MV *Iran Deyanat*, 130 kilometres southeast of Yemen.[1]
— *Vancouver Sun*, October 27, 2008

Two restless days later, the last of the food cargo is loaded into the holds
of MV *Abdul Rahman*. Our ship heads back out to sea in advance of the
rusted cargo vessel that we will escort to Somalia's battle-hardened capital.
We loiter just beyond the sheltered waters of Mombasa harbour.

"Thank God we're at sea," exclaims Marcus when I stop by the cabin
he shares with Kevin.

I look at him, perplexed. "Wow. I never thought I'd hear that from you."

"That whole water rationing thing was driving me crazy."

For the past two days alongside, the ship's supply of fresh water has
steadily dwindled. At sea, our engineers use the ship's systems to make
our own fresh water. Alongside Mombasa, however, we are at the mercy of
local water sources. One truck that had shown up on the jetty had refused
to wait until the water quality could be tested, while another had failed the
test altogether. As a result, each member was restricted to one two-minute
shower per day.

"One pusser shower a day doesn't cut it when you work out," Marcus
continues. "I was bathing myself with bottled water by the end, just to
feel normal."

"You're such a princess." I laugh, glancing around the cabin. "Both you
and Kevin. Look at this place!"

They have got to be the world's cleanest men. Shipboard etiquette dictates that cabins and mess decks be kept clean and tidy, but these two take neatness to a new level. The two racks stacked against the far wall, Marcus's above, Kevin's below, are immaculate. The crisp bedding is pulled taut. The single desk is spartan, graced with only a laptop and a bottle of body lotion. Two towels are the sole adornments on the closed lockers. The cabin even smells like a spa, diffused with a sweet aroma of mysterious origin. The pristine cabin is a clean cousin to the larger but malodorous Cabin 68 next door, which is crowded with six male sub-lieutenants.

"Yeah, Kevin and I are a pretty good match," Marcus says. "I probably couldn't live with anyone else on board." Then he grins. "You're just jealous that we have a cabin."

He's right; having a cabin at all seems like luxury compared to my mess deck accommodations. But I'm careful not to complain. Unlike other messes, mine, at least, contains only five other bodies I need to worry about waking. Inevitably I will need to visit the heads, a short distance down the flats, for my nocturnal bathroom break. Performing this soundlessly is a challenge. For one thing, the metal hooks connecting the curtains to the frame of the racks are poorly designed for a ship, and make a loud swishing sound regardless of how slowly and carefully they are drawn. And then I have to fumble for my shower sandals and try to minimize their slapping on the vinyl floor, the noise always magnified in my mind by concern for waking the others.

Accessing my locker is out of the question. For this and other transgressions, like leaving clothes on the deck or our beds unmade, we — the three female officers who live together in the mess with three female petty officers — have already been admonished a few times by the Mess Mother, PO Adams, a petite, fit woman in her late forties. We are guilty of some of the transgressions; others are pre-emptive strikes probably fuelled by the assumption that officers are used to living in cabins and relying on stewards to clean up after them, a service not offered to us in the mess. In fact, none of us has ever berthed for any length of time in a cabin — a comparative luxury with only one roommate and a sink of one's own. I've learned to move stealthily about in our darkened mess space. But having a personal refuge, a retreat from the ship's close quarters, is what I miss most.

~

MV *Abdul Rahman* steams toward us from the port of Mombasa. From a distance, the small vessel's navy hull and white superstructure appear freshly painted, masking years of wear and corrosion. Cranes fitted to the ship overhang cargo holds containing the World Food Programme aid, 5,400 metric tonnes of maize and soya meal — enough to feed twenty-seven thousand people for a year[2] — that *Abdul Rahman* will carry north and offload in conflict-ridden Mogadishu.

Most of the piracy is taking place in the Gulf of Aden off Somalia's north coast, far from the primary World Food Programme shipping route ranging from Mombasa, where the main food warehouse is located, to Mogadishu. Somalia's east coast, however, not far from where we now sail, has amassed its own impressive history of piracy incidents in recent years. These include indiscriminate attacks and hijackings of fishing boats, dhows, sailing yachts, and commercial ships, regardless of whether they carry food aid for the Somali population.

In an upswing of piracy in 2005, prior to the enlistment of naval escorts, several commercial ships carrying World Food Programme aid were attacked.[3] Pirates captured MV *Semlow*, a cargo ship carrying rice to Somali survivors of the Indian Ocean tsunami. During the time they held the vessel and crew for ransom, the pirates used MV *Semlow* to attack two other vessels, hiding their skiffs out of sight as they approached their new targets in what appeared to be a peaceful cargo ship. Then the privately chartered MV *Torgelow* was hijacked while carrying supplies for MV *Semlow*, recently freed from captivity.[4] The capture of another World Food Programme–contracted vessel, MV *Miltzow*, soon followed.

The Kenyan shipping agent responsible for these ships had mistakenly assumed that because they were carrying cargo for the benefit of the Somali people, Somali pirates would not touch them.[5] A published account of the MV *Semlow* hijacking from one of the Kenyan hostages is revealing: "They called themselves Somali Marines and said we were carrying illegal weapons, that was why they had boarded us. Our captain told them, 'No, we are carrying rice on a humanitarian mission for the United Nations, not weapons.' But the leader did not believe him. That was when I first became worried, because we were supposed to be helping the people [of Somalia].

When the pirates went to check the cargo holds, they saw we had only rice, but were still angry."[6]

These incidents caused several weeks of suspension in the delivery of seaborne food aid to Somalia, seriously hampering the World Food Programme humanitarian mission. Shipments eventually resumed, though, and in 2007 pirates followed up with three more attacks on vessels carrying food aid.

The threat of piracy has radically diminished the number of cargo ships willing to carry food aid into Somali waters. The day after pirates attacked another World Food Programme ship, MV *Victoria*, the agent of a second ship fully laden with food aid refused to let the vessel sail for Somalia.[7]

It's difficult to blame ship owners and vessel masters for refusing to sail into Somali waters. UN contracts are likely fairly lucrative, but for many shipping companies the payoff is probably not worth the skyrocketing insurance premiums and potential cost of a million-dollar ransom, much less the risk to the crew. Finding merchantmen willing to enter these waters is becoming increasingly challenging.

For the first time in its history, the World Food Programme has called on countries to provide naval escort for vessels carrying food aid. The French, Danish, and Dutch navies have responded with successive escort missions. Since the operations commenced in November 2007, no vessel under naval escort has been attacked by pirates.

Escorts ceased this past June, however, when no country stepped in to fill the gap left by the departing Danish despite repeated calls by the World Food Programme and the International Maritime Organization to UN member states. The UN agency was again forced to suspend the seaborne delivery of food aid for the two months following, warning that food shipments were at risk of ceasing altogether, owing to the unwillingness of commercial vessels to proceed into Somali waters without naval escort. By mid-August, the stores of food aid already ashore in Somalia would be depleted.[8] The Canadian government came to the rescue in early August, offering *Ville de Québec* for escort duty until the end of September.

For the most part, our mission is uncontroversial. Nobody claims that escorts are a long-term solution to the piracy plaguing Somali waters, acknowledging that it is the lack of effective government ashore that allows it to flourish. That the escorts do some good in the short term, even save lives, is hard to dispute. If the choice is between doing this and doing nothing, the Canadian government has chosen right.

~

While our ship was alongside in Mombasa, the CO, Jeff, and a few key members of the boarding team met to discuss escort procedures with the master of MV *Abdul Rahman* — the positioning of the ships, the speed of the transit, reactions of the armed boarding party and *Ville de Québec* in the event of an attack, and the turnover of MV *Abdul Rahman* to African Union forces stationed in Mogadishu. By the time our two vessels rendezvous in the waters outside Mombasa, the escort is ready to get underway immediately.

I lean against the wooden railing of the bridge wing as the boarding party's first wave — ten sailors identically dressed in tan coveralls and protective helmets, a single female among them — descend the Jacob's ladder down the side of *Ville de Québec*. Weighted down with well over a dozen kilos of personal body armour, weapons, and ammunition, they are sweltering in this equatorial heat, their faces already flushed as they settle into the boat for the short ride to the vessel idling a few hundred metres away. They've trained specifically for this mission over the past few weeks, focusing on how to defend the escorted vessel against attack. Although no World Food Programme vessels under naval escort have been attacked, there's a first time for everything.

The CO stands on the aft end of the bridge wing with the XO and Jeff at his side. His blue eyes track the RHIB as it jets through the dark water, its rubber hull bouncing off the chop. For this mission, as commanding officer, he holds ultimate responsibility for success or failure. A high-profile operation like this must be a captain's dream, but real lives — and real reputations — rest on it. But then, he has a long history of operational experience at sea. While he must be wary as we begin our first escort, his tall, erect figure against the railing reveals nothing.

Through high-powered binoculars that I struggle to keep trained on the shifting scene, I watch the coxswain expertly manoeuvre the craft alongside *Abdul Rahman*'s cargo deck where it is greeted by crew members. *Abdul Rahman*'s low freeboard enables the team to reach the cargo deck with only a few steps up the ladder that extends down the hull, so the boarding is relatively easy despite the chop. That low a freeboard would also make the vessel easy pickings for pirates.

Once the coxswain has safely delivered the team, he shears the RHIB away from *Abdul Rahman* and flies through the water toward us. The boat is hoisted aboard, a look of sea-sprayed vitality on the coxswain's face. With *Abdul Rahman* sailing tranquilly a few hundred metres distant, we begin our northbound journey toward Mogadishu.

~

It takes a few days to cover the five hundred nautical miles from Mombasa to Mogadishu. Periodically, a fresh team is ferried over to relieve the one on board *Abdul Rahman*. When they return, the teams report long stretches of boredom while ensuring they stay alert for waterborne activity, of which there is none. Within the ship, the crew manning the ops room and bridge remain vigilant but the routine continues unchanged.

Mid-morning on the second day of the escort, TiFou, the air detachment commander, ambles into the deserted wardroom. He spots me crafting my morning latte.

"How's it going, KGB? Pretty busy today?" he asks in his Franco staccato.

He rests his lean body against the bar on the opposite side of the cappuccino machine, awaiting his turn. Lattes are an on-board pleasure that we share. The regular coffee on board is adequate at best, but coffee quality isn't what drives this morning ritual. What does is the simple act of enjoying an espresso. It's a rare luxury that restores some normalcy to our shipboard lives.

"Yeah," I say, turning to smile at him. "But no busier than normal."

"Do you want to come flying this afternoon?"

The question catches me off guard. I had told TiFou some time ago that I'd like to fly in a Sea King, but had promptly forgotten about it. I'd never flown in a helicopter. Truth be told, I'm a nervous flyer in small aircraft, and I don't have much inclination to fly in one now — particularly not in a forty-five-year-old Sea King. Professionally, though, I need to understand what the flight crew see when they fly over these waters.

"Uh, sure," I reply, sounding more certain than I feel. "That would be great. I'll check with Jeff, but I'm sure he'll be fine with it. Thanks."

"No problem. Be ready to go at twelve-thirty."

At twelve-thirty sharp I show up at the air detachment room for the pre-flight brief. Reclining in theatre-style seats in tan one-piece flight suits, the Sea King's four-person crew focus on the white board. TiFou, crew commander, kicks off the brief, followed by Nathalie, the air navigation officer. Marcus, tilting back his closely shaven head as he downs a Red Bull in the seat beside me, is TiFou's co-pilot. Neil, a chatty and competent sergeant, is the crew's airborne electronic sensor operator. His job is to counter threats, such as anti-aircraft fire detected by the helicopter's sensors. The only other passenger is the videographer for Combat Camera, the military public affairs team embarked to provide images of the mission for the Department of National Defence and the media.

As the others leave after the pre-flight brief, Neil delivers the passenger safety brief to the videographer and me.

"You need to do exactly what the flight crew tells you at all times," he says in a lightning-fast monologue that makes it clear he has given this brief a hundred times before.

"You won't be able to hear each other in the helicopter." He hands each of us a camouflage green helmet equipped with a mike. "This is how you'll communicate with the crew during the flight.

"If we have to ditch, keep your belt buckled until we hit the water," Neil continues in his matter-of-fact voice. "Once we've hit and the helicopter is in the water and has turned over, undo your buckle, take a deep breath, and swim toward the opening in the helicopter that should be right in front of you. Don't inflate your life vest until you're outside the helicopter or you'll have trouble getting out. It's important not to panic."

Other than that, getting out will be a piece of cake. My palms are sweating. This is all happening so fast. The flight crew carries emergency oxygen in case they have to ditch and get trapped underwater for more than a few seconds, but that oxygen is only provided to trained personnel, a policy I don't quite understand. *Can't they offer passengers a quick tutorial and give us oxygen too, just in case?* Not that I would be the first to volunteer for dunker training, which is compulsory for flight crew and night-flying passengers. The training scenario simulates the environmental conditions inside a helicopter forced to ditch in the ocean after dark. The occupants must escape from the murky, inverted helicopter while submerged. The key is not to panic and merely follow the training instructions, but to me it sounds terrifying.

On another NATO mission a few years ago, Billy was air navigator in a Sea King that ditched in the Mediterranean. The crew barely escaped with their lives. From the little he's said, the experience was clearly traumatic. If a flight crew has the misfortune to undergo such trauma, Billy tells me they can then choose whatever posting they'd like, including work in another type of aircraft entirely. True to form, resilient Billy chose to stick it out with the Sea King.

As I struggle into my unwieldy helmet and clumsily attempt to fasten the chin strap, I can't shake my self-image as an uncoordinated, heavy-headed alien exploring new territory way beyond my comfort zone.

The master corporal and I follow Neil up the ladder into the dim, sealed hangar, and then through a door and into the blinding sunshine of the flight deck. There sits the hulking grey body of the Sea King. The thunderous whirring of its rotors obscures all other sound. Neil leads us to the helicopter, past TiFou and Marcus, already seated in the cockpit, past the navigation station behind, where Nathalie is stationed, toward the rear. We strap ourselves into the three seats that line the helo's port side and plug our mikes into the overhead outlets. Directly in front of us is a wide door, closed now, but our primary escape route if we have to ditch. *God I hope we don't have to ditch.* Just in case, I study the immediate area and run a quick analysis of potential impediments to self-rescue.

Neil's voice over the earphones disrupts my concentration. "Good to go back here."

"Roger." I recognize TiFou's clipped tone, and then Marcus's lazier drawl, as the pilots speak amongst themselves, but distinguishing their words through the radio distortion and the roaring of the rotors is a challenge.

As the helicopter lifts off and away from the ship, excitement over-rides my nerves. I can't see the ship from where I sit, but I sense us moving away from it, the helo floating weightlessly through the glimpses of blue I catch through the window. My excitement builds, bubbling up from my stomach.

Neil unbuckles himself and slides open the giant door. An impeccable canvas of endless blue sky and perfect clouds unfolds before us, and when we bank to alter direction, we glimpse dark ripples of the open ocean below. There's another feeling fuelling my growing euphoria, and with a start I realize what it is: a sense of freedom. Suddenly I'm limitless! The feeling of bursting my body's boundaries is both familiar and new — and glorious. For the first time since we set out to sea, I feel free. A giant grin spreads across my face of its own accord, the automatic response to my growing sense of well-being. I don't know if it's the contrast with the confinement of life at sea that makes this freedom so sweet, but all of a sudden it's clear to me. *This is why they love to fly.*

In the next moment Neil indicates that I should unbuckle my seatbelt. I stand up and he fits me into a safety harness. Then, at his direction, I sit cross-legged on the floor beside the open door. Clutching the door frame beside me, I gaze out at the clouds floating above us and then down hundreds of feet to the indigo of the Indian Ocean. Seated here, at the edge of a precipice, my occasional vertigo doesn't bother me at all.

I scan the distant water, looking for life in the form of ships or small skiffs, but it's empty. All I see is a dark blue expanse, broken by occasional whitecaps that hint at the choppiness of the sea below. The pilots must have eagle eyes ever to spot small-scale activity, even from these relatively modest heights, but they often do: fishing boats, small skiffs, the fin of a shark, the shadow of a whale swimming just beneath the surface. It takes a practiced eye to distinguish a small skiff hidden in the folds of a swell or to discern the activities of a barely perceptible fishing boat. The vantage point I have now gives me new respect for the work of the flight crews.

I am plugged into the radio outlet beside the door when I hear TiFou's tinny voice over the headphones. His speech is difficult to make out, but I hear the word *Jen* and a moment later Neil's hand is on my shoulder. I slide back from the door, unhook myself from the harness, and follow him toward the cockpit, where we stand directly behind TiFou and Marcus. I gaze, mesmerized, through the windshield as we race through a maze of clouds. Abruptly, Marcus lifts himself out of the co-pilot's seat, twisting around and smiling at me as he makes his exit.

"Have fun!"

This I make out loud and clear over my headphones, so I'm confused until Marcus beckons me to climb over the gadgetry between the pilots' seats and fill his vacated seat. *Right.* My heart races. I knew that the pilots sometimes allow passengers to fly the helicopter for short periods, but I had assumed that was only if passengers wanted to. I don't want to. I may have just discovered a new love of flying, but I'm quite sure it doesn't extend to actually piloting an aircraft. But it seems that I have no choice. Concealing my reluctance, I climb into the co-pilot's seat. TiFou has the best of intentions in giving me this opportunity, so I shoot him as sincere a smile as I can muster, but my gratitude is less than whole-hearted. My palms rest on my legs, sweaty with the return of my nerves. *Best to just get this over with as quickly as possible.*

Before me lies a bewildering array of displays and toggles. I grip the throttle with my right hand as TiFou instructs, staring out at wispy networks of cloud that have newly taken on a menacing cast.

"The throttle controls our altitude, which you can see recorded here on the altimeter." He looks over at me. "You control the throttle to start with, and I'll do the rest. Try changing altitude a little."

At first I decide it's safer not to move the throttle at all. After a few moments, though, curiosity overcomes me. I edge the throttle forward, just a touch. When I glance at the altimeter, I'm amazed to find that we've dropped 150 feet. I pull back on the throttle to restore us to our previous altitude, but I overshoot. The helo floats up, and then descends. Keeping it level seems impossible.

"Not as easy as it looks, is it?" TiFou laughs beside me. I suddenly realize I'm having fun. I laugh too, exhilarated.

Next he lets me control the throttle *and* the foot pedals, which control the rudder and determine our direction. My right foot presses down on the pedal, gently, and we slowly swing to the right as I pull up on the throttle. My attempts to control our altitude and direction simultaneously are ridiculous, but good-fun ridiculous, and TiFou is at the controls ready to take over the second the situation became dangerous.

After a good deal of cloud-chasing, and hero-photos of me piloting, I reluctantly relinquish my seat to Marcus.

"I totally suck!" I yell as I pass him, a grin plastered to my face. I've forgotten to speak into the mike, so I press one of the two buttons and repeat myself.

Marcus presses the opposite button on his mike. "You didn't do too badly. And you pressed the wrong button. You just radioed that to the ship." But he's laughing, and nobody is panicked. Adrenaline continues to pump through my veins, flushing my face warm with exhilaration. I linger behind the cockpit and stare ahead at the pilots' water view, more impressed than ever at their ability to search for waterborne activity while flying the aircraft.

A distant grey vessel, the sole sign of life that I've seen, grows gradually larger through the cockpit window. A sinking feeling lodges itself in the pit of my stomach. It's *Ville de Québec*. Time to return. Back to the routine, back to the ship's confinement, for who knows how long. But I do feel different now, armed with this uplifting experience. There is much about shipboard life that doesn't sit well with me, but opportunities like this almost tip the balance.

Vessels held by Somali pirates: *Stella Maris, Yenegoa Ocean, Thor Star, Bunga Melati Dua*

CHAPTER 12

MOGADISHU

On Aug. 21, armed attackers in speedboats swarmed and quickly hijacked the German cargo ship *BBC Trinidad* as it steamed through the Gulf of Aden.[1]

— NPR, September 29, 2008

My euphoria is short-lived. Moments after TiFou gently manoeuvres the Sea King onto the ship's flight deck and I return to my station in the communications control room, reality intrudes again. Pirates have hijacked three more merchant ships in close proximity to one another within the Gulf of Aden, all within the past twenty-four hours.

MT *Irene*, a Japanese-owned chemical tanker carrying sixteen Filipinos and three Croatians, was seized as she journeyed from India to France.[2] Iranian dry bulk carrier *Iran Deyanat* was carrying minerals and iron ore from China to Germany with a crew of twenty-nine when she was attacked. An Indian crew member later reported hearing loud gunfire: "Many of us ran out on the deck. We saw a group of men in two tiny speedboats close to the ship. The ship's radar had failed to pick them up. The men were firing in the air," he said. "There were sixteen of them. They threw a ladder fitted with grappling hooks over the side of the ship and clambered aboard. They stormed all cabins and herded the entire crew into a small room, and told the captain to cut the engine."[3]

BBC Trinidad, a German heavy lift project vessel, was the third vessel captured. Once alerted that his ship was being pursued by small boats, the master zigzagged, but failed to evade the predators. The pirates fired into the air once they were within shouting distance from the ship and ordered it to stop and surrender.[4]

This many hijackings in such a short span of time is unprecedented. In response, the International Maritime Bureau issues a flash piracy warning to all vessels sailing through Pirate Alley, advising masters to prepare for attacks and remain on alert for boats approaching at high speed. Ships unable to avoid traversing the area are advised to stay thirty-five to forty miles off the Yemen coast.[5] Even then, there is no guarantee against attack. While the northern passage gives Somalia a wide berth and is considered the safest route within the gulf, pirates seized MV *Irene* only a handful of miles south of this transitway.[6]

We've been in the mission area only a week and already the piracy has escalated alarmingly — from an attack every few weeks to three ships hijacked in a single day — likely owing to the advent of favourable weather conditions and the pirates' growing confidence. Naval vessels already patrol the Gulf of Aden in response to the piracy surge, but it's an impossibly large body of water to cover for the number of ships available. Unless they can respond to a merchant ship's distress call and reach the scene of an attack before the pirates board the vessel, there is little these sophisticated warships can do to quell the attacks without risking the lives of hostages. The next day, Combined Task Force 150 announces a Maritime Security Patrol Area — a narrow, navy-patrolled corridor through Pirate Alley that is the recommended route for merchant ships crossing the area. But this is still no guarantee of safe passage.

~

While things heat up in the Gulf of Aden to our north, the waters through which we pass remain eerily quiet. Ashore in Mogadishu it's a different story.

"Did you hear about that Canadian journalist who was abducted?" asks Kevin, craning his head around to look at me. His solid figure is stationed in front of the dimly lit wardroom's stainless steel milk dispenser, where he is preparing his nightly protein shake.

At the table beside him, I'm sipping a mug of hot chocolate. I look over at him. "Yeah, I read about it. It's terrible," I say, shaking my head. Amidst the ongoing conflict between Somalia's Ethiopian-backed Transitional

Federal Government and Islamist insurgents, aid workers and reporters are routinely killed or abducted and held for ransom. "But I just don't know what she was doing there in the first place."

"I know. Mogadishu's a hell of a place to volunteer to go to," says Kevin, just as Kate enters the room.

"Who's volunteering to go to Mogadishu?" she says with an ironic laugh as she grabs a glass of juice.

"A Canadian journalist. I just can't figure out what she was doing there," I reply.

Freelance journalist Amanda Lindhout, along with Australian photographer Nigel Brennan and their Somali colleague, Abdifatah Mohammed Elmi, and two Somali drivers, have been kidnapped in Mogadishu. They were reportedly travelling with only a security detail from the Transitional Federal Government, not the local militia detail considered imperative for accompanying foreigners travelling the stretch of insurgent-held road from the capital to a displaced persons camp a few dozen kilometres to the west.[7]

I don't know much about Amanda. She's beautiful in the photos posted on news websites. In one of them, a headscarf obscures her long dark hair, and huge brown eyes illuminate her pale face. She is only twenty-seven. I know little about her, except that she hails from Alberta and that Somalia is not the first hotspot she has landed in. She also worked in Iraq and Afghanistan. This isn't much to go on. What does seem certain, however, is that she chooses to work in dangerous places.

The newspaper articles on her abduction give a superficial explanation of why she was there — to report on the displaced persons camp — but say nothing of her deeper motivation for travelling to Mogadishu at a time of such severe unrest. As a Western woman, especially, the simple fact of her presence there would put her life in imminent danger. I can guess at possible motivations: an altruistic desire to tell a story that isn't being adequately told, to help effect positive change; a thirst for adventure, maybe bolstered by a sense of immortality; a drive to do something meaningful — or perhaps all of these had morphed together to validate the incredible risk. Or any one of a thousand reasons that may have been determined by Amanda's psychology, as so many of our choices, at least mine, seem to be driven by the psyche's drive for a defined life purpose.

Accounts of violence and kidnapping in Somalia are familiar territory for me now, but this one hits me like a punch in the gut and creates an internal conflict I can't resolve. It's a struggle between respect for Amanda's willingness to risk her life to tell an important and untold story, if that was her motivation, and utter dismay that she could be so naïve about her safety and willingly put herself into a situation that could cause herself and her family such grief.

The vehemence of my feelings about this, my critique of her actions, is probably inappropriate, but I feel a kinship with her that, in my mind at least, entitles me to examine her choices. She reminds me of me. At least, based purely on her choice of work environment, the idea of her I've become attached to reminds me of my younger self's idea, driven by family mythology and personal psychology, of a life worth living. Independent travels or work abroad, rendered superficially satisfying by exotic, occasionally dangerous, challenge. The list included Bosnia, Zambia, South Africa, Guatemala, and, nearly, Afghanistan and Sudan. None were as extreme as Amanda's chosen locale, though, and in the end I had to admit that none were rewarding just because they were difficult places to be or because the work sounded important. Any reward was temporary, enduring only while my self-image matched, however superficially, that of my mind's idealized heroine, and remained firmly entrenched in the realm of ego.

I struggle still to move beyond my blind romantic notions of alien lands and the promise they surely must hold. Instead, I try to base my travel and work choices on plans of substance revealed by objective research, trying to be honest with myself about which will actually make a positive difference, as well as the potential impact on my family — hoping that decisions so supported will lift me beyond the narrow perspective of my egocentric self and lead to greater fulfillment than I've found so far. I often fail. I'm not sure yet on which side of the spectrum this deployment falls.

Perhaps Amanda is wiser than I was at her age. Perhaps her reasons for being in Somalia have substance. Perhaps she, too, was in hot pursuit of a sense of fulfillment, based on something beyond herself, when she was abducted.

"Maybe she felt she needed to be there, to shed some light on what's going on," I say to Kate with a question in my voice, once I've caught her up on what I know of Amanda's circumstance. "There can't be many foreign journalists still doing that there. That's got to be important."

Another reporter in Mogadishu at the time of the capture tells of how Somali passengers at the Mogadishu airport approached him to express their regret about the kidnapped journalists, their gratitude for his presence, and their hope that he would tell the story of Somalia to the outside world.[8] But even if bearing witness was Amanda's true goal, I'm not convinced it would make the hell she and the others are going through, their sacrifices, and their families' sacrifices, ultimately worth it.

~

To draw close to Mogadishu is to enter a war zone. The next morning the crew prepares for the ship's approach — the nearest a Canadian military unit has been to Somalia since the Canadian Airborne Regiment's ill-fated mission ended amidst scandal in 1993. From the few journalists daring to remain in the country come reports of near-constant gunfights and other acts of violence. Insurgents attack the Ethiopian forces, as well as the Ugandan and Burundian troops that comprise the African Union Mission to Somalia (AMISOM), in a campaign to drive them from Somalia and force them to abandon the fragile Transitional Federal Government that they support. If this happens, there is little doubt that the Transitional Federal Government will fall to the insurgents in short order. Somali civilians are routinely caught up in shootouts that rage within the city at sporadic intervals. Already this year, hundreds of thousands of the capital's residents have fled the fighting for refugee camps in the surrounding countryside.

In this environment, the diminutive cargo vessel we are escorting will offload her food aid into Mogadishu's small, beleaguered port and from there it will be loaded onto World Food Programme trucks for distribution across Somalia. Most of the time the food makes it to the intended recipients, the most malnourished Somalis, usually found in the country's south. But occasionally hungry mobs loot the trucks as they wind through the capital.[9] At other times insurgents or warlords or bandits seize the food as the vehicles bounce down dusty roads in the country's south. Here, control of food equals control of the population. Four World Food Programme drivers have been murdered during such incidents over the past year.[10] The UN agency's mission will clearly remain in jeopardy long after our cargo ships have docked in Mogadishu's modest port.

The bong bong bong of alarms blaring throughout the ship jolt me upright at my desk. Like Master Seaman Davis and the other communicators sitting across from me in the communications control room, I instantly pull a white fire-resistant hood out of the flash gear bag I carry with me and tug it over my head, positioning the narrow opening in front of my eyes. The mesh that covers my nose and mouth stinks of mouldy sweat. I tug long white gloves over the tops of my sleeves and up to my elbows, then hurry to the bridge.

By the time I push through the door at the top of the ladder, the bridge is already crowded with the crew required for the heightened force protection state that is the ship's response to the multiple threat environment of Mogadishu. Piracy remains a danger in these waters. No attacks on shipping have recently been reported near the capital, but this likely reflects the scarcity of ships daring to draw close rather than a reduction of actual threat. From the storage box, I grab the dark green flak jacket and helmet that is this state's mandatory uniform for bridge personnel, pulling it on as I weave through half a dozen people to reach the port bridge wing. Even from this distance offshore, the anti-Western terrorist threat here is as unpredictable as it is real.

Islamist insurgent groups like Al-Shabaab, "The Youth," an extremist splinter group (rumoured to be aligned with Al Qaeda) of the Islamic Courts Union that ruled Somalia in 2006 before being defeated by the Ethiopian military, dislike foreign intervention in Somalia. What our ship is doing here is no secret. The Canadian government and the World Food Programme have publicly announced that *Ville de Québec* will be escorting vessels carrying food aid to Somalia. Only a few days before, Al-Shabaab posted to their website an expression of displeasure with a Canadian ship entering their waters, labelling us plunderers of Somali resources. Clearly, they and other insurgent groups are aware of our activities. We are a symbol of the West and of detested foreign intervention. The 2001 waterborne terror attack on USS *Cole* in Aden has also made us hyper-vigilant to the possibility of small boat attacks against us.

The captain, Jeff, and a half-dozen others lining the bridge wing scan the harbour and its sandy shoreline with binoculars. MV *Abdul Rahman* loiters off our beam, awaiting the AMISOM boat that will escort it the final stretch into port.

The harbour's light, hot breeze provides little reprieve from the heat baking my body under the weight of the flak vest. A single drop of perspiration runs its slow course down my ribs. With my naked eye I squint at Mogadishu in the distance. Clusters of low, whitewashed buildings line the coastline for several kilometres and rise in layers beyond, reminiscent of sea-breeze-swept Mediterranean towns. The edifices appear refreshingly clean and white and cool in the heat, not at all like the wartorn Mogadishu I've heard about. I eye the high-powered binoculars affixed to the bridge wing.

"Do you mind if I take a look?" I ask the port lookout as he pulls away from the Big Eyes.

"Not at all. Go right ahead, ma'am."

I press my eyes close to the lens and swivel the apparatus until it points at a white building ashore. I adjust the focus. As the details of the structure sharpen and I slowly scan the cityscape, I soon realize my mistake. The city I saw moments ago was a mirage. The buildings are not clean and white and breezy, but crumbling in various states of disrepair. The elegant shapes of some of the larger ones reveal their history as once proud, stately buildings, likely international hotels and government offices. Smaller structures are simple, single- or double-storey homes, now partially destroyed. The walls that still stand are sunken and scarred, pocked with crater-like holes from mortar shells, and with lesser damage from small arms fire. This, the harsh reality, which has now come sharply into focus, is the Mogadishu I've heard about, a city scarred by twenty years of intermittent civil war.

This city is one of the primary reasons why Somalia often tops the world's most dangerous country list and the failed state index. Prior to 1991, Mogadishu was a modern metropolis, with wide avenues and clean, dignified buildings constructed during the pre–Second World War Italian colonial period. The seaside city boasted a lively social set and a thriving restaurant scene that attracted vacationers and elite from all over Africa. People thronged the streets. The generous expanses of white sand beach were among the most stunning in the world.

Now, all I see are bombed-out buildings reduced to rubble, or else empty frames and solitary walls slowly crumbling in on themselves. Warring factions are often less than precise in their aim. Mortar shells and other indiscriminate fire have rained upon civilian neighbourhoods accused of sheltering one side or the other. Gunfights still erupt daily, interrupting periods of unpredictable calm in the city's streets. Countless civilians, including women and children, are killed in the crossfire, the poorest of them unable to flee the violence for outlying refugee camps. All this I've known from reading about it, but witnessing the devastation of once-lovely Mogadishu now, even from a few kilometres distant, brings the tragedy home in a way that no news article could.

The white sand beaches I study through the Big Eyes are still beautiful, at least from this vantage point, and sprawl almost the entire length of the city. Now, though, they possess an eerie quality difficult to pinpoint. I spot a lone dark figure walking along the water's edge and suddenly realize why the scene is so chilling. *There are no people.* Aside from the solitary figure, no people are walking along the shore; no children are playing on the beach or swimming in the warm clear water.

I adjust the Big Eyes. Now I observe the crisscrossing streets and the few wide avenues that rise from the shoreline and disappear into the jumble of skeleton structures that inhabit this city. Like the forlorn beaches,

Aerial view of the Port of Mogadishu during Operation Restore Hope, 1992.

the streets are devoid of life. Nothing moves. No pedestrians meander about, no cars are driven in the streets. Mogadishu is a ghost town.

A few moments of searching offers up a sign of life: a military truck winds up a low hill at a snail's pace toward a prominent set of white buildings that dominate the cityscape. The complex was clearly imposing at one time, but has suffered the same shot-up fate as so much of the rest of the city and retains little of its dignity. From this distance, with its sooty stains and gaping holes where windows once were, the building seems little more than a carcass. This is Villa Somalia, the Presidential Palace, the seat of government for Somalia's presidents. Driven out by violence, the interim government has relocated to Baidoa, the provisional capital, a city a few hundred kilometres to the northwest. The once-proud seat of Somali government is a forlorn, vacuous shell.

On the bridge, half a dozen sets of eyes now skim the harbour's ruffled waters for signs of either the AMISOM boat or fast-moving skiffs. Spotting a small boat at distance in even the slightest chop is a challenge. An occasional fishing skiff, nets cast, appears atop a swell as a tiny speck before disappearing with the sea's next undulation.

I examine the shoreline again. This time I focus on a low, flat building fronted by a prominent runway that runs roughly parallel to the water's edge. This is Mogadishu International Airport, established on what once must have been prime real estate, and serving as the main base of the African Union's Mission to Somalia.

At the north end of the runway is a decaying cargo plane missing an engine, its abandoned, come-here-to-die quality matching that of the ghost town it lies in. Later research will identify it as one of two Belarusian cargo planes fired upon by unidentified assailants in March 2007. This was the first one targeted, and the luckier of the two. It made an emergency landing and the crew and Ugandan peacekeepers aboard survived. Two weeks later, a second plane carrying humanitarian aid and parts for the damaged aircraft was shot down on its approach to Mogadishu, killing all eleven crew members.[11] The Belarusian airline that operated the two planes suspended its operations in Somalia and abandoned the damaged aircraft to its fate. Cargo planes and a few commercial flights continue to operate from the airport, but right now the only activity is the odd military truck moving about.

Past stretches of beach and rock outcroppings lies the port of Mogadishu. A few small boats are tied up at the solitary jetty. Only a single vessel alongside one of the port's six berths is large enough to carry significant cargo. This is MV *Abdul Rahman*'s destination. Here the vessel will unload its cargo of food aid onto the trucks that will carry it into the interior, and hopefully, if not disrupted, to its intended recipients.

Somalia's four deep-water ports — Kismayo to the south, Mogadishu in the central region, and Bossasso and Barbera on the northern coast — were developed in the sixties and seventies to facilitate international trade. Until that time, "lighterage" — shuttling cargo between ship and shore by barge in shallow waters — was the method used in various natural harbours along Somalia's coast. The 1991 civil war hit Mogadishu hard, however, destroying much of the port infrastructure and ultimately forcing the closure of both seaport and airport for more than ten years. Lighterage at nearby natural harbours again became the primary method of bringing goods ashore.[12]

In a second blow, the 2004 Indian Ocean tsunami further damaged port facilities. In 2006, the Islamists gained control of Mogadishu and reopened both the port and the airport. This allowed the resumption of commercial flights and the import of goods by sea. Now, of course, port usage is limited by the piracy threat and the unstable situation ashore — neither especially appealing to commercial vessels.

While researching for our approach, I was surprised to find a functioning website for the Port of Mogadishu. It told me that between thirty and forty-five vessels entered the port each month between January and May of 2008, before steeply dropping off to fifteen in June, just eight in July, and nine so far this month, the number correlating with the gradual increase in piracy. Nine of the fifteen vessels that docked in June were carrying food aid.[13] The World Food Programme probably pushed to deliver as much as possible before the cessation of naval escorts and the suspension of food shipments at month's end.

From his position on the bridge wing, Jeff spots the boat we're looking for.

"Captain, sir," he calls, binoculars pressed to his face. "I can see the AMISOM boat. It has an African Union flag flying and it looks like four people are on board."

The captain swivels the Big Eyes in the indicated direction and locates the black, rubber-hulled boat, a dark speck that my untrained eye can barely make out.

"Okay, raise the boat on VHF."

Jeff disappears into the bridge. A moment later, his voice is distinct on the bridge radio.

"AMISOM RHIB, this is *Ville de Québec*, over."

"HMCS *Ville de Québec*, this is AMISOM," comes a deep, heavily accented male voice. "We are on station and ready for escort."

Our security team disembarks from MV *Abdul Rahman* and the AMISOM boat leads the cargo ship gently away from us and toward the port. The bridge radio crackles to life.

"Captain," comes the voice of *Abdul Rahman*'s master, "God go with you on your journey."

"Thank you, *Abdul Rahman*," replies the captain. "God be with you as well during your time in Mogadishu."[14]

For what seems an eternity, we watch the vessel approach the port and tie up at the jetty. Hoping for the best, I mentally prepare for the worst. The situation is so unpredictable. We can assist with the security of the escorted cargo ship for their part in the World Food Programme mission, but after that no stage of this food delivery is guaranteed.

As we sail out of harbour and beyond the most dangerous waters toward Mombasa, the palpable tension of the bridge dissipates. Some distance out, our flak jackets and helmets come off, but as we settle back into our regular routines, the vague air of uneasiness proves impossible to shake off.

Vessels held by Somali pirates: *Stella Maris, Yenegoa Ocean, Thor Star, Bunga Melati Dua, Iran Deyanat, Irene, BBC Trinidad*

CHAPTER 13

ZANG ZA

Heavily armed Somali pirates have seized another Malaysian tanker
in the latest such attack in the waters off the Horn of Africa country,
a maritime official said on Saturday.[1]

— Reuters, August 30, 2008

Just ten days after the hijacking of MV *Bunga Melati Dua*, pirates capture
her sister ship, MV *Bunga Melati 5*, a second chemical tanker belonging to
Malaysia's leading international shipping line. The tanker and her crew of
forty-one were sailing through the designated security corridor in the Gulf
of Aden, en route from Saudi Arabia to Singapore. Crew members jogging
on the deck first spotted the pirate boats in nearby waters and waved to them,
thinking they were fishermen. The pirates met their friendly waves with a
spray of gunfire. The bridge watch officer manoeuvred the vessel erratically
to evade them, but the hijackers threw an aluminum ladder up the ship's
side and scrambled aboard.[2] Coalition naval forces patrolling in the security
corridor failed to reach *Bunga Melati 5* in time to prevent her capture.

Later, after their release, the tanker's crew will recount how pirates
allowed the Muslim prisoners to fast and pray during the holy month of
Ramadan, then shoved guns in their faces and threatened to kill them.[3]
Despite this optic, the hostages' safety was the pirates' ultimate bargaining
chip for the duration of ransom negotiations.

"After twelve days being there," stated Maheshwaran Muniandy, the
master of *Bunga Melati 5*, "I came to the conclusion that, intentionally,
they are not going to kill any of my crew."[4]

Shortly after the second hijacking, the Malaysian shipping company barred its vessels from travelling through Pirate Alley.[5]

~

In the few days' reprieve before our next escort, we settle into the at-sea routine. The World Food Programme escort schedule is planned weeks in advance but changes constantly, leaving a haggard Jeff to pick up the pieces in late-night planning sessions and relay the new, glued-together schedule to us in the nightly ops brief. The boarding teams rejoin their regular watches, but reserve the choicest time slots on the cardio equipment scattered throughout the ship to maintain their fitness regimen. TiFou and Billy and their respective air crews continue their twice-daily forays over calm, empty waters that seem unlikely sites for a pirate attack.

Each morning I research piracy and Somalia's state of affairs, find gaps in our knowledge, request information from ashore, then scramble madly each afternoon and into the evening to prepare the intelligence brief and dash with it through the flats and into the ops room.

"I'm sorry, I know I'm late," I say as I sheepishly deliver the thumb drive into the palm of a reproving PO Tremblay.

He glances at me but says nothing, his usually charming smile replaced by grim-faced no-time-for-niceties seriousness. But his lost shine is about much more than my tardiness. His once sparkling blue eyes, now underlined by deep pockets, have faded along with his grin. Lacking a second information management director on board, he's a one-man show. Eighteen-hour days are taking their toll.

I'm not always smiling either. Understanding the complicated geopolitical landscape of Somalia and its manifestations of insurgency, extremism, clan warfare, drought, and piracy is an ongoing task that keeps me up late at night — and even then I only scratch the surface. Computer-bound days, interspersed with briefings and meetings, leave my head heavy and my mind fogged. The essence of my job — trying to make sense of and anticipate regional events that might affect the mission — is fascinating to me. But the lack of downtime, the utter absence of variation in routine and setting, could transform the most enthusiastic sailor into a zombie.

The unofficial "morale police," the entertainment representatives in each mess, the cooks, the organizers of banyans, or flight deck barbecues, all endeavour to improve on-board living with "fun" activities intended to break up the shipboard routine. Becky, for example, selects DVDs from the ship's library for evening viewings in the wardroom, balancing dramas, romantic comedies, and thrillers, but only a few officers turn up. The rest of us are too busy or tired or sick of one another's company to bother. Thursdays are steak nights, a special treat for the meat-loving crew. Saturday is pizza night, sometimes delivered direct to our cabins or work spaces in exchange for donations to the ship's ongoing charity drive. Then there's the "duff," navy-speak for dessert. On the wardroom bar after meals lay a mind-blowing array of treats: freshly baked cookies and cakes, pies and puddings, sometimes even ice cream and ingredients to make our own sundaes, surprisingly effective morale-boosters for sailors on long deployments. That's why I don't understand the wardroom's No Duff Challenge. Taped to the wooden pillar that bisects the room is a neatly typed oath, the signatures of a dozen officers scrawled beneath. The officers who have enlisted in the No Duff Challenge, watched with eagle eyes by the rest of the wardroom, have vowed to eat no candy, dessert, or chips until the ship exits the Suez Canal on the way out of this theatre. The drive to get healthy is admirable, but ditching one of the rare pleasures on board would drop my morale faster than a lead weight.

We've just finished a Saturday night pizza dinner and I'm leaning against the wardroom bar, eyeing the sugary spread. Much of the duff has already disappeared. The longer this deployment lasts, the more pre-duffing (eating dessert before the main course) goes on.

"Hey Jen, doing a little double-duffing?" Kevin has materialized just as I reach for a second chocolate chip cookie.

I shoot him a guilty look. "I am. There's a lot of that happening these days."

"I hope you're doing Luc's workout tonight then." His face twists into a wry smile as he reaches for his second piece of pie. "It's your only saving grace."

~

Billy and I flop onto mats laid flat on the flight deck after another of Luc's body-blasting workouts. In an impromptu ritual initiated a few weeks before, we lie motionless as the rest of the group stow away the surrounding mats and return to the ship's confines. I gaze absently at the sky, darkened early now because of our proximity to the equator, and the day's stress falls away. For this rare moment I am entirely in my exhausted body. My million-mile-a-minute mind is empty of the thoughts that weigh heavy on my conscience: my ability to keep up this crazy routine, the flagging of my long-distance relationship with Scott, impending career decisions that will determine my next steps. These workouts *are* my saving grace, in more ways than Kevin knows.

I can just make out Billy's listless shadow beside me. We don't say much, but we both feel good in these moments. Bodies heavy against the deck, we breathe in the warmth of salty ocean air that transforms these gently undulating waters into the most restful place on earth. Not even the engines' constant drone can detract from our hard-won sense of well-being. It hasn't always been so, not even for easygoing Billy.

One night I wandered up to the flight deck on a quest for fresh air and privacy and saw a different side of him. Buried in darkness in his folding camp chair, he was staring out over black water.

"Hey Billy," I said softly, sitting down beside him on a black steel bollard used for anchoring lines. "Are you doing okay?"

For a long time he said nothing. Then, quietly, he began to speak.

"Two of my friends from back home have gotten engaged over the past week. Another buddy of mine is getting married and I won't be there for the wedding." He paused before continuing. "I feel like I'm missing out on so much in my friends' lives right now. I really miss everyone back home."

I was so used to Billy's stoicism that his confession took me by surprise. Because he didn't talk about it, that he was ever less than content on board never occurred to me. Now, lying on his mat, he seems his usual contented self. But that evening served as a reminder to question how much I really know about what goes on beneath his, or anyone else's calm exterior on board.

The flight deck door clangs open behind us. I hold my breath, hoping the intruder is the relief for the lifebuoy sentry, the invisible sailor standing watch at the ship's stern. Instead, a bulky silhouette shuffles toward us, back-lit by the single light over the door.

"Ma'am? Lieutenant Savidge?" queries a low male voice.

I pause, holding onto tonight's reprieve a second longer.

"Yes?"

"The ORO is requesting to see you in the ops room. He'd like you to come right away."

I exhale slowly. "Okay, thanks for letting me know."

He disappears back into the ship and I look over at Billy just as a thought strikes. I laugh out loud. *They're going to have a field day with this one.*

"Let the rumours begin," I say, and Billy laughs too.

"I'm sure it's not the first time."

He's right. It doesn't take much to start a rumour on board. A man and woman lying in close proximity on gym mats is x-rated as far as naval shipboard life goes. At the very least, Billy and I, found alone together, hints at secret romance.

The ship's strict no-fraternization policy provides fertile ground for rumours of undeclared relationships. To be fair to rumour-mongers, human nature makes it probable that for every declared relationship, there are three that are not. Deployments can be lonely; people who spend extended periods of time together will inevitably develop attachments, romantic or otherwise, regardless of whether they're declared even to each other.

Luc and Annette, a sweet-looking MARS officer with short dark hair, declared their relationship prior to the deployment and both were permitted to remain on the ship. But declaring a relationship is a crap-shoot. It removes the secrecy and associated stress, but it also means falling under the scrutiny of crew just waiting to see a slip in professionalism between the two parties — arguing at work, favouritism, or, God forbid, on-board physical intimacy. Luc and Annette have found themselves under the glare of a senior officer at least once, and that was when they were merely chatting in the same cabin, several feet apart.

Hauling myself off the mat, I wave a reluctant farewell to my most recent suspected lover.

"See ya, Billy."

"See ya, Jen."

I grab the backpack containing my naval combats — we must carry our fire retardant uniforms everywhere we go — and work my way through dimly lit flats to the ops room.

Several heads swivel toward me when I push open the heavy door, their inquisitive eyes giving me a once-over in my shorts and T-shirt — inappropriate attire for an operational environment. I tiptoe toward the ORO station.

"*Salut, Serge. Ca va?*"

"*Oui ...*" He turns in my direction and his eyes, too, flick over me.

"Sorry to interrupt your workout," he says, sounding slightly annoyed. "I didn't know if you were aware that another vessel was hijacked. *Carré d'As*. A French yacht."

I press my lips together. Another one taken.

"No, I hadn't heard."

The frequency of these hijackings is becoming absurd. It's difficult now to even keep up with the changing status of each stolen ship.

"Does the captain know?"

"Yes, he was in the ops room when we received the notice."

"I'm assuming she was captured in the Gulf of Aden?"

"Yup."

"Okay. I'll see what details I can dig up."

After a quick shower, I pull my uniform back on, plunk myself at my desk, and get to work. *Carré d'As*, a fifteen-metre Venezuelan-flagged yacht, was sailing from Australia toward the Suez Canal when pirates attacked her. The two French sailors — a couple, both sixty-year-old Tahiti residents — were captured along with the vessel they were delivering to France. For pirates, after having clambered aboard larger and faster vessels, a yacht is easy pickings.

The couple's daughter later recounts having received a call that the yacht's emergency positioning indicator beacon had been triggered. She eventually reached her father via satellite phone, and he told her that pirates were on board. She panicked upon hearing the news, but her father reassured her that everything would be fine, that the pirates were, in fact, "rather cool-headed."[6]

It's not difficult to fathom their daughter's anguish. She's not alone in it: pirates now hold well over a hundred hostages from eight vessels, most in the vicinity of the pirate stronghold of Eyl on Somalia's east coast. Families and friends of every hostage suffer a similar torment. Their loved ones might as well be on the moon for all they can do to help them. It's typically shipping companies and ship owners, not family members, that engage in ransom negotiations with the pirates. Family are held hostage by their own torment as they await resolution.

"Hi, ma'am. Would you like a caramel?"

Master Seaman Davis has materialized beside my desk with a bag of candies in his outstretched hand, loot from his wife's latest care package. It's late. The other communicators are sedate at their stations. I turn toward him with a tired smile.

"I sure would. I could use a sugar kick right about now."

The next day, I learn that, for the release of *Carré d'As* and her crew, the pirates are demanding nearly a million and a half US dollars and the freedom of the six Somali pirates captured by French commandos in the *Le Ponant* hijacking and now held in a French prison.[7]

~

In the waters outside Mombasa the next day, we rendezvous with our second escort vessel. *Zang Za San Chong Nyon Ho* is a cargo ship from North Korea. This in itself is a novelty. North Korea is a notoriously closed society, so the opportunity to meet its seafarers, particularly from a state-run shipping company, is rare.

The vessel is capacious, dwarfing *Abdul Rahman* and most other ships contracted by the World Food Programme. After loading food in South Africa, she carries enough in her holds to feed sixty thousand people for a year.[8] This is fourteen times the amount that *Abdul Rahman* carried to Mogadishu only a few days before.

I watch through the bridge window as *Zang Za* approaches. The ship is close to thirty years old, but is unlike the many decrepit ships in this part of the world. Her superstructure and catwalks are painted a fresh white that contrasts pleasingly with the burnt yellow of the funnels, each adorned with a painted North Korean flag.

The XO, helmet obscuring her short hair, embarks our small boat and shuttles to *Zang Za* amongst the black-clad boarding team's first wave. There she will brief the master on escort procedures. After weeks of what can only be mind-numbing administration as the ship's second-in-command, she is well-deserving of this interesting reprieve. The boat's grey rubber hull bumps gently against *Zang Za*. One after another, the sailors heave themselves and their fifty pounds of body-strapped gear up the ladder's wooden rungs, to be greeted at the top by a smiling North Korean crew.

The first NAST shift returns from *Zang Za* a long while later. Mike, the black-haired engineering officer and team lead, reports that *Zang Za*'s master is grateful for the escort, but most evident is his nervousness about taking his vessel in to Mogadishu. This is a significant common point of understanding, of clear rationality, that transcends cultural boundaries.

Our two ships advance on the port days later. A distance out, the bong bongs sound and we take up our force protection action stations. As our vessels draw closer, a cargo plane, made tiny by distance, makes its lonely approach to Mogadishu's waterfront runway, our first visual of the airport's ongoing operations. A few kilometres out, a shoreline scan reveals hints of life ashore. A handful of people in ones and twos wander the beach; a child plays in the water. A dozen residents — civilians, they look like from here — stroll along the wide avenue that leads up from the port toward the centre of town. Small wooden fishing skiffs are scattered before us in the waters that surround the city.

We saw little of this activity our first time here. It seems like a positive sign. Perhaps normal life is resuming, sneaking in a gulp of air before fighting drives it underground again. Or at least a sham of normality prevails for a few hours or days, while the relative peace endures. Life hasn't been normal here for a long while. An entire generation has grown up since Somalia's last stable government fell in 1991. For young adults who have only known a life that straddles lawlessness and clan-driven order, fighting and desperation *is* normal life.

At least that's what I extrapolate from what I've read. The Somalis I met in Canada were endowed with fine, noble features and effervescent smiles that drew me to them, as we are so often drawn to beautiful people, an archetype now impossible to reconcile with the ugliness of the violence ashore. But outsiders, Westerners, know few details of what transpires here: the diminishing number of journalists in the country translates into declining news coverage of the hard lives of Somalis struggling to get enough to eat, of refugees forced to flee Mogadishu's violence, of idle, rifle-toting youth with no education and bleak futures. What calamities do enter our peripheral attention usually have a hook — a UN worker killed, a foreign journalist abducted — tragedies befalling people more like ourselves. But even these events are old news in a country in which a lack of other sorts of opportunity has come to justify violence. We'll never get close enough to understand what life has become for the average Somali. Perhaps Amanda Lindhout did need to be here to tell the untold story. But to my chaotic mind, whether such a risky venture can rationally be judged worthwhile remains uncertain.

So I study Mogadishu through the Big Eyes mounted on the bridge wing instead. More than its inadequate lens separates me from the ruined city. From a few kilometres offshore, the broad strokes of life here are painted in clear relief, but the nuances of individual stories are lost behind crumbled walls.

Zang Za lumbers toward the black AMISOM boat that waits a few hundred metres away, her freshly painted profile sharp against the city's shambles. I imagine the frayed nerves of her North Korean master as he prepares to gamble on the fates of vessel and crew alongside this perilous port. In a week's time we will return to escort her back to Mombasa. Until then she is on her own. MV *Abdul Rahman*, shrunken next to *Zang Za*, lingers at the jetty where we left her a week before. Her food is not yet unloaded. Looting of the port's cargo handling equipment in the early nineties has left the facility at the mercy of private owners who loan inadequate equipment at their convenience, or to the glacial pace dictated by unloading by hand.[9]

From the bridge wing, the captain's eyes fix on *Zang Za*, one of the last commercial ships that will still go alongside here, as if he is willing her to stay safe. It's for her sake that he would wish it, would will it, but also for the sake of the World Food Programme mission, which is dependent upon the willingness of ships to deliver food here. And for the sake of those same hungry Somali civilians whose story Amanda came to tell. Only when *Zang Za* rounds the corner of the jetty and ties up does the captain — seeming reluctant in my eyes — signal to the officer of the watch to depart.

Vessels held by Somali pirates: *Stella Maris, Yenegoa Ocean, Thor Star, Bunga Melati Dua, Iran Deyanat, Irene, BBC Trinidad, Bunga Melati 5, Carré d'As*

CHAPTER 14

SHORE LEAVE

The two hostages, identified as Jean-Yves and Bernadette Delanne from the French island of Tahiti, were seized by pirates two weeks ago in the Gulf of Aden as they were delivering a 48-foot sailing yacht, the *Carre d'As*, from Australia to La Rochelle, on France's Atlantic coast.[1]

— *The Washington Post*, September 16, 2008

Our frigate slices through vacant waters back to Mombasa. The speed-time-distance painstakingly calculated by Eric, ship's navigator, has us cruising in right on time for the scheduled escort of the next World Food Programme ship. The sea just beyond the Kenyan port undulates softly beneath us as we wait, and then wait longer still, under clear blue skies. After consulting with MV *Golina*'s Pakistani master, alongside Mombasa port with his rusted cargobucket of a ship, the captain decides that we too will go alongside the next morning. The cargo ship is only partially loaded with the food that she will carry to Somalia. It's pointless to remain at sea, burning fuel. Besides, after weeks at sea since departing Crete, the crew is well past restless.

"Are you excited to go alongside, Jen?" asks Kevin between bites of chicken breast at dinner.

More relaxed and sociable than I've seen him in weeks, he even grins at Kate, his crew pilot seated on my other side, with whom he has an uneasy cockpit relationship. She smiles back, happy to be included in his good humour.

In truth, I'm ecstatic, barely able to restrain the inner voice that shouts *Going alongside! Going ashore! Getting off this claustrophobic ship!* I need to keep it from bubbling out of my mouth, which is now set in a tightly controlled smile. The prospect of time away and out of uniform thrills me like anticipation for a junior high dance.

"Yeah, I think I'm ready for a little time ashore," I say in measured tones, glancing at Jeff across from me. Even he has let his guard down a notch, now that the first escort has unfolded successfully. His brown eyes, unsmilingly serious when he's under stress and fed up with his underlings, now sparkle with humour.

"Oh, I think we all are," he says. "Looks like it might be time to gather a few more wooden giraffes."

The ship is alongside by late morning. By twelve, the garbage is landed and stores, mostly fresh produce ordered the day before, have been brought on board.

"Secure! Leave expires at 19:00 hours for ship's company not required for duty!" bellows an enthusiastic voice across the ship's pipe.

A palpable energy vibrates through the flats, emanating from the crew as they retreat into cabins and messes to prepare for forays ashore. Few on board have visited this continent. East African cities are not typical port destinations for the Canadian Navy.

This is my first time in Kenya. It's a world apart in my mind. The name itself came to represent the Africa I idealized growing up, on the basis of little more than Hollywood versions of the country. So going ashore here will be another first, one that will inevitably disappoint when measured against the image I've fabricated and that six months living in Zambia is only beginning to dispel.

Our freedom has been granted only until evening. At that time, MV *Golina*'s readiness for departure can be re-evaluated. By early afternoon I'm readied for my escape, my tan cotton skirt and T-shirt fly-away free against my skin. Sailors emerge into the flats disguised in shorts and worn-in jeans, their place in the ship's hierarchy for once invisible. Anticipation of relief from this pigeon-holed existence drives us outside in clusters, sees us impatiently filing up a crew-clogged ladder before bursting at long last onto a dazzling flight deck, our pale eyes squinting into the blinding African sun. The intense heat, without the sea-breeze buffer to which we've grown accustomed, instantly envelops us. Bizarrely, the newly erected white canvas awning on the flight deck and the quarter-master who lounges beneath look like a long-established part of this golden flight deck scene.

Word travels fast in town. Scores of vendors selling crafts already line the pavement beyond the ship's security cordon, its entrance controlled by a Kenyan port security guard with a semi-automatic rifle casually slung over his shoulder and an accompaniment of sailors.

I step onto the small bus hired by the ship to take us downtown. PO Marcotte stands in front of me, her long dark hair trailing down the back of her blouse. My eyes flit around the vehicle. On the dozen passengers, vibrant summer colours have replaced the drab blue and black tones of shipboard uniforms. A few are dressed down in T-shirts tucked into baggy jeans straining against beer guts, their lacklustre ensemble finished off with a pair of white running shoes, but most of the men and women are dressed stylishly and look more like young professionals than sailors.

The women have undergone the most dramatic transformation, their femininity restored. They are dressed simply enough, but the contrast between their capris or jeans with their sleeveless tops and the austerity of the uniform is sharp. It's like encountering colleagues in evening gowns. Those with longer hair allow it to cascade over their shoulders. Shorter cuts have been styled or tied back with clips and headbands and frame faces transformed into prettier versions of well-scrubbed at-sea visages. But the way they carry themselves is the most dramatic difference. It goes beyond confidence. Their feminine power, exuded in every proud movement of their newly defined figures, lies in having recaptured an expression of their individuality.

Master Seaman Davis sits across from me and behind a young naval communicator I recognize from the communications control room. They stare out the window as we roll through the port facility. We pass dirty warehouses and stacked containers of shipped goods that will eventually make their way inland and into neighbouring land-locked countries. Most of it will be transported on heavily laden lorries that travel the busy highway to Nairobi and onward to Kampala, some along the same rusted railway tracks that we now cross.

The bus soon leaves the griminess of the port and enters the dusty streets that lead into the heart of this city. After Nairobi, Mombasa is Kenya's second largest city, with a population of just under a million. Still, most of the buildings that line the clogged streets of the downtown core are simple single- or double-storey structures, small shops with bland, forgettable façades that impart the impression of a much smaller town. The grand hotels that cater to Westerners and wealthy businesspeople are found in choicer locations along the nearby coastline. The city may be a gateway to the tourism spread along Kenya's coast, but it is the inland capital of Nairobi that is the country's business and political centre.

We peer out the bus windows at pedestrian-crowded streets. Many of the women wear kangas, brightly patterned lengths of cloth, draped around their waists or over their heads and shoulders. Swarms of cars and trucks press in tightly around us. Matutus, the minibuses used for public transportation, are sorry-looking vehicles. Sagging and noisy, they are jammed full of passengers who would otherwise have to walk long distances in the oppressive heat. Their owners invest just enough money in their vehicles to keep them running, neglecting both comfort and safety.

Children greeting sailors in Mombasa, Kenya, August 2008.

Minibuses are a popular form of local transport in most developing countries. I rode them in Zambia. I was a reluctant passenger because of the close press of bodies from the inevitable overloading and the frightening safety record due to excessive speed or drunk driving or poor maintenance that frequently resulted in mass-casualty accidents. Besides, my fellow passengers never got bored of staring at me, not comprehending why a *mzungu*, Swahili for white person, would ride in a minibus instead of in the SUVs common to expatriates.

Only a metre and a half and a few millimetres of cloudy glass separate us now from passengers of the surrounding matutus. They gaze at us, dark eyes wide with naked curiosity at such a concentration of white faces, still a novelty here despite the regular rotation of Western tourists through Mombasa.

The bus has only two scheduled stops: at Fort Jesus, the stronghold built by the Portuguese as protection against foreign invaders in the sixteenth century, and the Castle Royal Hotel, a distinctive but now weary white-pillared structure with a colonialist flavour, in the centre of town.

Nearly all the passengers file off at the hotel with its spacious veranda fronting the street. I peek over its plant-lined barrier and into the open-air seating area. There, ship's crew already occupy a handful of tables, lounging beneath slowly rotating ceiling fans that provide the only hint of coolness in the still heat. There will be no escaping one another here, I think, surprised anew at Mombasa's small-town feel.

A group from the bus marches forward and past their fellow crewmen at the hotel. I fall in beside PO Marcotte.

"Do you mind if I tag along for a bit?" I ask, feeling my face getting hot. "I'll take off once I find another 'buddy' I can explore with."

The ship has imposed the buddy system, a system requiring sailors ashore here to travel in groups of two or more. The Command Team is conscious of the trouble to which our sailors, few of them seasoned travellers, could be exposed, ranging from petty criminality to terrorism targeting Westerners — not unheard of in East Africa. Locals are keenly aware that a Western warship is in town.

But I've planned poorly. By working a few extra hours, I missed the groups of other officers going ashore. Kevin had led Marcus and Billy off the ship's brow at a determined pace, his furrowed brow indicating, as usual, that he would wait for no man or woman in his escape from the ship. I would welcome the opportunity to wander around town alone, but it would set a poor example for the crew when I was inevitably sighted. Now, instead of allowing the crew to decompress, away from the ship and the officers that direct them, I'm forced to be their tag-along.

PO Marcotte is gracious. "That's no problem," she says, the slowness of her drawl at odds with her quick mind. "I don't mind having you around."

My shoulders relax; she might actually mean it. During the six weeks on board, my preoccupation with work has left little time for serious conversation in the communications control room. PO Marcotte is almost exactly my age. We get along well and we share the same work ethic. We even sleep in the same mess. But on-board socializing between officers and petty officers is discouraged, even if there was a common space to do so, inhibiting any opportunity for real friendship between us.

Our group, all dressed in pants or skirts that fall well below the knee out of respect for the city's predominantly Muslim population, weaves its way through chaotic streets crowded with pedestrians. Slowly the group spreads out and I soon lose sight of the lead sailor-cum-guide. The absurdity of the situation strikes me: we've escaped the ship's cloistered quarters only to squeeze en masse through Mombasa's narrow streets — exactly what Kevin was trying to avoid when he bolted. The idea of breaking from the group, abandoning any reminders of the ship, is a sweet siren song, its lure irresistible. With my trademark fast march I could blaze through town, headed nowhere and anywhere. It's not about a desire to embrace the local culture. A year ago, living in Zambia was all about that. Now, a simple desire to roam free, to have no strings attached, no obligations, trumps everything.

Instead, I stick fast to the group as we pass the fort, its crumbling yellow walls looming over us, then round a corner into a narrow shop-lined street. The modest shops occupy the ground floors of three-storey buildings, their entranceways cavernous against the sun's dazzle. Ornate balconies and rounded windows are decorated in various hues, typical of the Swahili architecture that characterizes the old town.

"Jambo!" calls out a shopkeeper in the common Swahili greeting, emerging from a dark doorway as we meander by.

"You from Canada? Came in on the ship today?" he continues enthusiastically. His smile gleams against his dark skin. "Come, just take a look inside," he says, gesturing toward the shop's interior.

I had not planned to advertise my association with the military, common protocol when travelling in foreign countries. But to deny it now, surrounded by this large group so obviously not from here, would be ridiculous. An influx of more than 250 people, almost all *wazungu*, does not go unnoticed in a city the size of Mombasa.

Instead, I mumble vaguely and shoot him a friendly smile.

For the next hour, I trail the others in and out of shops whose crowded shelves showcase variations on the same merchandise: wooden giraffes and hippos, colourful masks, carved boxes, hand-made chess sets. My shipmates are accumulating armloads of tall objects wrapped in news-paper. I suspect them to be the ubiquitous giraffes, destined to continue their infiltration of the ship.

I spy Maggie, a slightly built engineer of Asian descent in her late twenties, huddled with a cluster of ship's officers outside the next shop. She waves.

PO Marcotte is intently examining a carved wooden box.

"Sylvie," I say, smiling shyly. "I'm going to take off and leave you guys alone. Thanks for letting me tag along."

She glances up at me briefly. "Sure, no problem. See you later."

"How's it going?" I say, wandering over to Maggie. I notice a plastic bag under her arm. "Did you buy a wooden giraffe?"

"No. But I bought some cool necklaces and this really beautiful wooden hippo," she says earnestly.

Maggie and I wander away from the group. A small side street winds into another, narrower road that soon becomes a cramped laneway. On either side of us rise three-storey homes. Loaded clotheslines sag between open-shuttered windows. Below them, small children play in the dusty lane, imbuing it with the air of a private front yard through which we now trespass. The residents throw cursory glances our way as we pass through, but their attention, like our passage, is benign.

A cluster of kids, six or seven years old, dressed in dust-packed trousers and faded American T-shirts, karate-chop their way toward us. They kick their legs high as their arms slice the air before them, each faux-karate move synchronized with impassioned shouts.

Maggie laughs, her dark eyes crinkled in good humour.

"Jambo!" she calls out, her petite figure turning to face the approaching force. But they are too busy fighting the air, their jabs steadily gaining in enthusiasm, to reply.

I suddenly understand that the karate moves are for her. The children's limited exposure to other cultures is through film and television; karate is what they think of when they see Asian features. Maggie also recognizes this. The pure simplicity of their interpretation of her, this stranger in their city, their means of crossing cultural boundaries, is strangely touching.

"That's pretty good," she says to them as they continue to practise their moves. "Just like the movies." And she emits another light, cascading laugh.

~

Maggie and I climb up to the ship on a gangway made steep by the changing tide. At the entrance to her cabin, we wave goodbye. I find Kevin and Billy sprawled out on a wardroom sofa.

"We just motored all the way through this town. We went everywhere," Kevin explains without lifting his reclined head. "I'm pretty confident we've seen everything there is to see here. And now we have to stay longer!"

That's the first I've heard of this. "What do you mean?"

"The *Golina* is still loading and won't be ready until tomorrow," Billy says evenly, ever his unruffled self, "so we're here until at least the morning."

"I don't even want to go out tonight," says Kevin. "I've seen everything. There's nowhere interesting to go in town."

"Kevin!" I exclaim. "We've only been ashore half a day. You were bored at sea, now you're bored here. We're only here for one night — of course we're going out!"

He shrugs, indifferent to my outburst. Billy and I exchange exasperated glances.

Two hours later, Kevin having finally been persuaded to join us, our group leaves the bus and heads toward a low flat-roofed building. Club Florida beckons a pink neon sign in the black night, its design holding out the unlikely promise of palm trees, tropical drinks, and a fresh sea breeze. We descend poorly lit stairs, then pass through a dance floor, nearly empty but for a few lanky women swaying to eighties rock, and onto a depressing-looking patio. The promise is instantly dispelled. The patio's cement walls, spartan décor, and sparse clientele give the place an air of hopelessness. The few patrons aside from the dancers are solitary local men by the look of them. They study us as we settle into a large table facing the dance floor.

"Jen, I'm so glad you dragged me out tonight," says Kevin, his sarcasm softened by his characteristic chuckle. "I was so wrong about there not being good places to go to."

"Point taken," I grumble, disappointed myself. "But at least we get to hang out and have a few drinks off the ship."

A comfortable café where we could have a quiet drink and enjoy time out of uniform was more what I had in mind. Club Florida is certainly not that. This seedy club strikes me as a place where local and foreign men with money pick up women.

We nurse our beers, conscious that the two-drink-per-sailor limit for this operation remains in effect. The odd local man and a few groups of junior sailors from the ship occupy additional low-lit tables. The latter deliberately sit at a distance from us on the far side of the room.

"Jen, check out the dance floor," says Marcus. "One of your friends is making his move out there."

I follow his gaze to darkened figures swaying incongruously to a staccato hip-hop tune. My friend is an amiable junior sailor who frequently flashes me ingratiating smiles. Now he presses close to a tall local girl as they slowly rotate on the dance floor. She curls her extra inches of height around him like a protective shield, her long, graceful arms encircling him everywhere at once. Around them, other couples are similarly glued together along the length of bodies that wandering hands explore unabashedly. Several of the men are sailors from the ship. Their partners — clearly sex workers — are all well-defined curves poured into skin-tight jeans and short skirts, beautifully complemented by clear ebony skin and seductive smiles.

We watch from the table with morbid fascination as the couples conduct their mating rituals. The scene is at once tawdry and heart-wrenching in its display of raw human need. Over the year and a half that I've been separated from Scott, I've come to know first-hand the power of the human necessity for any form of intimacy. Separate from any judgment of how it ultimately manifests itself — people have different thresholds for holding out — is the recognition that this need is so innocently human.

We've been six weeks at sea now. For some of these sailors, it probably feels like six months. Some have wives or girlfriends at home, others are single. The crews of frigates sail an average of four to six months a year on deployments and exercises — a lot for a relationship to bear. Many sailors marry young and relatively quickly. An officer once referred to his rapid engagement immediately prior to the deployment as "securing his investment." It sounds callous, but he doesn't mean it to be. Many partners won't wait without a clear idea of what they're waiting for. The navy is a tough business for relationships.

"Man, no one wants to see that," says Marcus, as he watches one of the women take a sailor's hand and lead him through a side door and out into the warm night air. Minutes later they're followed by another couple, pressed tightly together, hip-to-hip, as they exit out the same door.

It's one thing to judge these sailors on their morality, and another to be concerned for their safety. The rate of HIV/AIDS and other sexually transmitted diseases amongst the general population in Kenya is just under 5 percent.[2] Among sex workers, the figure is much higher. The coxswain, Chief Richards, piped these details before granting shore leave, while the medical staff encouraged sailors to help themselves to free condoms offered in the flats outside Sick Bay. But there's only so much babysitting the ship can do. People will make their own choices. Need sometimes outweighs risk. I stare after another excited sailor and his new mate, seemingly oblivious to our prying eyes, as they disappear out the door.

Our group is quiet as we board the bus back to the ship. None of us want what we observed inside. But that doesn't stop a feeling of melancholy from creeping into my chest, reminding me of the void that my newfound friendships aren't able to fill.

Vessels held by Somali pirates: *Stella Maris, Yenegoa Ocean, Thor Star, Bunga Melati Dua, Iran Deyanat, Irene, BBC Trinidad, Bunga Melati 5, Carré d'As*

CHAPTER 15

FAREWELL

The ship was hijacked by 30 Somali pirates, who demanded a ransom as well as the cargo, the crew of the ship said. *Al Mansoura* was transporting cement and left behind 15,000 tons to the attackers.[1]

— *Daily Egypt News*

Our plans have changed again. It will be days before *Golina* is loaded to capacity. Instead of wasting time here, we'll escort *Zang Za* on her return trip through Somali waters and back to Mombasa.

By late morning we are steaming north toward Mogadishu. At lunch, a half-dozen officers are lounging on the wardroom settees. Laughter punctuates their animated conversation. Even Marcus, his full lips upturned in a hint of a smile, appears upbeat. The day ashore has done wonders for morale. Only the few officers consigned to the ship by their duties are noticeably tense.

"Hey," I say as I plunk down beside Jeff at the table, "I didn't see you downtown. Did you get ashore at all?"

"Jennifer," he says, his tone mock-serious as he turns his deadpan face toward me. "Some of us have work to do. We can't all go off and *play* whenever we'd like."

"Right. Guess you didn't get ashore. Again."

Jeff's packed work schedule constantly obliges him to forfeit time ashore, but he refuses to complain. His work ethic and his stoicism are two of the reasons I have such respect for him.

Across the table, Billy shakes his head.

"Jeff, you should at least take a break from shaving — it's very relaxing. I haven't shaved this puppy in weeks," he says mildly, stroking whiskers already blossoming into the full-blown moustache that is creeping down past the corners of his mouth.

Many of the men have allowed their moustaches to grow unhindered since the Suez Canal. They are getting shaggier by the day. Already I can barely recall the clean-cut military grooming with which they commenced the deployment. Growing facial hair while at sea is a naval tradition, a competition of sorts between the men, although victory is trumped by the real reward — skipping the requisite daily shave.

The result, a few weeks in, is a scruffy lot of vagabonds exhibiting a range of unbecoming facial hair, from full-on beards to boyish peach fuzz. A few, like Helmz and Billy and Kevin, are fashioning their lengthening whiskers into biker moustaches or long bushy sideburns or other equally unmilitary designs. Helmz's 'stache is so far the most impressive, lying thick and dark below his nose, then angling sharply downward to his chin and framing his mouth. The menacing look it lends him is comically at odds with his gentle demeanour.

The longer the hair grows, the more I miss the handsome youthful faces supplanted by these Neanderthal visages. The scruffiness is unappealing. For all my mild resistance to military conformity, I appear to have adopted its austere grooming aesthetic as my own.

Later, at the dessert bar, I confide my dismay to Kate. She is in enthusiastic agreement.

"Seriously, I'm sick of looking at it too," she says, her dark eyes glowing as she beams a rare, delightful smile. "Maybe the girls should start a leg-hair-growing competition — or better yet, armpit hair — and see how the guys like that."

The guys around the bar stare at us blankly, clearly not amused at the prospect.

These relatively rare interactions with women, with Kate, Maggie, and PO Marcotte, leave in their wake nostalgia for genuine female connection. Billy, Marcus, and Kevin — by now we are close friends. But close female friendships offer an intimacy that those with men only occasionally do. At times on board, I feel the absence keenly.

~

From our idling position beyond the harbour, which is empty but for a few small fishing skiffs, the bridge watch focuses on MV *Zang Za*. At this distance, there is no sign of the master's previous angst, but I find myself concerned nonetheless. The ship slowly draws away from the Port of Mogadishu's single jetty and glides through quiet chop toward us. From the bridge wing, the captain's eyes are trained on *Zang Za*. The XO, her blond hair peeking out from beneath her ball cap, stands beside him. Nobody utters a word. But there is an almost palpable collective sigh of relief, of empathy for the North Korean crew as their ship safely exits from five nerve-wracking days alongside this no man's land.

I pass Jeff later in the captain's flats.

"To clarify the schedule, as it stands now at least," I say, leaning my back against the bulkhead so as not to block the well-trafficked corridor. "We're escorting *Zang Za* back to Mombasa and then immediately picking up *Golina* for the transit to Mogadishu?"

"Not exactly." Jeff pauses, his face serious. "We just found out that *Zang Za*'s master has cancelled his contract with the World Food Programme. He had some pretty significant security concerns alongside Mogadishu."

"We just found out?"

"Yeah." Jeff lets out a small laugh. "I think he wanted to make sure we would still escort him out, even though he's no longer under WFP. I can't say I blame him."

The master's security concerns are on the mark. In this weapons-rich capital, the modestly trained port security guards assigned to his ship would be useless against a concerted and unexpected attack by any number of armed factions. *Zang Za* will no longer travel to Mombasa to pick up her next food shipment as scheduled, but will now head due east to the relatively safe waters of India. The loss of one of the few vessels still willing to brave pirate-infested waters and a lawless city to deliver food is a blow to the World Food Programme mission. And to ours. Since *Zang Za* carries nearly twice the metric tonnage of smaller cargo vessels like *Abdul Rahman*, her abandonment of the mission is a real setback. But the master's change of heart is hardly surprising. *Ville de Québec*'s sailors can protect ships from piracy during the at-sea escort, but we can do little once they proceed into port. The battle zones in Mogadishu are fluid. It's not improbable that insurgents might choose to target the port in an effort to control this coveted gateway of supplies into the city.

A few dozen kilometres off the coast, we part ways with *Zang Za* as she follows her eastbound route. Attacks off the east coast have been rare over the past six months. But the vessel has not yet escaped the danger zone. In a twist of fate, six weeks later, Jeff receives a distress call from *Zang Za* as she sails through the Strait of Malacca. An important shipping lane between West Malaysia and the Indonesian island of Sumatra, the strait has a history of often-violent attacks by Indonesian pirates. The North Korean master's email, addressed to Jeff, quickly gets to the point: "Now, armed pirates are attacking to my vessel, please urgently arrange rescue to us."

Proud *Zang Za* is under attack. Her master's fears have materialized, just not in the waters off the coast of Somalia. The Straits of Malacca lie nearly four thousand nautical miles to our east — well beyond our range. Jeff relays *Zang Za*'s distress call to anti-piracy authorities near the strait. There is nothing more we can do.

~

At long last, with enough sorghum in her holds to feed five thousand people for a year, MV *Golina* is ready to leave Mombasa.[2] The diminutive cargo ship that now sails toward us projects decrepitude. Rust creeps uncontested up the once deep blue of her hull. A small liaison team from the ship, led by the captain, has already met with *Golina*'s master, a Pakistani mariner with decades of experience in the region and none of the nervousness of *Zang Za*'s master. Somalia's war-torn capital is no novelty for him. His vessel and her seasoned Pakistani crew sail into Mogadishu several times a month, though only occasionally carrying UN food aid.

The escort to Mogadishu is uneventful, a voyage that quickly falls into the monotony of routine. *Golina* sails coolly into port and ties up at the jetty. We buzz back to Mombasa. With no escorts scheduled for the next week, a few days to rejuvenate alongside after four nearly unbroken weeks at sea seems like a distinct possibility. The ship's grapevine fuels the rumour.

But plans and timing alter quickly on this continent. The captain likes to be prepared for anything that might either serve the mission or set it back. Keeping our schedule unpredictable is also wise. It hinders the word-of-mouth network between Mombasa and Mogadishu that could alert would-be pirates about our movements and responsiveness to pirate attacks, and when we are in port and no threat to anyone. Command has been careful to make no promises. Amid wardroom grumblings, the captain elects to remain at sea. I know that the success of the mission is — has to be — his priority. I should know better than to entertain hopes.

Marcus is vocal about this latest development.

"You fishheads just love being at sea," he complains as I fiddle with the cappuccino machine.

I glance up, surprised to be grouped again with the fishheads.

His warm brown eyes narrow. "At this rate, we probably won't go alongside again until October. There's no point even planning for anything."

Kevin chortles beside him, his blue eyes level with mine across the bar.

"It's not like there's anything to do in Mombasa, anyways," he says. "We may as well stay at sea." He has spent enough time on board U.S. navy ships to be acclimatized to shipboard life.

I can't decide which attitude is worse. Exasperated, I glare at them both.

"You guys aren't helping the situation. We will go alongside, eventually, and there *are* things to do in Mombasa. How can you even say there's not, Kevin? Before all this happened, you were planning to vacation around there in a few months' time, and on your own dime."

In secret, though, I share Marcus's concern. The prospect of being incessantly cloistered in these narrow spaces for the next few months is enough to drive anyone mad.

The capture of another vessel quickly brings me back to reality. Pirates board the Egyptian-flagged cargo ship MV *Al Mansoura* in the Gulf of Aden, taking hostage her twenty-five Egyptian crew.

The following morning we leave hastily to rescue *Golina* from her perilous berth. We are receiving consistent reports of seaborne attacks and hijackings farther north in the Gulf of Aden, of battling in Mogadishu and attacks on aid workers in southern Somalia, that remind us that the unpredictable environment in which we're operating could quickly deteriorate.

My soft rap is tinny against the door of Jeff's cabin in the officers' flats.

"Come in," says a quiet voice after a few seconds' pause. I push aside the heavy navy curtain over the door, which allows a modicum of privacy, and tiptoe in.

On either side of the room are bolted two plain desks equipped with laptop computers. Jeff is seated at the one on the right, focused on his computer screen. Papers spill across the second desk belonging to TiFou.

To the left of TiFou's desk, a small metal sink with a square utilitarian mirror above it is secured to the wall. Two racks are attached, bunk-bed style, to the bulkhead opposite me. Blankets are draped over the curtain rod affixed to the ceiling that surrounds the top rack on two sides, creating a fort-like enclosure — the Time Machine itself — within which TiFou gets his pilot's beauty sleep. With such shielding from the outside world, it's impossible to determine if he is, at this moment, hidden inside.

The bottom rack, Jeff's, is folded neatly back against the bulkhead in the style of a mini Murphy bed. This instantly converts it into a settee appropriate for daytime use as a working space. Large drawers underlie the settee, while the remaining storage space consists of two lockers on opposite sides of the room. Unlike the crowded mess decks, the privacy and personal space these small cabins afford is luxurious.

Few personal touches adorn this cabin. Cold and clean, the spartan décor is in keeping with most of the ship's spaces. The photos tacked to the bulkhead beside Jeff's bed are notable exceptions. Two baby boys, one dark and one fair, gaze out in various states of mischief. Every day, Jeff's wife emails him new photos of the twins — only six months old when he left Halifax.

I lower myself onto the settee and cradle my covered coffee mug. Jeff waves me over to his computer, and as I hover at his shoulder he clicks through the newest photos of his sons. In one image the two boys are crawling, laughing at one another with open mouths across the few inches that separate them. In another the dark-haired baby has pulled himself up to standing in his crib, gripping the rails as he stares up at the camera with wide brown eyes. In a third image, his fair brother is settled back in a chair, chortling with glee.

"Pretty cute, aren't they?" Jeff says, with the soft look playing across his face that he wears only when speaking of his children. Then, to camouflage the paternal pride that motivates these photo displays, he says "You girls love this stuff."

His devotion to his sons is moving. I nod my agreement and smile warmly back at him. "They're adorable. You must really miss them."

Jeff doesn't answer. Instead, he focuses on shutting down the slide show.

I return to the settee. Out of the corner of my eye I spot a wooden monkey tucked into the corner of Jeff's desk. I lean closer for a better look. The monkey is small, the size of a chipmunk, and its dark, sleek body rests, Buddha-like, on its haunches. A long tail extends upward in a smooth arc.

"I like your monkey," I say with an ironic smile. Jeff has endlessly mocked the host of African carvings that have invaded the ship since our first alongside in Mombasa, so I have to ask. "Did you suddenly develop an affinity for wooden monkeys or something?"

His eyes twinkle. "The Maj hates monkeys. He had a bad experience with a monkey in Thailand."

At that moment, TiFou shoves the curtain aside and walks into the cabin, stopping just inside the door.

"Are you talking about the goddamn monkey?" he asks, a severe look on his thin face. "This morning I woke up to find it perched on the edge of the Time Machine, staring at me as I slept."

Jeff is laughing soundlessly at his desk, clearly enjoying himself. By the end of the deployment, Jeff will host a large monkey family on his desk for the express purpose of taunting TiFou. One he will even rescue from Helmz and Mike, who abuse it by using it as a door-knocker, and take under his protection.

"It's not funny." TiFou's eyes drill into Jeff. "I hate monkeys." With that he exits the cabin.

After a moment of private speculation on the origin of his monkey hatred, I get to the purpose of my visit.

"Jeff, I just wanted to give you a quick summary of recent piracy activity, to make sure you're up to speed." I wait for his nod before taking a notebook from my breast pocket and glancing down at the scribbled references in it.

"All of the activity that's occurred over the last four days has been in the Gulf of Aden. Still no piracy activity reported off the East Coast, in the area that we're transiting. Pirates continue to hold hijacked ships in the vicinity of Eyl or Hobyo, coastal villages in Puntland, approximately three to five hundred nautical miles north of Mogadishu." This is much farther north than we are likely to sail while carrying out escort duties.

"As you know, the cargo vessel *Al Mansoura* was hijacked four days ago. No further information on that attack." I look up to see Jeff nodding. "Over the last three days, three more attempted hijackings in the Gulf of Aden have been reported. A general cargo ship and a tanker were fired upon in separate incidents. Pirates also attempted to board a liquefied petroleum gas tanker. These all occurred in the same area of the gulf, closer to the Yemen side, so it's likely the same pirates lying in wait for passing ships. The piracy activity is on a steady rise and shows no signs of abating."

I look up from my notes.

"That's it?" Jeff says. We look at each other and laugh drily.

~

The Crossing the Line ceremony is set for the next day. Finding time for the two-day event in the midst of an ever-changing escort schedule has been tricky. We have already crossed the equator eight times. Now it's just one more ship's routine that has ceased to be novel. To already initiated cynics like Kevin, holding the ceremony belatedly seems pointless.

"The moment has passed," he says. "If you're not going to do it the first time around, why bother?"

"It's naval tradition!" I protest self-consciously, loath to show Kevin that a part of me remains attached to the idea of the ceremony. No steadfast adherent to tradition, I still abide by the philosophy of trying everything once — at least the things that won't kill me.

"I'm sure it's no big deal, but I don't want to have *not* done it."

Like me, Billy and Jeff are Pollywogs. The next morning, the Shellbacks invite us to breakfast in the junior ranks mess. Standing in the galley lineup outside the cafeteria, we watch as Shellbacks-cum-chefs flop servings of cold green eggs, bright pink hash browns, and sickly looking bluish sausage onto our plates.

"Enjoy! Eat it all up!" says one Master Seaman Shellback, grinning as he hands me a heaping portion.

Part of the initiation ritual is the obligatory consumpton of unappetizing food, but the rainbow of food arrayed on my plate is not bad compared to the gastronomic nightmares at other ceremonies I've heard about. Beside me at the cafeteria table, Billy gobbles down his portion as if it's the best of gourmet cooking.

His thickly lashed eyes flick up to see me watching him.

"What? It's not bad. The eggs are cold, but whatever."

Shellbacks of all ranks patrol the dining area to ensure that we Pollywogs demonstrate a healthy appetite. Across from me, Jeff indicates with his eyes, not as subtly as he intends, that I should look under the table. There he holds a plastic bag containing his unwanted food. Into it go my eggs and hash browns. I'm enjoying the blue sausages, so I keep those on my plate.

The main initiation ritual is planned to take place the next day on the upper decks, in conjunction with a barbecue on the flight deck. The prospect of open air, sunshine, and dressing down in shorts and T-shirts is, as usual, absurdly exciting. But the sea is pitching and rolling as I spill from my rack the next morning. I fight the moving ladders to reach the bridge. Ominous grey clouds dominate the sky, dumping heavy rain over the ship and into the growing swells. Soon the officer of the watch pipes the cancellation of the ceremony in a voice devoid of emotion.[3] My heart sinks and I stare out the bridge window. I'm embarrassed at my disappointment. The defused anticipation leaves an empty feeling in my chest, and I resign myself again to the monotony of life at sea.

Vessels held by Somali pirates: *Stella Maris, Yenegoa Ocean, Thor Star, Bunga Melati Dua, Iran Deyanat, Irene, BBC Trinidad, Bunga Melati 5, Carré d'As, Al Mansoura*

CHAPTER 16

ASHORE AGAIN

Somali pirates have hijacked a South Korean cargo ship off the coast of the Horn of Africa nation with 21 crew members aboard, a regional maritime official confirmed on Wednesday.[1]

— *Xinhua*, September 11, 2008

By the time we arrive in the environs of Somalia's crumbling capital to rendezvous with MV *Golina*, the resilient little vessel has endured a full week alongside as her cargo was unloaded, her hardened crew seemingly indifferent to the city's anarchy. Now, the backdrop of Mogadishu hazy behind her, she trails the AMISOM boat and its rifle-toting soldiers to reunite with us at our position. Soon our two vessels are plotting a careful course back to Mombasa.

That same day, pirates hijack another ship, MV *Bright Ruby*, with twenty-one crew. The South Korean bulk carrier was transiting through the Gulf of Aden en route from Europe to Asia when she was attacked. Her captors now force her to sail southbound toward their coastal stronghold of Eyl.[2] Dangerously, accounts of hijackings have begun to lose their shock value. New attacks on shipping are reported almost daily in what have become the world's most dangerous waters. Three serious attacks on commercial ships have occurred in the last two days alone, their capture averted only by the swift reactions of crews alert to signs of an assault and a prompt response by coalition ships and aircraft.

With the crew of *Bright Ruby* added to the tally, Somali pirates now hold ten ships and close to two hundred hostages — a multinational sampling from Pakistan, Bangladesh, France, India, the Philippines, Malaysia, Nigeria, Iran, Ghana, Slovenia, Russia, Croatia, and Thailand.[3] That's a lot of countries to upset. India, Russia, and Malaysia are already signalling their intent to add warships to the increasing numbers of coalition vessels dedicated to anti-piracy tasks in the region. The additions will increase the danger to pirates, but perhaps not enough to act as a serious deterrent, given the enormous economic payoff from ransomed ships.

The very next day, MV *BBC Trinidad*'s German owner pays a ransom to the pirates who have held her for twenty-one days. The exact amount is undisclosed, but the owner admits to paying over a million dollars to release vessel and crew.[4] The ransom is delivered in hard currency carried in two suitcases, taken by helicopter from Nairobi to Mombasa, then delivered by tugboat to the pirates aboard the hijacked ship by a British security firm. Beyond providing an incentive for pirates to continue to hijack, the payment of ransom increases the pirates' capacity to purchase faster boats and more weapons, making them better at what they do.[5] But what choice do the shipping companies have when lives are on the line?

~

"Mail!"

Jean sweeps into the wardroom with an armload of packages piled to his chin. Large padded envelopes rest atop boxes weathered in the globetrotting chase from Canada to our latest port. Becky follows behind, her arms gripping a second avalanche of mail. It's just an hour since we arrived in Mombasa for three full days alongside. We had been looking forward to this barrage of mail. On the coffee table in front of Kevin, Jean piles several packages, presumably filled with magazines and photos and sweet treats.

"Thanks, Jean," says Kevin, glancing casually at the parcels before returning his attention to a magazine.

"You're so lucky!" I say ardently, eyeing his treasure from my place on the settee. "Who sends you all these care packages?"

"A few of my lady-friends are very good to me." He looks up at me and chuckles, his twinkling eyes defusing the envy in my stare.

"Jen, you have a package here," calls Jean from across the room.

My head snaps up from my mug of tea and I am instantly at the bar, eyes wide.

"Ha! I finally got a care package!" I bellow to anyone who will listen, grinning broadly.

"Marcus, did you see this?" I hold up a medium-size white box and he nods back encouragingly, his tightly pressed lips containing a smile.

This is nearly unprecedented. I've so far received only one care package, sent upon request by my parents. I settle back against the faux leather of the settee in preparation for a prolonged ceremony. First I examine the dirt-streaked exterior of the package. The return address is that of Melissa, a close friend and fellow naval officer. A surge of affection for her grips me.

After cautiously slicing open the box with a ship's knife borrowed from Helmz, I carefully lift out the contents. I unscrew the top from a bottle of body lotion, breathing in its mildly sweet coconut aroma. Next I pull out a delicately feminine camisole, then a teal blouse for hypothetical nights on the town. Assorted candies and chocolate fill up the next third of the box, underneath which lie five pairs of lacy underpants in vibrant pinks and purples. Girlishness is not my thing, but I'm nevertheless in love with it all, with these bright antidotes to the ship's grey sterility.

I pull out the card last. Sarah, another close naval officer friend, has also contributed. She and Melissa are both beautiful, intelligent women who excel at their military jobs. Reading their sweet words of encouragement and support, I realize how much I miss them, and how well their strong feminine presence would counterbalance the heavy weight of shipborne testosterone. Carefully I repack the box for further examination in my cabin.

At short notice, Becky has organized one- and two-day safaris only a few hours outside of Mombasa. Billy stands beside me as I scrawl my name beneath his on the signup sheets in the second deck flats.

"Awesome. It's going to be a good time," he says as our palms slap weakly together in a mock high-five. Kevin and TiFou have signed up for the same overnight trip. Marcus's duty watch restricts him to the ship.

That evening, the five of us take a chartered bus to Mombasa's north shore. I glance out my window at scenes of haggard women trudging home from work, of inscrutable faces staring at us through the windows of packed minibuses, of children playing in dusty side streets. I'm ashamed to admit that at this moment I have little interest in the local culture. All I want is to be off the ship and somewhere that demands little of me.

We hop off the bus at the Diani Reef Beach Resort. Inside, the foyer is dominated by white marble and modern oak furniture enlivened with tasteful groupings of tropical foliage. Clean, airy, and insulated, it feels worlds away from the poverty and chaos of Mombasa. Spacious lounges open onto an extended outdoor patio — just the sort of space we've been craving. Moving past the open-air bar and sprawling pool, we seat ourselves at one of the tables scattered across a palm tree–sprinkled lawn. Beyond the lawn lies an enticing expanse of pristine beach. Warm gusts from the sea whip my hair into my face. We are the restaurant's patrons. A Kenyan waiter dressed in a pressed white uniform, his manner deferential, approaches to take our drink order.

"Is it usually so quiet here?" I ask, gesturing at the empty tables spread across the large property.

"This year, yes," he sighs. "There are not very many tourists coming here since the election violence last year."

Kenya is one of the most stable countries in East Africa, but opposition supporters rampaged in reaction to manipulation of Kenya's 2007 presidential elections, which resulted in over a thousand deaths and displaced hundreds of thousands of people. I was in Zambia at the time. Some Westerners, including Canadian interns working under the same CIDA-funded program that I managed, enjoyed an easy escape route from the instability and were evacuated from the country. Until now I had given little thought to the effect of the exodus and the lingering fear of renewed violence on a tourism-dependent economy like Kenya's.

We are each silent as we relax into the luxurious space and temporarily relinquish the obligations that bind us — to the ship, to our families, to our partners, to one another. I breathe in deeply. Behind us, the sun sinks into an ocean that seems only a distant cousin of the body of water that hosts our ship.

Kevin, Marcus, Billy, TiFou — their faces have already settled into expressions of utter contentment. We are all absorbed in the moment but blissfully aware of three full days of freedom stretching before us. The time cloistered aboard ship has given me a new appreciation of space, personal time, and even of money. This reprioritization of values justifies spending an exorbitant amount of the hardship, risk, and foreign service allowances granted on these infrequent reprieves. We will head back to the ship tonight, though, content to savour the reward of returning to this luxury for another two days.

~

At five the next morning, two safari minibuses park outside the ship. Bleary-eyed, I board the first, which is loaded with junior sailors. By the time I realize my mistake, the officers' bus is full. Kevin is gracious enough to join me, while Billy, Jeff, and TiFou ride in the other. I discover that Kevin is a morning person. He spends the next hour trying to engage me in a one-sided debate on U.S. politics, his Chicago twang becoming more pronounced with growth of enthusiasm for his topic. Not a morning person, I barely manage a grunt in reply. Finally I can handle it no longer.

"Kevin!" I snarl, snapping my head toward him. "It's six in the morning! This is what you want to talk to me about at this hour? Really?"

He chuckles, displaying his gleaming teeth. "Fine. What do you want to talk about?"

"That's the point — preferably nothing. It's too early for talking."

Soon the point is moot. The astonishing amount and variety of wildlife in Tsavo East National Park seizes our attention. As the truck trundles down dusty roads, we gaze astonished through open windows at the wide expanse of savannah stretching before us. Giraffes, zebras, elephants, and baboons wander casually by in no particular hurry, or else pause to feed on the sparse foliage, apparently oblivious to our intrusion. Less abundant are the lions. They stretch out long, lazy bodies in ones and twos under the rare shady spots in these dry grasslands — beneath a stunted tree or in the shadow cast by a slab of concrete, incongruous in this wild landscape. Already, the mid-morning sun is scorching the barren plains. We are so immersed in watching these animals, so excited to witness all this wonder that is so natural here, that everyday distractions simply fall away.

Over lunch at the safari lodge, the officers around the table are animated.

"Did you see that lion just strolling around? That was incredible!" Kevin exclaims with his blue eyes wide and excited. All traces of his cynicism have vanished.

"How about that baboon that came right up to the window? Those things are fierce-looking," says Billy.

In sharp contrast with the general weariness that had settled over everyone on the ship, all eyes around the table now shine with the exhilaration of new experience. The magic of African wildlife has caught everyone by surprise. Witnessing the beauty and grace of these animals in their natural habitat is life-affirming. The reality of violence and suffering in Somalia that has infiltrated most of my waking moments over the last months now feels distant.

Later, against a backdrop of elephants ambling in a slow-moving line toward a nearby watering hole, I snap photos of Kevin. When I review the images on the camera's tiny screen, there is his smile, glowing against his tanned skin and his new golden moustache. His physique, always deliberately arranged, is unfailingly framed at a flattering angle.

I roll my eyes and laugh. "God, Kevin," I say, "you have this golden smile, and you're so perfect and posed — in every single photo." I glance up at him. "It's like you've been practising in the mirror." He laughs, too, knowing not to take himself too seriously.

"What?" he says, grinning and shrugging, "I like to look my best at all times. And I can't help it if the camera loves me."

Later, as the day winds down, the distant form of a hyena materializes, its spotted dirty yellow body bounding through the tall, dry grass, roundish ears barely visible above it. The playful air is at odds with the reputation of a species known for zeroing in for the kill.

"Kevin," — I nudge him gently with my knee and point at the scavenger — "He reminds me of you — a playful, independent opportunist. You're like a golden hyena." I'm picturing a clever hyena with a mischievous smile. He chuckles, oddly pleased with the comparison.

He decides that I'm a lioness, the elusive creature that has held me riveted since my first Zambian safari, so I'm flattered, even though I know the allusion is more to my unruly mane of hair than to a brave heart or any other noble quality. Unbeknownst to our friends in the other safari truck, we decide that TiFou is a temperamental monkey, Jeff a wise giraffe, and Billy a gentle panda bear — this last a bit misplaced in Africa, but the only fitting comparison for our placid friend. Marcus, absent from this safari, and missed, is a fiery and impetuous baboon.

At the safari lodge, our thatch-roofed accommodation pods, supported on stilts, are connected by long breezy walkways. With the few other guests, the ship's crew migrate to an open-air bar as the sun sinks into the distant trees. The elevated veranda overlooks a watering hole cleverly incorporated into the precincts of the lodge so we can watch the stream of elephants that wander in and out in orderly lines, drinking their fill and then moving on in the fading light, oblivious to our overhead vigil. For once we are all silent, leaning our hips against the bamboo railing, beers in hand, mesmerized by the spectacle below.

Except for the skeleton crew of the duty watch, the ship is a ghost town when we return the next day. Marcus finished his duty watch that morning and is restless to leave. Within an hour of arrival our little group has again escaped on a bus heading to the north coast, where we check into the seaside resort we visited two nights earlier.

My room, opened up by its high ceilings and light décor, is luxurious and pristine. A majestic walk-in mosquito net surrounds the king-size bed. I immediately dive through the opening onto a soft mattress with a white feather duvet and lay my head on one of the many delicate cushions lining the headboard. Then I make my way to the balcony overlooking an impeccably manicured tropical garden and inhale the fragrant blend of flowers and greenery and ocean, another very welcome contrast to the overcirculated air of the ship. In the shower, finally, the balm of steaming water caresses my skin and begins to loosen each muscle in my back. This space is magic, and I seriously consider closing myself in for the night. Leaving this quiet haven seems like pure squandering. Overcoming my resistance, though, I dress for dinner, pulling on jeans and a black blouse. By the time I have untangled my wet hair I am a thousand times renewed.

In the lounge, the men are leaning back on carved teak furniture, sipping scotch on the rocks. Kevin, TiFou, and Billy are casual but stylish in jeans and button-down shirts. Marcus is sleek in tailored slacks, a fitted light pink shirt. I detect a whiff of cologne. After an elegant dinner, we stroll toward the wide stretch of white sand beach, pausing on the gently lit garden path to listen to the sound of rolling water invisible in the darkness ahead.

"Let's go swimming!" I blurt out, giddy with excitement, as we reach the beach and kick off our shoes. My outburst sounds childish, I know, but I feel like a child in my appreciation of this moment, the sudden sublime joy of being a sailor on shore leave with an entire day of freedom stretching ahead, and with these friends.

Billy rises instantly to the challenge. "I'm in," he says, his dimples deepening.

"Sure, why not," says TiFou.

"He loves this stuff — of course he's in," says Marcus. He rolls up his shirt sleeves.

Kevin is the only holdout.

"I'm out. See you guys later," he says, picking up his shoes and trudging along the beach toward the hotel.

"What's with him?"

"I think he just wants to take advantage of the Internet connection to Skype his friends back home," replies Billy. Kevin, too, is feeling the effects of separation.

Soon the four of us are floating in the warm saltwater and bobbing with the gentle swells. The glow of the half-moon reflects off the water. In its modest way, it dazzles us into a state of unadulterated delight.

"This is amazing!" I call out as a wave lifts me off the sandy floor. "Marcus, I bet you're loving the navy now! Where else would you get the chance to do this?"

"Fair enough. I can't argue with you on that," he replies, a smile in his voice.

Eventually we tire of our cavorting and return to our rooms just after the twelve o'clock curfew that the ship has imposed on crew sleeping ashore. As I open my hotel room door, I half-expect the phone to be ringing off the hook, a duty person on the other end — perhaps even Kate, tonight's duty air officer — frantically attempting to confirm that I'm safely tucked into bed. But it's silent. Subject to a curfew in my thirties after years of solo travel occasionally deepens my perplexity at the occupation in which I now find myself. At the same time, I know that not all of the ship's company are mature or experienced enough to safely explore a poor, insecure region like East Africa. The two-drink rule and the curfew are meant to limit the chances of sailors getting into trouble while blowing off steam in foreign ports after confined periods at sea. The curfew now seems a small price to pay for our relative freedom.

I sleep fitfully in the king bed. The content of my dreams is hazy, but they leave me with a warm feeling that eludes me on board ship. While I revel in the peace and security of the resort, pirates attack and board MT *Stolt Valor*, a Hong Kong–flagged chemical tanker, in the Gulf of Aden. The twenty-two crew on board are now hostages.[6]

Vessels held by Somali pirates: *Stella Maris, Yenegoa Ocean, Thor Star, Bunga Melati Dua, Iran Deyanat, Irene, Bunga Melati 5, Carré d'As, Al Mansoura, Bright Ruby, Stolt Valor*

CHAPTER 17

MEDIA

The chemical tanker MT *Stolt Valor* was hijacked from the Gulf of Aden near Somalia on Monday, Andrew Mwangura, East Africa Coordinator of Seafarers Assistance Program (SAP) said.[1]
— IBN Live, September 18, 2008

Tom, the Canadian Forces' public affairs officer who embarked in Souda Bay, towers over the other officers. At six foot five, he is constantly ducking his head to avoid collision with the ship's low bulkheads and now stands with a mild stoop that a month on board has rendered semi-permanent. His occupation is seemingly at odds with his low-key personality. Tom mediates between an array of reporters interested in the mission and the command team, organizing media interviews with the captain and other crew that are later conducted via satellite phone or in person in Mombasa. With the marked rise in hijackings over the past few months, piracy is fast becoming a hot topic with the media.

The military padre and medical doctor, who also embarked in Souda Bay, have similarly non-disruptive personalities. The doc and moustached padre are more than a decade older than most of the officers and keep to themselves when off the ship. On board, both provide personal counselling when sailors require it and make a point of remaining accessible.

Mid-morning on Sunday I slip into the wardroom for my ritual coffee. The room is nearly vacant. Only the padre remains, tentatively perched on the couch. A joyous melody, sung in an unusually pleasant alto, floats from the speakers beside the TV.

"Hello, Jennifer," the padre says amicably, turning his pleasant gaze away from the screen and toward me. "How are you this morning?"

"I'm fine, thanks, Padre."

As always, his kind, hungry eyes search my face in anticipation of meaningful dialogue. He often seems to want to chat while, perhaps in a subconscious reaction to his profession, I rarely want to communicate anything beyond superficialities. My glance moves past him and latches on to the television screen. Only now do I notice the content: a background graphic of wind-blown meadow fades into an orange sun sinking into the sea, while words play across the bottom of the screen. *I'm searching for a way ahead, and I know it's through You ...*

I now realize that I'm listening to the lyrics of a jazzed-up religious hymn flowing through the room. It could be easily mistaken for a pop song, so catchy is its melody and so modern its influences.

"Oh, right. You're doing the Sunday service in here. What time is that at?" I ask carefully, so that I know when to steer clear of the wardroom. Military padres fall into their religious denominations, but the services they hold are designed to be accessible for all those seeking religious or spiritual guidance. The world's religions are well-represented among military members.

The padre has watched me absorb the lyrics and now misinterprets my interest. "Are you planning to come to the service, Jennifer?"

I stare at him, alarmed, before I again manage a neutral expression. Though I have little interest in attending a service, I have nothing against religion in particular.

"I don't think so, Padre. I have a lot of work that can't wait," I say, attempting a sweet smile. "How's the crew turnout?"

"It varies from week to week, depending on what's going on in the ship. But we usually get a few."

A timid knock draws our attention to the open door. A young girl stands there hesitantly, obviously self-conscious about stepping into the wardroom. We beckon her in. I recognize her as one of the junior sailors, a former nun, I hear, who, with her shock of wavy hair and angelic face, fits that image to a tee. She quickly busies herself with setting up the service as I make my escape.

~

A half-dozen news reporters embark in Mombasa, a ragtag group from Reuters, AFP, CBC, and the *London Times*. They will accompany us for the four days of escorting *Golina* to Mogadishu for a second time and then back to Mombasa. Tom manages their movements and tours throughout the ship, coordinates their interviews with the crew. He even arranges for them to ride in the helicopter during routine flights. The captain understands well the public affairs function: for an uncontroversial mission like this one, media coverage is a positive thing.

The journalists are welcome in all three messes. Most stick close to the wardroom for the initial days of the escort, since the only activity observable from the bridge is *Golina*'s modest silhouette steaming off our beam with her cargo of sorghum, corn soya blend, and vegetable oil. From the get-go, sociable officers with time on their hands like Manny and Jean chat easily with the outsiders lounging comfortably on the settees. For the rest of us, the journalists' invasion of our tight space is an inconvenience to some and, to others, a welcome diversion from routine. Their presence infuses the wardroom with new energy. The few reporters I chat with are interesting and interested, especially the CBC's David McGuffin, a modest man with a kind face. The lone female among them, an attractive French girl in her mid-twenties with long dark hair, emanates a keen vitality, at least according to the male officers. New female blood on board makes her the talk of the ship. But most of us feel constrained while guests occupy our coveted space, unable to speak freely for fear of the complaints they might record. We clear out of the wardroom once we finish eating.

Holed away in the communications control room, I read voraciously on the Somalia-based events that took place during our time ashore. Each day has brought new tragedy: the looting of a truck carrying food aid by hungry mobs in Mogadishu, the effects of the worsening drought in the country's south, the assassination of an aid worker by Islamist insurgents, the indiscriminate killing of civilians in the shelling of Mogadishu's Bakara Market, an insurgent attack on AMISOM troops, another hijacking by pirates. Even at this distance, the situation is heartbreaking.

But I'm only reading words on paper. How to fathom such suffering? I can't get close enough to truly understand what it does to a person.

Part of me doesn't want to, knows better than to approach the experience too closely, understands that it can change a person. But another part craves real comprehension of the depth of this human misery. I can continue to do my job without knowing it, but I have an inkling that deepening my understanding to a level more profound than that of the intellect would provide a bridge to genuine human compassion. Still, I have no illusions. Grasping any land-based reality while on a ship kilometres offshore is virtually impossible, and there are no Somali safaris. Just ask Amanda Lindhout.

Perhaps that truth was what she was seeking when she made herself so vulnerable in Mogadishu. I wonder if the embarked journalists have any desire to experience that rawness, or if some of them have already, perhaps, been forced to shed their idealism along the way, the idea that it is worth the risk. Or perhaps they are content to remain on board and tell the story of piracy, of conflict, and of drought, from this relatively safe distance.

As I sip my morning coffee, I read about Mogadishu airport, now serving as AMISOM's main base. Islamist insurgent group Al-Shabaab has demanded the airport's closure and now threatens to shoot down any planes flying in.[2] Nobody believes the threat is empty. The damaged cargo plane abandoned on the tarmac provides ample evidence that insurgents have done it before. Rocket-propelled grenades and surface-to-air missiles capable of bringing down aircraft are in abundant supply in this weapon-ridden city.

Commercial and military flights operate out of the airport on a daily basis. Al-Shabaab claims that the airport is used by Ugandan and Burundi mercenaries — a reference to AMISOM soldiers — amongst other "infidels."[3] Airport officials indicate that they have no choice but to cede to the closure demand. The airport occupies what must have once been prime seafront real estate adjacent to Mogadishu harbour and just a few coastal kilometres from the port where MV *Golina* will unload her cargo. Most of the twenty-two hundred AMISOM troops, including our friends in the escort boat that will accompany *Golina* into the port, are based there. Shutting down the airport will close down an important supply route for local businesses and AMISOM alike.

In somewhat more positive news, soldiers belonging to the underwater combat unit of France's Special Forces have stormed the leisure yacht *Carré d'As* and rescued the two French hostages held for the past two weeks. The French decided to take action as the hijacked vessel approached Eyl, the pirate stronghold, where, had the hostages been taken ashore, their rescue would have been much more complicated.

During the previous night, a helicopter from French frigate *le Courbet*, which had been shadowing the pirates and their hostages, ferried the commandos close to the hijacked yacht. There they parachuted into the dark ocean and swam toward *Carré d'As* with the aid of night-vision goggles. They surprised the pirates after silently climbing aboard with ropes and grappling hooks.[4] Upon waking, one pirate reached for his gun and was instantly shot. The six others, along with the rescued couple, were taken to the frigate. From there they will be transported to the French base in Djibouti and then on to France to stand trial.[5] Only France has taken such an aggressive approach to rescuing hijacked vessels in this region. After April's special forces helicopter assault, as pirates from the *Le Ponant* incident fled ashore in their jeep, France is now two-for-two — and is encouraging other nations to take the same aggressive stance toward pirates menacing their vessels.

~

The embarked reporters record every detail of the ship's approach to our battle-torn destination. They seem to be all places at once, their khakis and faded button-down shirts incongruous against the austere naval backdrop: peering through bridge windows at an urban sprawl made hazy, its violence whitewashed by distance; leaning against the bridge wing railings with cameras rolling, bedecked with flak vests and helmets; observing from the boat deck as our RHIB retrieves the embarked team before *Golina's* final push into Mogadishu port.

On the bridge wing, a British freelance journalist whom I had noticed in the wardroom introduces himself. He's probably only in his late thirties, but the hard-living evident in his face ages him ten years.

"I'm Tim," he says, leaning against the wooden railing beside me. "What do you do on board?"

I hesitate. "I'm the intelligence officer."

He visibly brightens, a slight smile playing across his thin lips.

"So where do you get your information from?"

I return his smile. "Here and there. You know how it is."

"But you must have sources in Mogadishu telling you what's going on there, right?"

He's clearly fishing, but his bantering tone and obvious questions suggest that he doesn't actually expect to make much headway. He's just fooling around. At the same time, he would not hesitate to use any information I let slip in his follow-on article about the escort mission.

"Nothing really of interest," I tell him, smiling back to let him know I'm on to his game. "But what about you? Have you been to Mogadishu before?"

He laughs good-naturedly, recognizing the reversal in tactics.

"Yes, a few years ago, in between the worst of the fighting. I used to come here periodically," he says, growing more serious now, "when it was still reasonably secure for foreign journalists. There's not much reporting from here now."

I stare out at the spread of crumbling buildings, set in a distant crescent against the shoreline. "I've heard it used to be a really attractive city. Do you know if there are any remnants of that remaining, any part left untouched by the fighting?"

"I don't think there is. All of the buildings are falling down, just in shambles. Shot up, looted. It's very sad. You can see reminders that the city was once beautiful, but there's little of that left."

The African Union boats and their armed soldiers, detailed to escort MV *Golina* the final leg into port, are late. Several sets of bridge binoculars scan the harbour for signs of the black inflatables. The green and white African Union flag that flies from the boats' stern and the bright orange lifejackets of their occupants, attire foreign to Somali fishermen operating sporadically in the area, will make the pair difficult to miss, once they're launched from shore. But there is no sign of them yet. Jeff finally reaches the AMISOM contingent commander by satellite phone. The apologetic colonel reports that the past few days have been tough ones: two AMISOM troops have been killed by insurgents, and his soldiers, in a perpetual wait for reinforcements, are stretched particularly thin given threats against the airport and increased violence throughout the city. The closure of the airport may further delay their ability to obtain reinforcements.

A short while later, two AMISOM RHIBs carrying beleaguered soldiers motor into range and begin to escort MV *Golina* toward port. A high-powered skiff near the shoreline moves toward the rusted ship's position. The intentions of those aboard the skiff are impossible to ascertain. They could be merely preparing to fish, but as the world's media looks on from the bridge wings, one of the AMISOM boats, its crew unwilling to take a chance, surges forward to obstruct the vessel, manoeuvring aggressively toward it and preventing it from drawing close to *Golina*. I can't see the faces of the skiff's occupants from the bridge, but I imagine expressions of surprised dismay — regardless of their intentions.

I'm at my computer later that day when a message flashes into my inbox. It's a piracy alert: Greek chemical tanker MV *Centauri* and her twenty-five Filipino crew have been hijacked.

"Shit," I say under my breath as I read further details of the attack.

"What is it?"

I must have muttered more loudly than I thought. I look up to find Jeff's quizzical gaze resting on me from the desk opposite.

"Oh, I didn't even realize you were in here. There's been another hijacking, MV *Centauri*."

"In the Gulf of Aden, I'm assuming?"

I slowly shake my head, keeping my eyes fixed on his.

"No. This one happened off the east coast, well to the northeast of where we are now. Still far away from what has been our escort area so far."

But getting closer, I think to myself. "It's the first reported hijacking off the east coast since May. Now that the monsoon season off this coast is coming to an end and waters are beginning to calm, we could start seeing more attacks in closer proximity to our escort area."

"Better let the captain know," says Jeff calmly.

I find him in his cabin. "Captain, sir, a commercial ship, MV *Centauri*, has recently been hijacked — off the east coast this time, about 350 miles northeast of Mogadishu. It's the first reported attack off the east coast since the spring."

He sighs, then looks astutely up at me from his seat at the table. "Okay. Any additional information?"

"Apparently the alarm on board the *Centauri* was sounded after a watchman noticed a small vessel rapidly approaching. The ship tried to outmanoeuvre them but two boatloads of pirates with rifles and RPGs, of unknown origin, still managed to throw up ladders and board the tanker.[6] That's all I have so far."

"Okay, thank you," he says to dismiss me. He has much more than just this to deal with; fatigue is evident in his face. In addition to his heavy responsibilities, I suspect that he reads for hours each day to stay attuned to the evolving situation ashore and at sea.

Short hours later, pirates capture another ship, this time in their more usual hunting grounds. Pirates board bulk carrier MV *Great Creation* as she transits the Gulf of Aden en route from Tunisia to India, and augment their growing hostage collection with the twenty-five Chinese and Sri Lankan crew.

~

After racing south to Mombasa to drop off the media, *Ville de Québec* beelines it back to Somalia to escort *Golina* on her return journey. The situation in Mogadishu has further deteriorated in the few days we've been gone. A plane from Puntland has landed at the airport despite Al-Shabaab's threat to shoot down any incoming aircraft. It touched down safely, but the landing provoked a barrage of mortar fire from Al-Shabaab insurgents and return fire from AMISOM and Ethiopian troops. The ensuing battle killed dozens of innocent civilians.[7] The scene was repeated the next day with the landing of another aircraft.

Later that day, I check in with Serge, the on-watch operations room officer.

"Hi, Jen," he says, glancing up from behind his computer screens. His grey moustache, expanding now, competes with his glasses for dominance of his compact face.

"Hi, Serge. Just doing my check-in. Anything going on?"

"We've had reports of another hijacking. *Capt Stefanos.*"

"Where? In the Gulf of Aden?"

"Off the east coast."

Damn. Another one.

Pirates in multiple speedboats boarded the Bahamas-flagged bulk carrier MV *Capt Stefanos* and took her nineteen crew hostage. *Capt Stefanos* is now the second ship captured off Somalia's east coast in recent days, attacked in approximately the same location as MV *Centauri*.

The attacks are still hundreds of kilometres from our typical escort track, but the distance is closing. Pirates continue to prove themselves capable, and, more importantly, adaptable adversaries. With their opportunistic spirit and ever-expanding range of operations, estimating where they will next turn up is more of an art than a science — one that has stymied scores of analysts, including myself. Perhaps more pirates are getting into the game. It surely appears to them a winning one. Heightened naval activity in the Gulf of Aden might also be encouraging pirate groups to resume activity off the east coast, where they run less risk of naval intervention. For the past few years, merchant ships have steered well clear of Somalia's east coast whenever possible, leaving pirates with fewer targets. Still, the last two hijackings prove that enough vessels continue to transit off the east coast, even when they pass hundreds of kilometres offshore to avoid the high danger area, to make targeting them worthwhile. More attacks off the east coast, with a renewed potential to impact our escorts, are sure to follow.

Later that night, Jeff is tapping away at the communications control room workstation opposite me, chewing quietly on Master Seaman Davis's bonbons.

"Combat," I call, leaning out from behind my desk, "our next scheduled escort is still *As Salaam*, right?"

"Yup," he says, not looking up from his screen. "She's coming up from South Africa and we're RVing with her at sea."

I raise my eyebrows. "So we're not taking *Golina* all the way into Mombasa?"

Now his brown eyes meet mine.

"No. We'll get close, but we've had to deconflict the schedule. *Golina* should be fine the rest of the way to Mombasa. We need to ensure that we're ready to escort *As Salaam* when she finally comes."

The priority for *As Salaam*'s escort is clear after a review of her capacity: the nearly fourteen thousand metric tonnes of maize in her holds, even more than *Zang Za*'s single load, will feed sixty-nine thousand people for a year.[8] Of the vessels that the World Food Programme has managed to enlist, *As Salaam*'s capacity enables her to carry the heftiest load of food yet. Ensuring that her master feels safe under escort will encourage him to accept subsequent contracts and increase the UN agency's chances of getting food to people who desperately need it. And MV *As Salaam* is our last scheduled escort prior to the wrap-up of our mission; it would be nice to finish on a high note.

Somali Coast, September 2003

They motor out in the early morning, the sun low in the sky. Their two skiffs are equipped with powerful outboard engines, replete with fuel and water canisters, a grappling hook, bundles of khat, some meagre rations. They even carry nets and lines — fishing gear to enable them to claim legitimate activities. Each of the ten young men carry an AK — a requirement, along with seafaring abilities and personal connections, for employment with this crew. Abdi's heart is racing. This is his first operation. His apprehension is matched by excitement, by the promise of something new.

Fishing skiffs and houris dot the surrounding waters. Their skiffs continue on until they are past the bulk of the small fishing boats, moving beyond into great expanses of empty ocean, save the occasional fishing trawler in the distance. The young men beside Abdi chew khat as they ride, leaning against the sides of the fibreglass boat. Abdi, his eyes wide, nervously scans the water.

Beside him, Mohammed, his eyes glassy from the narcotic, lets out a boisterous laugh. "Abdi, there's nothing to worry about! We know what we're doing. Just do what we talked about and you'll be fine." Abdi only nods.

The skiffs parallel the distant coastline for most of the day before they find a suitable target. A lone trawler, its white paint faded and nets inboard, moves slowly through the smooth water ahead. A few crew with Asian features move about on the deck, working the nets. The two skiffs abruptly pick up speed and rapidly approach the trawler on either side. The crewmen look up, startled, but it is already too late. The boarding is so quick Abdi is barely aware of what is happening. The grappling hooks are thrown up the trawler's low sides, then Mohammed and two others from his skiff are already hauling themselves over the deck with their rifles. Abdi stares, paralyzed with fear.

"Abdi, go, go!" yells the driver from his seat at the rear. Abdi's heart is pounding now, and a surge of adrenaline flows through his body as he shimmies up the rope and onto the deck. Two of the others are already in the small bridge and, holding the master at gunpoint, have seized control of the trawler. Mohammed stands on the deck, pointing his rifle at the two hapless crewmen.

"Below, below!" screams Mohammed in Somali, gesturing with his rifle to a hatch in the deck. The crewmen are clearly terrified, their eyes bulging, but they do as they are told and open the hatch, disappearing below decks. Mohammed follows them down a few steps, Abdi following closely behind, his father's rifle pointing downward. There are a few more men in the crew's quarters, immobile in the small space. Abdi recognizes their fear from his own only a few minutes before.

"Don't move," screams Mohammed in Somali, his contorted face barely recognizable. The faces of the crew reveal their confusion, so Mohammed switches to broken English, Abdi recognizing the few words. "If you move we will kill you!"

Then he turns to Abdi and shouts in Somali. "Point your rifle at them! They need to know we are serious!" Abdi complies. From the crewmen's petrified expressions, though, he has no doubt the crew are taking them seriously.

Abdi can't believe this is real. He knows nothing about these people who are now terrified of him. Right now he doesn't care. The experience, completely new to him, is at once terrifying and exhilarating. All he has to do is keep it together and do his job as the vessel is steered toward shore.

Vessels held by Somali pirates: *Stella Maris, Yenegoa Ocean, Thor Star, Bunga Melati Dua, Iran Deyanat, Irene, Bunga Melati 5, Al Mansoura, Stolt Valor, Centauri, Great Creation, Capt Stefanos*

CHAPTER 18

AS SALAAM

Heavily armed Somali pirates have hijacked more that 30 vessels off the Horn of Africa country this year, making its waters the most dangerous in the world.[1]

— Al Jazeera, September 18, 2008

"As all of you know, *Ville de Québec* is scheduled to conclude our escort mission in a few days time," blares the captain's tinny voice through the piping system. Billy and I are loitering in our usual post-dinner positions in the wardroom, considering the duff trays at the bar before we make our selection. Like most of the ship's company, we know what's coming next.

"No country has stepped forward to provide a naval vessel to take over the escort mission when we leave," the captain continues. "Without a naval escort, the World Food Programme will be unable to sustain the delivery of food aid to Somalia."

Billy and I exchange a knowing look across the bar, our helplessness in the matter rendering us indifferent to its outcome.

"Already, the World Food Programme has reported that merchant vessels have begun cancelling their contracts in anticipation of a lack of naval escort and the increase in risk from piracy." The shipping companies are right to be concerned. So far, pirates have steered well clear of naval escorts, but without them vessels carrying food aid into Mogadishu would be sitting ducks.

And then, the expected *coup de grâce*.

"The World Food Programme is very grateful for our efforts, and has asked Canada to extend *Ville de Québec*'s escort mission until October 23, which our government has agreed to. We will not be staying beyond that date."

My eyes flicker around the room at faces resigned to change. A few raise their eyebrows, revealing that the announcement has sunk in, but few register surprise. Marcus's lips curl slightly to signal dismay as he leans his muscular frame against the wooden bar. Kevin appears indifferent, continuing to flick through a *Men's Health* magazine that has magically appeared. Once the captain finishes speaking, chatting gradually resumes, but it is hardly the expected hubbub of conversation given this latest news.

"Guess I'm not going to Europe in October," Marcus says nonchalantly. It's not that he isn't disappointed — he had plans to bring his fiancée over from Canada for leave once the escort operation wound down, operational requirements permitting — but he had already anticipated these last-minute changes. Like all of us, he was careful not to raise his hopes.

Jeff wanders to the bar and stands beside me. "Had you planned on taking off for a few weeks, once we were back in the Med?" I ask. He looks at me with deliberate patience and answers in a mock-serious voice.

"Jennifer, don't you know by now that I have no time for such things? There's work to be done. Of course I wasn't planning on cavorting around Europe!"

Then his tone softens, and all at once he is serious. "I'll just take the mission leave when I get home, see the boys and Teri then." His face shows what he does not say. Leaving small children behind once is hard enough. Twice might be intolerable.

Kevin glances up from his magazine, unperturbed.

"I may be flying back to Canada early anyway," he says with a slight shrug.

"What do you mean?" I say, alarmed.

"I've already spoken to the Maj. He feels badly about me being here on my shore posting, so he's going to see if they can switch me out with someone back at the squadron." This news takes me by surprise. Kevin long ago lost interest in our Mombasa port visits, but I never thought he would just leave. Now that his early departure is a distinct possibility,

I feel unreasonably crushed. He has become my sounding board. I'm more dependent on his friendship than I'd realized.

"But it wouldn't be the same without you here! I can't believe you'd leave us!" I mean every word, but this sentiment is unlike me. My contentment on board is worryingly fragile.

Marcus chimes in. "Jen, don't you think that's selfish? Maybe you should support Kevin to do what's best for him." He's absolutely right, of course, but in truth, I can't help being hurt by Kevin's lack of allegiance to us.

"Don't worry, Jen, it's a long shot," Kevin says calmly. "I doubt I'll be going anywhere. It's just that now we're not even going to have the European port visits, and I'm kind of done with this back and forth."

Little more is discussed about the mission extension. What's left to say? The government's decision to keep us here was the right one, the only one. In the communications control room that evening, I email Scott in Jerusalem to tell him about the extension. We had tentatively planned to meet in Europe in October. That won't happen now. *What's new?* is his reply. With both of us on deployment, our schedules are inflexible, meaning we won't see each other until sometime after my return to Canada. But we've gotten used to being apart over the past year and a half — too used to it. We both volunteered for our deployments, though. It seems unfair to complain now.

~

Another vessel is hijacked off Somalia's east coast the next day, three hundred nautical miles east of Mogadishu. Early indications warn that this one will be trouble. MV *Faina*, a Belize-flagged roll-on roll-off vessel designed to carry wheeled cargo, is transporting large quantities of Russian-made tanks, weapons, and ammunition. The cargo was loaded in Ukraine, but conflicting reports cite its destination as Mombasa or, alternately, conflict-ridden southern Sudan, in contravention of the UN arms embargo.[2] Whatever the intended destination, this sensitive cargo now lies in pirates' hands. There's no telling where such quantities of armaments could end up. The last thing Somalia needs is an influx of heavy weapons to further arm its fighting factions.

MV *As Salaam* sails into view the following day. Painted in clean, solid hues of white, black, and deep red, she's an impressive-looking ship. I watch from the port bridge wing as our grey RHIB bounces through white-capped chop to ferry the XO and a NAST team leader over to brief the ship's master on standard escort procedures. Once the first wave of the NAST has boarded *As Salaam*, we begin our quiet voyage north toward Mogadishu. The boarding team, switching out periodically, maintain vigilant lookout over empty waters.

Back on *Ville de Québec*, I'm bored too. The days flow together. Long periods of work, nearly indistinguishable from the next, are sewn together with short reprieves spent in my rack and punctuated by attacks on shipping. Tonight yet another vessel seizure is reported. MV *Genius*, a Liberian-flagged chemical tanker, is taken hostage in the Gulf of Aden with her nineteen crew. It is the ninth hijacking this month alone. But the monotony of routine too seldom broken still remains.

Workouts remain our savior. Luc leads his evening classes on the flight deck, when operations permit. We run on the treadmills in the dark flats, like the caged mice that we are, or climb steadily to nowhere on the step machine in the crammed hangar. A small gym with weight machines and a few free weights lies aft on two deck, but the excessive heat trapped in its cramped quarters dampens its appeal.

One evening the sea is rougher than usual. Not puke-in-the-flats rough, but rough enough so that our metal home rolls shallowly from one side to the other, unbalancing me as I wander the dark flats in gym gear and mount the treadmill. Light leaking out of the engineering offices' closed doors provides the only source of illumination. The treadmill picks up speed, nearly pinwheeling my legs with each gentle tip forward, then back again with the sea's rhythm, forcing me to grasp the railing. That I'm even trying this is ridiculous. Last week I toppled clear off a not-so-stationary bike on another rough day. But it's as much the psychological as the physical release that I am unwilling to relinquish.

Billy's casual gait is recognizable even in the dark as he covers the distance between his cabin and the air detachment room farther aft. There the air crew spend free time watching DVDs or playing Guitar Hero when not prepping for a flight. I loosen my death grip just long enough to wave as he passes in front of the treadmill.

"That looks a little tricky," he says, watching as I nearly fall backward with the ship's sideways roll. "We're watching *Entourage* in the ADR if you want to join after your run."

"Thanks," I reply. "I would, but I still have some work to do tonight. Next time, for sure." It might be some time before I have an evening free, given the near-constant drama in this part of the world. Still, the stamina that helps me endure these long days may well run out before then. Already, post-workout periods are stretching longer, delaying my return to the communications control room.

In the wardroom, still glistening with sweat, I gulp down some water. Helmz stands beside me in gym gear, playfully stroking his biker moustache. Kate sits in a corner of the room where she reads a magazine. She doesn't look up. I have heard rumours that she has broken up with her boyfriend back home. Respecting the vibe she is putting out, I decide to leave her be. Kevin bustles into the room full of purpose and homes in on his daily protein shake fix. We say little for the few minutes that we linger, relishing the normalcy of quiet company, and of momentarily adhering to no agenda. Out of uniform with the lights low, the relaxed atmosphere — so highly charged during the day — is a welcome change of pace.

Then, after a hasty shower, it's back to the communications control room. The capture of MV *Faina* and her game-changing cargo has been the buzz in the media for the past few days, and has finally cast Somalia's piracy into the international spotlight. Pirates have anchored the vessel off the east coast, not at Eyl this time but near another coastal town called Hobyo. U.S. Navy destroyer USS *Howard* is closely monitoring the vessel.[3]

All of this is unfolding just a few hundred kilometres to our north, not far from the anchorages where crews of hijacked ships wait out their fate. Recent UN resolutions now allow third party countries to combat piracy in Somali territorial waters and even on land. But aside from the forays of the French, no direct action against the pirates has been taken by any military force. The situation quickly becomes complicated once the lives of the hostages are under threat, and questions without answers are raised as to who has legal responsibility for captured pirates. It's clear that the long-term solution to the piracy problem is to re-establish security and stability, and to return the rule of law in Somalia — complex issues unlikely to be soon resolved.

What would it be like to live each day in wartorn drought-ridden Somalia with such uncertainty, such insecurity? Here, on board ship, life is the opposite. Shipboard life dictates a stable regime of almost unwavering predictability: Wakey wakey, hands to breakfast, watch turnover, hands to cleaning stations, stand easy, hands to dinner, watch turnover, stand easy, hands to supper, watch turnover, hands to cleaning stations. And on it goes. The ship can even hold sailors accountable for transgressions of the Code of Service Discipline, the military's own justice system, charging, trying, and sentencing them, all within the confines of the vessel. Before this voyage is over, the Code will be invoked on *Ville de Québec* more than once.

In Somalia, the absence of effective federal law enforcement has led to a breakdown in order: criminals rob and rape their captives; kids with AK-47s shoot innocents through car windows; pirates hijack and take hostages with impunity. A complex system of warring tribal, religious, economic, and ideological loyalties and governance systems has turned the country into what appears to the outsider as a free-for-all. The law of survival of the fittest reigns supreme.

Today, pirates release two of the hijacked vessels, *Bunga Melati V* and *Al Mansoura*, and their unharmed crews in return for ransom payments likely in the millions of dollars. The temptation of that kind of payout is easy to comprehend. If I had little prospect of earning a legitimate income, if my family was impoverished and my children malnourished, if I could find no other conduit for my youthful energy, if the solution to all of my problems was sailing past just over the horizon, and if attacking it carried little chance of consequence, I might be a pirate too.

But even if the individual choice to become a pirate might begin as a game of survival, it most likely becomes distorted along the way. By most accounts, piracy has become associated with a distinct way of life, most notably in the coastal village of Eyl. The village has become a de facto support base for the hijacked vessels anchored nearby while ransom negotiations are underway. Suddenly wealthy young men are pumping money into the economy. For the locals to decline that money would be next-to-impossible in a country where income is so hard to come by, even if they were morally opposed to the source. The pirates — typically young, in their late teens and twenties — sometimes buy flashy cars, big houses, marry multiple wives in elaborate weddings — all status symbols of the financial success they have achieved through their crimes.[4] Money gives them power, and power is addictive — just like khat, the mild stimulant that the pirates are said constantly to chew. It lends them much of the misplaced courage required to do what they do.

~

The captain leans forward against the bridge wing railing, his face an expression of calm intensity. The bridge watch is quiet behind his substantial form. He studies MV *As Salaam*'s slow progress toward the port of Mogadishu in the company of the AMISOM boat. *As Salaam*'s master is nervous, of course, but the captain has given his assurance that we will return in a few days' time to escort them on their outbound journey. The escort mission has gone smoothly so far, but I see reflected in the captain's intelligent, knowing eyes, every time we brief him, a keen awareness that there is still so much that can go wrong.

September 2003

Word of their return with the captured trawler spreads quickly through the village. Asad, deeply ashamed of their newfound livelihoods, will no longer permit Mohammed and Abdi to stay in his home. The owners of the trawler, still anchored in the bay with its crew after a few weeks, have not yet paid their fine, despite the cellphone negotiations of their interpreter — a former schoolteacher — with the ship's owner. This means that Abdi has not been paid either. For the stretches when they are not standing guard over their captives, he and Mohammed find refuge in the home of Elmi, one of the more established members of their "coast guard" group.

That evening he and a handful of young men board the skiff for their next long shift aboard the trawler. They climb the ladder up the hull, their automatic rifles slung over their backs and carrying food prepared by local vendors. The other, more senior members of the security watch retreat immediately to the bridge. Abdi knows they will spend the dark hours chewing their leaves and exchanging stories of bravado on the seas. He himself has accumulated neither stories nor bravado, and would have had little to contribute if he had been invited to the gathering.

Instead, he and Dalmar, another junior member, descend the short ladder into the cramped crew quarters below, shaking the hands of the two holders they relieve. There the half-dozen crew huddle together on the benches, one or two on their beds, as if cold despite their shirtsleeves and the warm night. Their brown faces range from young to middle-aged. Their eyes search Abdi's, looking for some form of recognition, of connection, before switching focus to the rifle he cradles in his arms. He keeps his face deliberately blank. He's spent days, weeks with them by now. Although they share only a few words of English, he can sense when they are nervous or exhausted or angry or resigned. Sometimes they use raised voices with one another, arguing unintelligibly over something one of them has said. He overrides them with an angry bark to be quiet. Sometimes he raises his rifle threateningly at them, like he has seen the other holders do, though he is always more nervous than angry. Dalmar will kid with the captives sometimes, cracking a joke at their expense and unbalancing them. They never know what to expect — Abdi can see it in their faces — and they alternate between confusion and fear in response to Dalmar's mood.

Abdi would never strike a hostage, much less shoot one, although he knows he can't reveal this to them. "They are up to no good today," Mohammed told him as he relieved him on duty one day. "The older one refused to answer my questions as to why it is taking so long for his company to pay the ransom." Abdi descended the ladder to discover that one of the hostages, an older man, had a bulging bruise on his forehead. The man fixed onto him with fear in his eyes, retreating back as far as he could on the bench.

Several weeks later, the company pays the fine — not as much as expected by his superiors, but it seems an enormous amount to Abdi. He and his fellow holders line up on the small deck to collect their share from Aweys, their group's leader. His eyes widen as the bills are counted into his palm. His payout is more money than he has ever had at one time. The skiff takes him ashore, and he immediately packs a small bag for the trip to Baladweyne. He can hardly wait to share this windfall with his mother.

Vessels held by Somali pirates: *Yenegoa Ocean, Thor Star, Bunga Melati Dua, Iran Deyanat, Irene, Stolt Valor, Centauri, Great Creation, Capt Stefanos, Faina, Genius*

CHAPTER 19

BREAKDOWN

The MV *Faina* is surrounded by U.S. warships and a Russian frigate is heading toward the scene, raising the stakes for a possible commando-style raid on the ship.[1]

— *Taipei Times,* October 12, 2008

Outside of Mogadishu the next day, our ship meets up with Jordanian-flagged MV *Victoria* as she leaves port. The compact cargo vessel is not on contract to the World Food Programme, but the UN agency has requested that we escort her back to Mombasa — likely because of their shared history, perhaps in hope that the vessel might again be enlisted to deliver food.

In May 2007, *Victoria* was attacked by pirates off Somalia's coast while transporting World Food Programme aid. The little vessel had just delivered four thousand metric tonnes of food to the port of Merka, about one hundred kilometres south of Mogadishu, and was en route to Tanzania. Upon receipt of the distress call, the Merka-based agent responsible for arranging the shipment immediately sent two boats armed with guards to prevent the boarding. The ensuing gunfight caused the bandits to abort their attack, but not before they shot one of the guards, who later died in a Merka hospital.[2]

This past May the vessel was again attacked, and fared less well. Pirates hijacked her, with her twelve-man crew, only thirty miles from where we now sail. Although not under contract to the World Food Programme at the time, she was carrying four thousand tonnes of donated sugar to

Mogadishu.[3] Her captors anchored her in coastal waters near the town of Hobyo, a few hundred kilometres north of the capital. A week later the vessel and crew were released, probably after a ransom was paid. She continued on, with Somali soldiers aboard, to discharge her cargo in the battle-torn capital. That day, Islamist fighters attacked Hobyo-based pirates. Four pirates and two Islamists were killed in the attack.[4]

Judging from the traumatic experience of another hijack victim, MV *Semlow*, the master and crew of *Victoria* are demonstrating impressive resilience in continuing to sail these waters. Hassan Adallah was a merchant sailor on MV *Semlow*, a ship hijacked while under contract to the World Food Programme. Pirates held him hostage for over a hundred days. Hassan described his terror when the pirates became frustrated with the pace of negotiations: "They took their weapons and began to shoot up the ship, smashing the windows, and we were very afraid. They said we had to tell the owner to pay the ransom or something bad would happen, and we worried they might … execute someone." After his release, the shipping company compensated him with one hundred American dollars. He has not been able to hold down a steady job since.[5]

~

Something is wrong.

At first there are only whispers in the communications control room, the occasional overheard snippets that only when pieced together in the context of the mission form a worrisome picture. As drafters of messages that leave the ship, the naval communicators are among the first to learn any news, though they are expected to treat their knowledge with discretion.

In the wardroom I find Jeff and Mike, our lead marine systems engineer, two people who can confirm or deny the truth of this latest rumour.

"Is it true that we're having some mechanical issues?" I ask.

Mike looks up from the settee, his dark puppy dog eyes clear of stress. His leadership aura, impressive for someone only in their late twenties, lies in his exceeding competence and ability to perform under pressure. Mike's is not the rigid world of the bridge, though, where a ship driver's error, or even hesitation, creates instant and palpable tension. He heads up a department of diesel mechanics and engineering officers who manage the mechanical functioning of the ship: the diesel generators that provide power to the engines, the diesel and gas engines that propel us, the black water system that flushes our waste, the water purification system that filters our drinking water, the damage control system that allows us to fight fires and floods. His department operates largely behind the scenes, at least until something goes wrong.

"Yes, we are," he calmly replies.

"So what happens now?" I look pointedly at Jeff.

He returns my gaze, brown eyes unblinking. We're both thinking of MV *As Salaam*, awaiting our escort from Mogadishu after a tense week alongside.

"We're waiting for direction from Ottawa."

Now that the other Canadian ships have departed the gulf and are en route home, the captain reports directly to the commander of the Canadian Expeditionary Forces in Ottawa. The captain will provide significant input into the decision, but, as MV *As Salaam* awaits our arrival, the orders will come from Ottawa.

"We're waiting to hear whether the necessary repairs can be done in this part of the world before any decisions are made," Mike explains patiently. "Ottawa's working on it."

At the evening brief, Mike relays options to a worried captain. There may be a local solution; both Nairobi and Dar es Salaam, Tanzania's capital, offer possibilities. But our own engineers will have to verify the suitability of those solutions in person. They will fly out from Mombasa tomorrow.

The ship's course remains unclear, but one thing looks certain: we will be neither returning to Mogadishu nor escorting cargo vessels until we are fixed. The risk while escorting vessels is simply too great. Any reduction in the ship's capacity to operate effectively could leave us unacceptably vulnerable in a highly dangerous region. It's a chance that, understandably, Ottawa is not willing to take.

As he addresses us, his legs braced against the rocking swells, the captain's heavy voice matches his concerned expression. He looms before us at the rear of the ops room, which has drawn a larger than usual crowd tonight in anticipation of significant news.

"We will be returning alongside Mombasa while a decision is made about how to address the mechanical problem."

He doesn't yet acknowledge that we won't be returning to Mogadishu to escort *As Salaam* back to Mombasa. He doesn't need to. His tone says it all: that he considers the success of this mission his personal responsibility, that its failure is untenable, that breaking his word to *As Salaam*'s master, deserting him and his crew alongside one of the world's most violent cities, where it is dangerous to stay and more dangerous still to leave, cannot possibly be the only option that remains.

A final decision will be made in the next few days, once our engineers have reported back on their findings in the neighbouring capitals. But the last weeks of the escort mission, with the hard-won extension, are ticking down. Frustration at having to go back to the jetty, at the disruption to the planned escorts, and especially at the abandonment of *As Salaam*, makes me feel truly connected, for the first time, to the reason we are doing this. The escorts need to continue; that food needs to reach Somalia. Lives are on the line. This waiting seems such a waste. We all want to complete the job we started.

~

When we return to the ship after a few days ashore in Mombasa, we learn the plan: *Ville de Québec* will immediately head toward Dar es Salaam, 170 nautical miles south. There, our own engineers will carry out the repairs as quickly as possible while we remain alongside. Only then will Ottawa give the go-ahead to resume the mission.

Jeff is in frequent contact with *As Salaam*'s master as we cruise toward Tanzania's capital.

"They left port and are anchored in Mogadishu harbour now," he tells me when I spy his tall figure in the gloom of the ops room.

He hesitates before continuing. "But the master is too scared to leave the harbour itself." It's difficult to say which would be the greater risk: remaining alongside, at the mercy of armed gunmen ashore, or at sea, at the mercy of pirates-in-waiting.

"God, poor man." I shake my head. "Poor crew!"

It's now confirmed: Ottawa will not permit us to escort *As Salaam* out of the danger zone until the ship is repaired, which, including the transit time to Dar es Salaam, could take a week or more. With the relative risks difficult to evaluate, *As Salaam*'s master has a tough decision to make about when to depart the insecurity of the harbour for the insecurity of the waters beyond Mogadishu. The captain has already contacted the few Allied warships that are in the area. While they could monitor communications as the vessel departs the harbour, none are able to make her escort their primary mission. *As Salaam* is on her own.

Seated before me at the evening brief, the CO's face is drawn, his blue eyes weary. I'd spent the afternoon researching the locations of pirate attacks that have occurred off Somalia's east coast over the past year, studying the scant information I could find on pirate groups active south of the capital in the direction of Mombasa, where *As Salaam* will be heading. The slides I'm presenting now are the best I could do with the available, if incomplete, information.

"While there were a few, sporadic attacks off Mogadishu's coast prior to May this year," I say, "there have since been no reported attacks between Mogadishu and Mombasa, where *As Salaam* will have to transit." I glance up from my notes to look at the captain.

"As you know, sir, there have been several recent incidents of hijackings and attacks off the east coast, indicating a resurgence of piracy activity in this area." I use a laser pointer to indicate the location of these events. "However, these attacks have occurred offshore, considerably north of Mogadishu, likely by pirate groups based in Harardheere, not in the vicinity of *As Salaam*'s route. Pirate groups operating south of Mogadishu are not known to be currently active."

I take a deep breath before continuing. I'm confident about my research but aware of the fallibility of my analysis, since the pirates are constantly adapting their tactics, expanding their range, to respond to opportunity.

"Given the lack of recent piracy activity or indications of active pirate groups along *As Salaam*'s planned route, it's unlikely that *As Salaam* will be attacked as she transits southbound toward Mombasa." There. I said it. The assessment seems reasonable enough, given the information I have to work with.

The captain lets out a short, unhappy laugh. "Are you briefing this to make me feel better?"

I shake my head no, of course not, that's what my research bears out. But both of us know that there is nothing predictable about piracy here;

its only predictable element is its ability to surprise, to respond to opportunity. Mine is an educated guess at best.

~

The next afternoon, I pop into the ops room for my usual check-in. The captain and Jeff hover behind the ORO station, where Denis sits before his glowing terminals. Tension hangs thickly in the recycled air. The captain's face is haggard, heaviness of spirit personified. Something is clearly amiss.

A hard ball lodges itself in the pit of my stomach. I'm afraid to ask. Finally Jeff leans over and hands me a piece of paper. On it is printed a brief email sent to his account. The handful of words says enough:

> Dear Sir,
> We are under attack by pirates. Your help is requested.
> Regards,
> Master
> As Salaam

The master's email is eerily calm, unlike the helpless panic that erupts from my belly. My assessment was wrong. The worst-case scenario is actually happening. God, how naive I was! Of course word would spread that a lone cargo ship was waiting at anchor in Mogadishu harbour. Of course word would spread that we were alongside Mombasa and are now heading south instead of north. Pirates could easily figure out that *As Salaam* would be unescorted. And it doesn't take an organized gang to launch an attack, just opportunists with a fast boat and some weapons. It doesn't matter that nobody seems to blame me for the faulty assessment. I blame myself.

"*As Salaam* is quite far south off Somalia's coast," says Jeff, pointing to a blip on the electronic chart. "The captain has given the order to head back up north, toward her position, at thirty knots."

Ottawa has supported the captain's recommendation. The risk to the ship must have seemed worth it, given *As Salaam*'s ordeal and the jeopardy to the mission. I flick my eyes to the electronic chart where an LED blip marks our own position. The port of Dar es Salaam is approximately a ten-hour transit from Mombasa at our typical cruising speed. But in order not to overstrain our crippled engineering systems, we have been moving at half that, which has still put us only a handful of hours from our destination — and far from *As Salaam*.

October 2003

Only a little money remains after his visit to Baladweyne. His mother, newly recovered from a bout of malaria, was able to purchase some chickens, a few goats — luxuries she has not enjoyed since his father was alive. She set aside money for the children's school fees out of Abdi's earnings. For the first time in a long while, a smile lit up her exhausted face.

But when she asked the inevitable question, Abdi could not bring himself to lie to her. "Hoyo, I work to stop foreign fishing boats from stealing our fish," he said, not meeting her gaze. "We have to defend our waters."

Her smile quickly faded. "How do you do that?" Her voice is suspicious. His astute mother awaited his answer, but she had already guessed, or perhaps had heard through the close-knit clan network, and was deeply shamed.

"But Hoyo, we do good things. We spend money in the village. We buy food and livestock and cigarettes in the market for the ships that we hold. People, our cousins, are better off." But his attempts to explain were in vain.

"Your abo was an honest man," she wept. The children huddled nervously around her. "You were always a good boy. Now you disgrace him with what you do." Still, she had no choice but to take the money, and Abdi returned to his coastal village with a sour taste on his tongue.

In the market, Abdi heads straight to the women selling bundles of khat, fresh and green, from small trolleys. He has chewed it a few times when guarding the hostages, unable to turn it down when the other holders offered, but immediately disliked its unpleasant flavour. Now he buys a large bundle. He sits down in a rusted lawn chair next to Mohammed and a few other young men under the small bit of shade cast by a makeshift shelter. They drink sweet tea and cram bunches of the green narcotic leaf into their bulging cheeks, telling bravado-filled stories of their exploits at sea, of how they spent their money, of the women they'd like to marry. Abdi, slowly discovering the appeal of the stalks' bitter taste in his mouth, joins in.

Vessels held by Somali pirates: *Yenegoa Ocean, Thor Star, Bunga Melati Dua, Iran Deyanat, Irene, Stolt Valor, Centauri, Great Creation, Capt Stefanos, Faina, Genius*

CHAPTER 20

THWARTED

The second Malaysian International Shipping Corporation (MISC)
tanker, hijacked in the Gulf of Aden by Somali pirates, has been freed.[1]
— *Bernama,* September 30, 2008

Even at our current maximum speed, it will be hours before the ship is
close enough to launch the helo toward the stricken vessel's position, and
even longer still before the ship arrives on scene.

"I can't believe that pirates attacked *As Salaam* in that location," I say
dazedly, slumping into an operator's empty chair. "No attacks have been
reported that far south."

Even as I speak, I know I shouldn't be surprised. The pirates have
been consistent only in their demonstration of resourcefulness, oppor-
tunism, and adaptability. Whether the attack was orchestrated by one of
the organized pirate groups that typically troll for victims farther north,
or by local opportunists handy with a boat who learned through local networks that a vessel would be transiting unescorted, the result is the same.

"What has *As Salaam* reported about the attack?" I ask Jeff, desperate
to put it into context.

"Four pirates in a single speedboat fired at the ship and tried to board
her," he tells me, his long face expressionless. "The master carried out
evasive manoeuvring and has managed to deter the boarding — for the
moment. The boat has fallen back now but is still trailing *As Salaam.*"

That *As Salaam* was able to defend herself from the pirates' initial
attack is good news. But pirates are known to follow commercial vessels

for hours, attacking repeatedly until they find a weak spot that allows them to board. *As Salaam* remains in danger.

As we speed north, Jeff remains in close contact via email with *As Salaam*'s master. The master's reports, unemotional and detached, offer details of the attack: In the early afternoon, the officer of the watch spotted a small speedboat approaching off the vessel's port beam, only a short distance away. The fibreglass boat was equipped with an outboard motor and had four occupants. One of them manned a gun mounted in the boat's bow, the others toted machine guns. The officer of the watch immediately sounded the ship's alarm to alert the crew of an impending attack. The vessel's security staff hustled their way to the bridge wing. The pirates fired upon *As Salaam*'s bridge, taking wide aim at the master and other officers struggling to evade them. The young men then pulled their boat alongside the cargo ship and attempted to throw a tall ladder up her side so they could scramble aboard.

In response, the master manoeuvred the ship hard to starboard, then to port, but failed to knock the attacking boat off-kilter. *As Salaam*'s saving grace was that she was light in the water after having dropped her cargo in Mogadishu. In ballast, her deck rose high out of the sea, complicating her attackers' boarding. When *As Salaam*'s manoeuvring failed to deter the attack, her security staff fired at their aggressors from the bridge wing. They may have injured one or two of the pirates, forcing the boat to fall back off *As Salaam*'s quarter. Although the initial onslaught was thwarted, the pirates continued to follow their prey from a distance, likely gearing up for another attack.

As Salaam's crew did not have to wait long. After trailing the besieged ship, the skiff again approached, this time off the opposite quarter. The boat closed in on *As Salaam* and the security guards again fired at the pirates, at closer range now. The pirate boat again fell back.

Though the initial attacks may have been thwarted, there's no telling when the pirates might stage another, and we're still too far away to be of help. The captain has focused all efforts on reaching and assisting the distressed ship. All I can do is report to our support staff ashore the information that I gather about the attack, and try to ascertain with which group these particular pirates might be associated.

On a break, I make my way aft through the main flats and up the ladder that leads into the hangar. The steel door onto the flight deck clangs against the exterior bulkhead as I swing it open. My feet fall softly against the rough non-skid surface of the flight deck. Save for the white noise of the ship's engines and the soft lapping of the sea against our hull, the evening is blissfully silent. I breathe in the salty air and attempt to shake off the tension gripping me like a vise. About ten metres away, a lifebuoy sentry looks out over the ship's stern. From here he's only a shape darkening with the day. Here, at least, I can nearly maintain the illusion that I am alone.

I perch on a steel bollock on the port side and stare out at the dusk. It's my favourite time of day. The sky glows a deep burnt orange that rapidly fades into darkness. The warm evening air is soothing, inappropriately so. It captures none of the human calamity happening under this same sky just a few hundred kilometres to the north.

~

The pre-flight briefing for the first helicopter flight is held in the air detachment room. I stand to the side, along the bulkhead beside the three short rows of movie seats where the first air crew sits. When my turn comes to brief, I tell the air crew — TiFou, Marcus, Nathalie, and Neil — what I know of the *As Salaam* attack. Their faces are serious as they focus on me, absorbing each word.

"The occupants of the single skiff have already fired several times at *As Salaam*'s bridge with machine guns," I say, meeting Marcus's eyes. "There appears to be a heavier gun mounted on their bow. *As Salaam*'s crew did not report seeing a rocket-propelled grenade, but we know that it is common for pirates to carry these — and to fire them. As you know, pirates in these waters have fired upon helicopters." These weapons, particularly the rocket-propelled grenades, pose a threat to low-flying aircraft like the Sea King.

"Thanks, Jen," says TiFou with a nod.

"No problem," I reply, but what I have told them feels woefully inadequate. I wish I had more details — every detail — about the risk my friends will be facing. That I was wrong in my last assessment has been preying on my mind.

A few hundred kilometres from the distressed cargo ship, we launch the helicopter. As the helo zips ahead, our frigate continues to transit toward *As Salaam*'s position at a maximum speed that still seems painfully slow. After an hour and a half that feels like three, the radio in the ops room crackles to life.

"*Ville de Québec*, this is D2F," comes Nathalie's voice across the frequency. "Reporting on station at *As Salaam*'s last known position, over."

"This is *Ville de Québec*," responds Annette, the on-watch shipborne air controller. "Roger, over."

The tension in the ops room continues to mount. Standing back from the ORO station, I watch as the captain listens intently to the radio exchange between Annette and Nathalie, his tall frame leaning forward. His face is etched into tired lines. Dark circles under his eyes show his exhaustion. I know that he has complete confidence in TiFou and his crew. It's the unknown element that is the stressor: Do the pirates intend to continue targeting *As Salaam*? Will the hover of the helicopter in the darkening sky serve as deterrent? What about potential threats to the Sea King itself?

The Sea King is flying over an empty expanse of water where little is illuminated. Its bright lights overhead are flashes in the dark. The air crew will be searching black water for an improbable visual fix of *As Salaam*'s position. The cargo ship's navigational lights will not be illuminated, to stymie the pirates' efforts to get a bearing off the vessel and relaunch their attack. But tonight, with the moon bright and the sky clear, conditions favour both pirates and Sea King. From the co-pilot's seat thousands of feet above the water, Marcus spots the wake created by the distressed ship as she moves through the sea.

Nathalie calls the master of *As Salaam* on the radio to relay the helo's presence. To a hyper-alert crew watching for an impending pirate attack, the illuminated Sea King would be difficult to miss. The air crew fires bright flares into the night sky, alerting *As Salaam*'s crew and any loitering pirates that military assistance is close by. In the dark night, no one but the pirates can know if their unlit, invisible skiff has left the area, or if they are merely awaiting the next opportunity to attack. The master's last report indicated that they have seen no sign of attackers for the past few hours. But pirates have demonstrated resilience and patience in other attacks. Determining whether they have truly given up their assault will be impossible until daybreak.

For a prolonged period, the Sea King orbits the area around *As Salaam* then returns to the ship and touches down on the flight deck. TiFou's crew is replaced by Billy and his — Anne, Kevin, and Tom — and the helo lifts off once more and races to the distressed vessel, orbiting again. After the helo has again touched down on *Ville de Québec*, we finally reach the stricken vessel. Our frigate immediately takes up the escort posture off *As Salaam*'s port beam with lights ablaze and weapons illuminated — removing any doubt among pirates that a warship is on station.

Throughout the dark early morning our two ships continue sailing toward the haven of Mombasa. At break of day, the bridge watch again scans the horizon with the Big Eyes mounted on the bridge wings. I hurry up to the bridge to peer out at the surrounding waters. There is nothing unusual to look at. No sign of pirates. *As Salaam* steams a few hundred metres off our beam, as tranquilly as if yesterday's attack had never happened. The sea's calm and the gentle morning light belie yesterday's drama. The captain is up here, of course, sitting back in his chair on the bridge's port side. The circles under his eyes have become cavernous. He must have been up all night, keeping watch. I sense that he feels keenly our inability to have prevented yesterday's attack, our absence when *As Salaam*, at long last, plucked up her courage and departed Mogadishu. Losing *As Salaam* to the pirates would have plagued him.

The boarding team has been embarked on *As Salaam* since first light. Jeff is with them, speaking with the master and crew about the details of the attack.

"They were clearly shaken up yesterday, during the attacks," he tells me upon his return. "But they seem okay, now that they're out of danger. They were able to speak calmly about it."

Jeff is most impressed by the records kept by *As Salaam*'s officers. In their reports, the locations and details of the attack and the actions taken by the crew are neatly marked on their chart and annotated clearly in their logbook. No detail has been ignored in their immaculate records.

As Salaam's master will agree to stay on with the World Food Programme mission only if he is guaranteed military escort, an understandable condition given what he and his crew have just endured. Outside of Mombasa, we part ways with the resilient cargo ship. She heads into the safety of the Kenyan port, and we resume our voyage to Dar es Salaam.

December 2006

This time Abdi is the first to scramble aboard. It's dangerous, but he is an experienced attacker now, and he will be given a new SUV for doing so. Grappling hook thrown up and over the cargo vessel's side, fuelled by khat, he climbs up the rope and onto the deck as the driver of the first of the two skiffs struggles to keep the boat close in. He takes stock of his surroundings. Two dark-skinned crewmen peer around the corner from the forward side of the deck, then, with alarmed faces, disappear from view.

Behind him, his colleagues scramble onto the deck one by one. Abdi shoots in the general direction of the bridge, and then, when an inquiring head emerges, fires at it a series of random, imprecise rounds. He leads the trio up the stairs, taking them two at a time. They burst into the bridge door before the astonished crew has a chance to bolt it against them.

"Stop the ship, stop the ship!" yells Abdi, anger in his voice. He waves his AK in the faces of the crew, who stand, frozen as startled deer, inside the bridge. After a half-dozen hijackings and prolonged negotiations, his English has improved enough to relay the necessary commands. From the corner of his eye, he can see a figure laid out on the deck, a small dark pool spreading around him.

The man he presumes is the master gestures to one of the men, saying something in a language foreign to Abdi's ears. "The ship is stopped, no more shooting," he says now, holding up his hands in a gesture of surrender. But his voice is angry. "Look what you have done!"

Abdi, his rifle still trained on the master, glances at the body of a young man, unmoving on the deck. His midriff is soaked in blood. His eyes, glassy now, remain open. A bullet must have ricocheted off a hard surface and into the bridge. He didn't mean to do this.

Fear grips Abdi for the first time since his initial hijacking, when he was only a novice. "It is not my fault," he shouts, the anger in his voice belying the panic growing inside. But he quickly clamps down on his distress. They can't see his weakness. He waves his rifle at the master once again. "I will shoot you too if you don't listen!"

In the master's eyes is a mix of sadness and fear as, for a few seconds, they directly meet Abdi's gaze. It is too much. Raw rage floods his body.

"Don't look at me!" Abdi screams. His arms raise and descend with speed, the butt of his rifle connecting with the master's head and bringing him to the deck.

Vessels held by Somali pirates: *Yenegoa Ocean, Stolt Valor, Centauri, Great Creation, Capt Stefanos, Faina, Genius*

CHAPTER 21

DAR

Somali forces on Tuesday freed the 11-man crew of a hijacked ship and captured the 10 pirates who seized the vessel last week, according to the foreign minister for Puntland, a semi-autonomous region of northern Somalia.[1]

— CNN, October 14, 2008

Only last March I passed through Dar es Salaam with the Canadian interns whose work placements in Zambia and South Africa I was supervising. We were headed to Zanzibar, the tropical island off Tanzania's coast known for white sand beaches and turquoise waters. There we decompressed, examining the development challenges that six months of working with local grassroots organizations in southern Africa had revealed with startling clarity. An absence of donor commitment to the locally managed, long-term programming required for social change to occur was among the most significant challenges. But to me the most disquieting obstacle to development was the massive shortfall in education and the aftereffects that rippled through generations. In Zambia, these hurdles were immense. These same obstacles in Somalia, but this time against a backdrop of insurgency, famine, and clan warfare, seem insurmountable.

But now, as our ship breezes into the port of Dar es Salaam, not far from hot, chaotic Malindi Wharf where the interns and I caught the small passenger ferry to Zanzibar, I'm caught at an intersection of space and time — of my two worlds — that transcends the six months separating my visits here. A realization, a key understanding that I could not fully grasp when I was in Zambia frustrated with the constant struggle for resources, strikes me: impacting a single person's life can be a force for positive change. Our actions may not create change on the desired scale, or as quickly or as permanently as we'd like. But, in the best way we know how, we have to keep trying to make a difference, to improve on previous mistakes. The World Food Programme shipments may only serve as a temporary fix, once they reach the intended recipients ashore, possibly after warlord militias and insurgents have taken a cut. But the food has undoubtedly saved lives. *That matters*, even though it is not enough, and despite falling well short of the permanent, elusive solution that is required in Somalia to combat chronic insecurity.

Entering this port city, I'm again overwhelmed by the sense of moving from famine to feast. Compared to the relative backwater of the Zambian capital of Lusaka, Dar es Salaam — Dar to the locals — felt like a modern, bustling metropolis. Now, the expansiveness of Dar's port, with the large city spreading behind it, casts Mombasa in a similar light.

By a stroke of luck, or perhaps higher-level UN intervention, the port authority grants us a berth the next day, allowing us to bypass the port's notoriously long waiting times. How long it will take to carry out the repairs and allow us to complete our mission is anybody's guess. The best that our engineers can do is to finish the repairs as quickly as possible. Long days blend into long nights as the ship's engineers carry out their work, oblivious to the rest of the crew's forays into the city or ferry hops to Zanzibar's pristine sands.

"Are you sure you don't want to come ashore with us?" I ask hopefully, pushing aside the curtain and leaning into Kevin's cabin. But by this stage in the deployment, Kevin has lost all interest in leaving the ship. He's ready to go home, although he still does not know whether he will be allowed to leave the deployment early.

"I'm tempted only so that I can take a good shower in some hotel room," he says, reading *Men's Health* magazine in his rack. The logistics officers have failed to locate a fresh water source — one that meets stringent Canadian Forces health standards — that can be pumped on board. We are again forced to ration our remaining fresh water. "Besides, I've seen enough wooden giraffes," he continues, "and I have Guitar Hero to keep me busy."

~

For the first time since the deployment began, Jeff has a few hours to spare. Billy and TiFou have taken the ferry to Zanzibar for a few days away, and Marcus is on duty. So it's only Jeff and I who catch the ship's bus to an open-air mall populated almost exclusively by expatriates and well-off Tanzanians. We dine on the outdoor veranda of a Japanese restaurant on the mall's upper level, next to a dark wooden staircase that descends to the main floor. A few junior ranks from the ship glance at us from the stairs. I give a little wave.

Unrestrained now by ship etiquette, for the next two hours Jeff and I give vent to our grievances, though I myself have surprisingly little to complain about. I work long hours, but I'm well supported on board, in large part owing to Jeff's confidence in me. As for him, he works longer and harder than anyone, with the exception of the captain and XO. He deftly handles the stress caused by the demands placed on him, so he's entitled to let off the steam he has contained until now about dynamics at work and unpredictable World Food Programme scheduling.

When the waitress, a young Asian woman, comes to our table, I order a few types of makimono, sushi rolls typically made with seaweed.

"I'm sorry," the waitress says in halting English, her brow furrowed, "we don't have any seaweed."

Out of nowhere, a black rage rises in me and spreads like wildfire through my core. "You're a Japanese restaurant and you don't have any seaweed?" I say angrily, indignant at this failure. I have no doubt at my right to be angry. "Really? Isn't that what Japanese restaurants do?" A devastated expression on her face, she apologizes and scurries off.

Jeff is staring at me, unblinking. "Wow. I've never seen your furious switch flipped before," he says in fascination, a bemused smile playing across his face. "That's a new side of you."

"A Japanese restaurant without seaweed? Does that seem reasonable to you?" I reply irritably, unrelenting.

"It's a Japanese restaurant in *East Africa*," Jeff asserts, his tone full of dry amusement.

Upon hearing this, I immediately deflate. Of course he's right. And my reaction, becoming so uncompromisingly angry at something so trivial, *is* uncharacteristic. I flush hot, suddenly and deeply embarrassed.

"I'm really sorry," I say to Jeff. "I guess I'm under a little more stress than I realized."

"It's not me you should apologize to," he says, still gently amused.

When the waitress returns, I smile brightly and speak to her in gentle tones, but she is nervous and avoids eye contact. Who can blame her? I wouldn't trust a Cheshire cat either, once I had seen behind the grin.

~

After a last day ashore spent lazing poolside at a hotel in downtown Dar, I return refreshed to the ship. Led by Mike, the ship's engineers are less than refreshed but uncomplaining. They've worked a straight round-the-clock week to effect the repairs. We depart the next morning.

I'm making my usual coffee in the wardroom when Helmz saunters in.

"Hey, Helmz," I call out from behind the cappucino machine. "Did you have a good time alongside?"

"Hey, Jen," he says, wandering over to the bar. "It was fine, though I didn't do much there. I was mostly working." He pauses a moment before continuing. "To tell you the truth, I wasn't that interested in going ashore. I'm ready to get on with things, to get back home." I hear this sentiment from various crew members over the following days. At four months out, everyone seems ready to finish the mission and return to their families.

As our grey hull motors toward Mombasa, I find my own mixed feelings beginning to surface. I have found aspects of the mission challenging from the start: the constant and last-minute changes, the long hours, the utter lack of privacy. But as I sort through the latest piracy reports at my desk, it strikes me that part of me thrives in these conditions. The hours and the uncertainty burn me out, but the flipside of these same factors — the adventure, the sense of purpose, being part of something bigger, the camaraderie, and my surprising degree of autonomy — they fulfill me. All this is what I, what many of us in the military, signed up for.

Apprehension about the mission's end and return to normal life begin to haunt me. I have restless dreams that leave me tossing in my narrow rack. I've never craved stability or predictability, but now I find myself clinging to what I suddenly realize is of great value. In a few weeks, I'll leave the good friends I've made and the solid place

I've found among peers, to return home to Victoria, where most of my shorebound friends are now busy raising their own families. Scott will remain on deployment for an indefinite length of time. My family is spread across the country. I won't be working right away, so I will have none of the structure that I've built my life around for the past six months. But what scares me most is losing the coveted sense of purpose that I have found here.

None of my peers in the wardroom, excited about reunions with partners and children, seem bothered by any of this. Jeff continues to show off the photos of his beloved babies that his wife sends daily. Helmz is looking forward to seeing his fiancée and getting married the following summer. But I know that returning home after a deployment can be tough on both children and partners who have to readjust their lives around a returning spouse — and also hard on military members readjusting to family life and its obligations. It is typical to feel an overwhelming sense of purposelessness upon return from a busy deployment. The change in daily tempo, the transition from a clearly defined role into two months of unstructured leave, and thereafter into what can feel like less rewarding work, often creates restlessness and anxiety.

Despite my apprehension, there is probably a reason why deployments typically last only six months: the lack of work-life balance is not sustainable for much longer, at least not without serious ramifications. By this time, the stress of deployment on many of our relationships is beginning to show, though it's rarely talked about. A life at sea, particularly during long-term deployments, is never easy on families or relationships. Scott and I had neglected ours over two years of mutual but separate deployments. We made the mistake of believing that a declaration of commitment would keep our relationship strong, but it quickly became clear that investment in time and energy were essential elements. Reciprocal visits, frequent phone calls — these we too often neglected. The strain had begun to show when we were together briefly last Christmas. Now, almost a year later, the constant nurturing that a relationship requires, nurturing of a kind impossible to provide while on deployment, is clear to me. Strong relationships last over six months apart, but may be weakened nonetheless; weaker ones do not. Just like everyone else, I need to get home to establish some balance in my life. What that will look like is a mystery to me.

~

Upon our return to Mombasa, we find that tentative plans to escort another three merchant ships to Mogadishu and Kismayo, a port town on Somalia's southern coast, have been cancelled. The helo had conducted reconnaissance of the area, flying close to facilities that were reported to be under Al-Shabaab control. Vessel delays meant they would not arrive before the end of our mission. *As Salaam*, it turns out, is the last ship we will escort. The mission feels truncated, abbreviated as abruptly as it was extended only a month before. Mostly, though, I am grateful that we are not *As Salaam*'s last escort. After her well-fought battle, she and the other commercial ships still willing to sign on to a World Food Programme contract will be escorted by our replacement for the mission, Dutch frigate HNLMS *De Ruyter*.

The World Food Programme escort scenario now differs starkly from that of a month ago. Then, not a single country had offered a warship to relieve us on the escort mission. Now, the unprecedented number of attacks over the past months, including the ongoing high profile hijacking of MV *Faina* with her contraband cargo, has launched piracy and its impact on global shipping into the spotlight — even amongst the Western world's general public. Warships are now lining up to escort World Food Programme–contracted ships to Somalia. It's no secret that the escort

The crew of MV Faina *and her captors line the decks in response to a U.S. Navy request to check on the hostages' health and welfare, November 9, 2008.*

mission is a band-aid solution that ignores the roots of the piracy problem ashore in Somalia, but at least the escorts will provide a short-term fix until a more permanent one can be found. In addition to the Dutch ship, a floating multinational NATO Task Force is en route to carry out escorts and other anti-piracy tasks in the Gulf of Aden. Then, in December, the European Union's first-ever naval task force will commence another escort mission. Suddenly everyone is in the escort game.

"Sir, with so many ships carrying out World Food Programme escorts, it's the coordination that will be critical to mission success," declares Jeff, by now an escort coordination expert, in the evening brief. The captain, the lines and contours of his face shallower now that the immediate crisis has passed, nods in agreement.

HNLMS *De Ruyter* has beaten us alongside to Mombasa. We berth directly behind her, the smooth metallic finish of the sleek new frigate's angular lines rising over our humbler vessel.

"You know you have a speaking part, right?" Jeff says, as we follow the captain the short distance along the jetty for a mission turnover meeting with the Dutch officers. My body tenses at his words and I turn my head toward him.

"What do you mean?" The stress is obvious in my voice. "I thought I was only meeting with my counterpart over there."

"It's not a big deal," says Jeff. He laughs openly now at the expression on my face. "You just have to give an intelligence overview. You know your stuff, so what are you worried about?"

He clearly doesn't understand. Not a big deal for him, sure, but impromptu briefings are not my thing. A structure, a plan to follow, keeps me firmly in my comfort zone.

After we cross the jetty, a Dutch officer leads us through the ship's spacious and immaculate flats through which tall blond sailors of both genders are passing. We emerge into a meeting room. There, eight Dutch officers, including the ship's captain, operations officer, and communications officer, are lined up near the doorway to shake our hands. Once introductions are complete and we are seated around a table, our captain gives a brief overview of the escort mission, then hands over to Jeff for a more in-depth briefing. As he launches into his effortless spiel detailing escort operations, I discreetly write a few notes on how to approach the intelligence overview.

The situation ashore and at sea in Somalia is complex, involving clan-based, political, and religious loyalties. So much happens on a day-to-day basis there. Whether it's the latest battle between insurgents, government forces, and AMISOM peacekeepers, or the most recent pirate hijacking, it's difficult to provide adequate context for such a complex confluence of forces. Instead, I decide to make it easy. When my turn comes, I have nothing scripted, but at least I have a plan in place of how to begin approaching this vast subject.

"As you no doubt already know, the situation ashore and at sea in Somalia is a complex one," I begin nervously, glancing around the table where ten sets of eyes are fixed upon me.

"The current social, political, and economic situation in Somalia affects the success of our mission in three major ways," I say, gaining confidence. "The first is the piracy that threatens the commercial ships we escort on behalf of the World Food Programme. The second is the insurgency ashore that could threaten our own ships and helicopters as we approach Mogadishu, the African Union peacekeepers that escort the ships on their final leg in, or the commercial vessels as they unload their food cargo once in port. The third is the threat situation in Mogadishu and in southern Somalia that impacts the distribution of food aid and thus the viability of the larger World Food Programme mission." No longer nervous, I'm almost enjoying myself, and the genuine engagement of the Dutch officers around the table is invigorating. The extent to which I do enjoy my work on this mission, and my apprehension about its impending conclusion, strike me anew. I'm envious of these officers who have the experience of a mission before them.

That evening, our ship draws away from the jetty in Mombasa for the last time. I tuck myself into a corner of the bridge wing as the officer of the watch directs the letting go of lines. The captain remains pensive and watchful in his chair on the bridge's port side. Behind us, we can hear the shouting of the Dutch ship's crew as they line their bridge wings, bidding us farewell. Through the bridge window, the Port of Mombasa grows smaller, its rusted cranes and stacked containers now looking quite familiar. With distance the decrepit ships tied alongside concrete jetties regain some of the illusory romance that comes with their transience, the promise of changing horizons as they voyage around the world. They remind me of a tune, indelibly fixed in my memory, that a childhood friend used to sing:

> *Barges, I would like to go with you.*
> *I would like to sail the ocean blue.*
> *Barges, is there treasure in your hold?*
> *Do you fight with pirates brave and bold?*

But pirates have now lost their exoticism, and the thin veneer of romance associated with ports and cargo ships has been stripped away by the filth, crime, corruption, and backbreaking labour that goes with them. Men working the ships in this part of the world remain apart from their families for months, even years, to keep a job that pays enough to support them. But despite what I know of the industry's dirty underbelly, the allure of ports and merchant ships refuses to dissipate entirely. I have learned the difference between a barge and a frigate, but I *am* a romantic, I know, and a fool to boot.

Vessels held by Somali pirates: *Yenegoa Ocean, Stolt Valor, Centauri, Great Creation, Capt Stefanos, Faina, Genius, Wael H, Action, Shri Shiv Shamboo, African Sanderling*

CHAPTER 22

THE RED SEA

The Philippine government on Thursday said that another group of 21 Filipino sailors had been taken as hostages by pirates who hijacked a Japan-operated bulk carrier Wednesday off Somalia.[1]
— *Pinoy Abroad*, October 16, 2008

We steam north along Somalia's east coast, accompanied by the occasional fishing skiff. As we pass Mogadishu, which projects an illusion of calm from this safe distance, we close up our huge battle ensign to the top of the mast in a gesture of farewell. Across the VHF comes the crackle of Somali voices from the Mogadishu Port Authority, thanking us for our efforts.

Soon we will leave the Indian Ocean and enter the Red Sea. We'll leave behind us the ten commercial ships and their crews that pirates continue to hold, anchored off strongholds at Eyl and Hobyo and Harardheere as they await the conclusion of negotations and the payment of ransoms. Also left behind will be Amanda and her four co-captives. Little news has been heard of them since they were kidnapped in Mogadishu two months before. After a few short weeks in the Mediterranean, we will head home; they may never return home. Abandoning this forlorn stretch of ocean now, when we are among its few willing visitors, feels like betrayal.

Three NATO task force ships are heading toward us en route to Mombasa. In addition to the Dutch ship, these vessels will join in escorting merchant ships. The captain, Jeff, and I will travel via helicopter to the task force flagship, Italian destroyer ITS *Durand de la Penne*, to provide a mission turnover brief.

I'm in my rack by midnight the night before the brief. My restless body jerks me awake every few moments, forcing me back from the edges of sleep. The rack creaks with each movement, increasing my fear of waking my messmates, particularly Becky, sleeping soundlessly in the rack above. My mind is agitated, recycling the usual: end of mission, impending loss of purpose, apprehension at leaving new friends I've come to rely on, lack of structure and support network awaiting me at home. My anxiety grows. Only a few hours before Wakey Wakey do I finally allow myself to fall asleep.

By the time the pre-flight brief concludes the next afternoon I am exhausted.

"Drink this," Marcus says, retrieving a Red Bull energy drink packed with caffeine and sugar from his locker. "This should help you out." Against my better judgment — two other disastrous experiences with Red Bull deprived me of two days' sleep — I force myself to swallow the sickly sweet contents.

Seated in the rear of the helo flown by TiFou and Marcus, my delight to be flying again is tempered by mild apprehension at the coming meeting. I'm alert now, thanks to the Red Bull and the scream of the propellers. I've written a few notes, but I sense that I'm off.

Thirty minutes later, TiFou sets us softly down on the flight deck of the Italian ship. A small delegation of officers of various nationalities greets us and leads the way through the hangar, into a series of flats and then into a spacious room dotted with white tablecloth-covered tables. As we enter, we are greeted by a lineup of middle-aged men in stiff uniforms, representing the leadership of this NATO task force. The hasty introductions do nothing to help us distinguish one grey-haired man from the next. Our captain is seated at the head table, Jeff and I at a table near the front. I study the room. Only a few officers appear to be younger than forty-five. I am the only woman present.

I had expected an intimate, relaxed setting for the mission turnover, like the atmosphere on the Dutch ship. Instead, the air is thick with formality. The unsmiling faces surrounding us offer little reprieve from the tight clutch of military etiquette. I feel a mild panic unfurl in the bottom of my stomach, but I suppress it with soothing mental assurances that I know my material. Besides, I've prepared some notes. I can handle this. Jeff's noble face beside me maintains its confident lines.

When an Italian officer with a welcoming smile offers us cappuc-cinos — real Italian coffee! — the opportunity is too good to pass up. I nod an enthusiastic yes, oblivious to the effects of caffeine already running rampant through my bloodstream. It has left me jittery and distracted. I gulp down the frothy coffee, convinced that the more alert I am, the better I'll perform. Jeff is looking at me quizzically, his mouth upturned in a bemused smile.

I beam back at him. "This coffee is delicious!"

At an invisible cue from somewhere in the room, the chatter cuts out and quiet descends over the space. An Italian officer at the elevated head table introduces the captain in thickly accented English, who then stands up and graciously introduces Jeff and I — describing us, to my consternation, as indispensable to the success of the mission. Jeff speaks first, about the guts of the mission — the operational side, the planning, the challenges of an ever-changing shipping schedule. He is eloquent and to the point, barely referring to the notes laid out on the table in front of him. As he speaks, the anxiety that started in the pit of my stomach climbs steadily until it reaches my head. I'm practically vibrating, so agi-tated am I at the prospect of speaking next.

When the moment comes, I rise to my feet and turn to face the crowd. They are probably gentle enough, in reality, but the dozens of pairs of eyes staring out at me now appear as austere as their uniforms.

"Intelligence-wise, there were three main areas we focused on which could impact the escort mission," I say in a thin, shaky voice. Having for-gotten to breathe, I now take big gulping breaths before I can continue.

"The first was the threat of piracy against commercial ships in the area, including the vessel we were escorting. The second ..." Here I pause, having suddenly lost my train of thought. "The second was, um, the threat from ashore, that could impact both our ship as well as, uh, a ship in port."

I struggle on against the flush of heat that has travelled from stomach to my face, inhibiting my ability to construct complex sentences. My hands clutch the notes at my side, but I'm past the point of using them intelligibly. Instead, I bumble my way through rambling, half-coherent sentences that I neglect to connect to the larger mission, forgetting a thought before I can carry it through to its logical conclusion. At one point, when I've let all the threads go and am wondering how to extract myself from this situation, a wave of dizziness washes over me and I nearly pass out. *What is wrong with me?* I catch a glimpse of the captain's long face, looking startled, but the rest of the faces are a blur. As soon as I can wrap up my ridiculous five-minute blurt, I sit down hard in my seat.

Through my mortification I can feel Jeff gazing at me, as if he were driving by the aftermath of a car wreck, but I can't yet bear to look at him and confirm my humiliation. Not that I need it confirmed. My heart is racing and my legs are jittery. I've overdosed on caffeine. Public speaking in this environment gives me a legitimate reason to be nervous, but nowhere near to this extent. What a stupid mistake. The only mitigating factor is that most of my audience speaks English as a second or third language. Perhaps they have attributed the incoherence of my ramblings to their own limited comprehension?

The captain succinctly closes off the session, in contrast to my blustering, and then, mercifully, we are forced to leave quickly to get back to *Ville de Québec* before nightfall. Only the captain has the dunker training required for flying in a Sea King after dark.

At the end of the hangar stands Marcus, his skin tanned against his beige flight suit. He's been chatting with members of the ship's crew as he and TiFou wait to fly us back to our ship. The sight of his friendly face is reassuring in my mortification.

"Hey, how did it go?" he asks quietly as I approach behind the captain and Jeff.

I shake my head. "I choked."

"I'm sure it wasn't that bad," he replies generously.

"It was. Ask Jeff." At this, Jeff turns around and grins widely at the two of us, laughing soundlessly.

The captain is ahead, climbing into the Sea King, and doesn't hear this exchange. I haven't been able to look him in the eye since the event. Now, after the fact, what the audience thinks of me — people I'll never see again — is not my concern. I do worry about losing the captain's confidence, as I have great respect for him, but it's not my place to bring it up with him. The din from the propellers precludes any talking during the flight back to the ship. Instead, I make wild choking gestures at Jeff to pantomime my performance while through the windows, warm dusk transitions into night.

Then, from out of nowhere, a truth slams into me with the uncompromising impact of a wrecking ball: my mortification is pure self-indulgence. A waste of energy. The unexpected speaking fiasco is just a tiny piece, irrelevant to the mission's objective of helping people to simply survive, of getting food to those who need it. That's what it's about. My individual failings are a mere blip in the overall mission.

~

Our steel hull slices through the tranquil waters of the Red Sea, a 2,250-kilometre-long stretch of water that will take us beyond the piracy of the Gulf of Aden to the relative freedom of the Suez Canal's far side. At the XO's initiative, the logistics officers organize a Red Sea rig dinner.

At this event, officers are permitted to wear a relaxed wardroom dress, traditionally permitted only while passing through the extreme heat of the Red Sea, considered sufficiently remote from England to allow some leeway in officers' dress.[2] For our officers, Red Sea rig consists of white short-sleeve uniform shirts and black wool pants complemented by cummerbunds — the usual black replaced by bright red ceinture fléchées to symbolize our connection to Québec — tied around our middles and descending halfway to the floor. The look reminds me of a pirate costume, and I'm unable to dispel the vision of red bandanas wrapped around the officers' heads, a patch over one eye. In contrast to our usual drab naval combats, we look sharp in our uniforms tonight, glowing with colour and vitality. The men's hair is gelled just a touch, enough to give flair to hair devoid of style after months at sea, their clean-shaven faces mercifully smooth once again. Hints of cologne wafts among them. Light makeup and a subtle new energy transform the women into uniformed beauties. Evenings like this are a welcome extravagance contrasting with the usual austerity at sea.

The cooks and stewards have prepared a decadent array. Lobster tail, shrimp, devilled eggs, and other hard-to-come-by favourites adorn the table. For dessert there are truffles, delicate cream-infused pastries, and chocolate-covered strawberries. Jean stands tall behind the table with a proud expression.

"Jean, this is really spectacular," I say, looking up at him with a smile. "The spread is amazing. You guys have done a really great job."

"Thanks," he says, beaming. "My team worked really hard to make it perfect." Jean has worked magic in foreign ports to miraculously secure whatever supplies the ship needs, usually at short notice. Tonight's feast is no exception.

After months of a dry at-sea wardroom, the bar is reopened for the occasion and Martin, a young officer, serves drinks. We dine buffet-style, sipping on the first, then the second of our allowable drinks. I feel the tension in my body falling away.

"I almost feel like an adult again," I say to Kevin, who is enjoying his wine beside me on the settee, "being allowed to drink on board and all."

Kevin grins back at me with a flash of white teeth and a low chuckle. "Yeah, the dry bar was making this feel almost like an American ship. Cheers to the Canadian way!" he says, raising his glass.

The tall figure of Jean appears, looming over us.

"The captain would like to invite all of the officers to the bridge for a glass of port."

"Sounds good to me," responds Kevin. Then, more quietly to me, "seeing as I just finished my second drink. Another sounds perfect!"

I glance at my barely touched second drink, then set it on the table beside me. "I'll come back for this."

We file up steep ladders and through the dark flats and emerge onto the starboard bridge wing, unlit against the clear star-clustered night. The warm air wafting off the calm Red Sea caresses my bare forearms. Tiny lights twinkle on the distant shore of what must be Saudi Arabia's long coastline.

I can make out the dark silhouette of a man carrying a tray as he steps outside. He is at my side a moment later, offering me a small plastic glass of port. I smile in thanks, although he can't see my face, and sip the sweet liquor. I've never truly enjoyed port, but now I appreciate its warm flow as it slides down my throat.

The captain is speaking with a group of officers at the forward end of the bridge wing. He and I have lots of face time — at least one brief a day — so I leave him to talk to those he seldom sees. I look around and realize that I am part of a circle of officers that has spontaneously formed on the bridge wing's aft end. The black outlines of Marcus, Kevin, and Billy are barely distinguishable beside me. Eric, on the other side of the circle, strums his guitar. The notes coalesce into a gentle melody that renders all conversation extraneous. I breathe, pulling the air deep into my lungs, responding to the gravity that wants to pull the air deeper still. My body relaxes, feels part of the universe.

Suddenly, inexplicably, I can sense my friends' beings around me, despite their cardboard cut-out silhouettes. Their openness is utterly without fear. I learn more about them in that moment than I have in the past five months, with nobody saying a word. They sense it too. Eric continues his strumming, singing now until we have no choice but to sing along, mumbling through words we don't know by heart, a rare show of closeness on board ship.

Sailing an exotic sea under a clear night sky with friends by my side — there is nowhere I would rather be at this moment. The navy's romantic promise, the reason I signed up, is fulfilled in a flash. I don't want the moment to end. None of us do, and it's this wave of innocent longing that leads to what happens next.

"I'm heading down," says Kevin, and he disappears immediately into the darkness. Marcus, Billy, and I are among the few remaining on the bridge wing.

"I guess it's time," I say. I want to prolong the moment but I know it has already passed.

"Good night," I call out to the shadowy figure of the officer of the watch as the group of us slip through the bridge.

"Night," comes the reply.

As we enter the wardroom, I expect to see it nearly abandoned as usual, perhaps one or two bodies sprawled across a settee. Instead, the area has been transformed into a dance floor, on which a half-dozen officers are grooving to upbeat tunes pumped out of the stereo. Air det and navy, francophone and anglophone, are having fun together in a way that I've never seen on board this ship. I assumed that Kevin had disappeared to his cabin in his usual style, but he's dancing with Becky, both clearly enjoying themselves.

"Check out Kevin, the social butterfly," I say to Billy with a perplexed grin.

"Yeah, he's really turning over a new leaf. Who knew?"

As the dancing continues, so too does the flow of alcohol. Multiple bottles of wine, most of them empty, line the varnished wooden bar.

Behind the bar, Martin enthusiastically serves drinks. Of the fifteen or so officers in the wardroom, almost all have a drink in hand. Some are in clear transgression of the two-drink rule.

"Hey, do you want a glass of wine?" Martin asks with a giddy smile as I approach the bar.

I hesitate for barely a moment.

"Sure, why not?" I reply. We've broken the back of our mission. Now that the pressure is off, we have reason to celebrate.

What is confusing is that no one is curtailing the serving of alcohol. My slightly tipsy brain tells me that if alcohol continues to be served so publicly, the powers that be must somehow have allowed it. Rules are generally followed so rigidly on board that such blatant, unauthorized transgression seems impossible. Other officers, gladly helping themselves to a third, fourth, fifth glass of wine, don't appear to be concerned. Later, I realize that we drew confidence from one another, convincing ourselves that if others were doing it, it must be okay. For now, we luxuriate in forgetting that we are military officers obligated to live by shipboard rules.

Partway through my drink, the faintest of pipes floats through the pulsating music. "Lieutenant Savidge, CCR, shore call, Lieutenant Savidge." Feeling hazy from alcohol, I leave the party in full swing and head to the coxswain's office on the deck below, where I have arranged to take the call. I pick up the phone and Scott's voice comes across the line in its deep, reassuring tones.

"Jenny. It's Scott."

So foreign is the sound of his voice in this context that for long seconds I am speechless. A silent pause hangs on the line. The two of us have not spoken in three months. Communications have simply been too difficult while we are both on mission — or that is at least the excuse we have used — so we arranged for Scott to call on the ship's satellite line. His voice, usually so clear, is muffled and distant, despite being quite close to us on the other side of the Suez Canal.

"Hi!" I finally get out, the single word jolting me back to reality. "I thought you had forgotten to call me. I forgot about the time difference."

"No, of course not. Are you okay? You sound a bit strange."

"It's been kind of a crazy night. Crazy, but good."

"It's been a long time since we've talked. How are you?"

I'm unsure of how much I should say. "I'm okay. I should be glad that the mission is done. But you know, I'm a little apprehensive about heading back home."

"I would have thought you'd be glad to get home. It sounds like it's been a pretty tiring go."

Bit by bit, the deep, competent voice that I have always loved starts to feel like home again, transporting me, briefly, away from this place.

"Yes. But you won't be there. I don't have any plans when I get back. I'm worried about not having a sense of purpose."

"You'll figure it out," he says. "You always do. There will be an adjustment period, but that's normal." He hasn't said anything I don't know, but coming from him it's reassuring. And I feel closer to him, and to home, than I have for ages.

On the way to my rack an hour and a half later, the alcohol worn off, I peek into the wardroom. The dimly lit space has been cleared out. Relieved to find the show over, now that I'm sober, I begin the trek to my mess and find officers emerging, one by one, from the cabins lining the flats.

"What's going on?" I ask a tousle-headed Billy as he opens his cabin door with sleep-heavy eyes, still pulling on his flight suit.

"I don't know. A meeting's been called in the wardroom."

"At midnight?"

This is not good news. As the wardroom fills with officers, I seat myself at the table in the back beside Kevin and Marcus.

"Can you believe the fishheads got us out of our racks to come to this meeting?" says Marcus disapprovingly. Then he looks at me more closely. "Why do you seem different?"

"It's nothing," I say. But I do feel different. The phone call has had a grounding effect on me. Scott's phone call was a reality check, a reassuring reminder that there is life beyond the mission. This is what our loved ones do for us, offering comfort and a way back home, even though the path is often fraught with lost sense of purpose. "Do you know what the meeting's about?"

"No. But we can probably all guess. Look who's heading it up."

Seated in the middle of the settees packed with officers is Danielle, the lieutenant assigned the unenviable task of investigating officer on board.

Her smooth hair is pulled back into a neat bun. Her furrowed brow and serious expression contribute to the air of the disciplinarian that she now adopts. She begins to speak in a low monotone that displays her lack of enthusiasm for her task, locking eyes with each of us in turn. "I've been designated as the investigating officer on board. I'll be looking at allegations that excess alcohol was consumed in the wardroom tonight."

"Those of you who had more than two drinks this evening have until 0700 tomorrow morning to come forward to either myself or the Doc," she continues in her calm voice. "I will be conducting an investigation. You should know that there are many witnesses to the events. Those who come forward will be treated more leniently than those who don't."

"Jen, were we not allowed more than two drinks?" whispers Kevin mischievously, leaning in to me. His grin tells me that he's still a little tipsy.

Unable to contain myself, I laugh, then rush to stifle it with my hand before Danielle zeroes in on us.

Kevin's not the only tipsy one. As some of our colleagues pose questions to Danielle, a retching sound, quiet but distinct, can be heard to the right of the table. In full view of everyone, Martin is on his knees throwing up into the empty blue recycling bin against the wall. Two sub-lieutenants are desperately attempting to curtail his performance. In between bouts of retching, clearly still drunk, he looks up at the meeting with a silly grin that is his attempt to feign normalcy. But then he's at it again, heaving into the bin.

"Danielle, do you still need Martin to see you in the morning?" says a deadpan Jeff from the settee, which elicits more titters from Kevin and I. Jeff had taken the ORO watch so that Serge could attend the Red Sea rig dinner and had been unaware of the entire fiasco until the meeting.

If not for my own modest transgression of the two-drink rule, I should be anxious for my friends, but the absurdity of the situation strikes me full force. Laughter threatens to bubble from deep in my belly. I push it back down with difficulty. Beside me, Marcus and Kevin are making decidedly less effort to restrain themselves. The other officers are attempting to maintain decorum, staring straight ahead and paying unnaturally close attention to what Danielle is saying about the consequences of their actions, trying to maintain a detachment from the puker. It's been a long time since I've seen anything this funny.

Still, as the officers disperse back to their racks with their morning deadline, I'm nervous. It was only luck that the phone call pulled me out of the wardroom early and kept me from finishing a third drink, after my dose of port on the bridge, and then moving on to more.

"Kevin," I whisper through clenched teeth, a ventriloquist in my effort to be discreet. "Are you going to confess tomorrow?"

He swings his blond head toward me with wide, incredulous eyes. "Of course not. Why would I do that?"

"Well …"

"Oh my God, you're considering going forward!" whispers Kevin, halfway between a sneer and a laugh. "Are you crazy?"

"Isn't it the right thing to do?" I say, genuinely confused.

Here Marcus, standing on my other side, chimes in. "Seriously, Jen, it's not a good idea. You barely even had more than two drinks."

Then he pauses. "You know, about someone in your situation, they don't really want to know."

That night, I toss sleeplessly in my rack, considering Kevin and Marcus's arguments. A short while ago I would not have considered failing to come forward, so indoctrinated was I with the idea of complete obedience, a trait nurtured in childhood and reinforced by the military ethic. Transgressing rules has always made me uncomfortable. In childhood, at home, I was honest to a fault; in school, I was quiet and well-behaved. I played by the most important rules and aimed to please. What I realize now, though, lying awake in the dark, is that the spirit of a rule is more important than the letter. For officers, the military training system implies this, attempting as it does to instill the values of integrity and honesty without providing a prescriptive answer to every scenario. New recruits are taught to follow rules blindly and obediently; junior leaders are taught to trust in their own low-level decision-making but to still follow without question; officers are taught to lead by example and trust in our own reasoned decision-making processes. The very best officers possess qualities, whether derived from their personalities or gained through experience, that can't be taught. They inject creativity into their decision-making. They accept risk. They balance the best interests of those they lead and those they serve with that of the overall objective. If they do all this well, it's because they have a grasp of what is important in the bigger picture.

That perspective and vision is critical to effective leadership, whether in the military or the civilian world. Being able to discern what is truly important, as an officer and a human being, is perhaps more valuable. I was not drunk or disorderly. Given my role on board, I am of more use to the captain and to the mission as an upstanding officer than as a slightly tarnished one. It's a small step taken in what might seem a self-serving scenario, but this discernment frees me from my pedantic reasoning and represents a significant change in my perspective as to the kind of officer, and person, I'd like one day to be.

The next day, a notice is posted above the bar with a list of eight officers who are not, for the duration of the deployment, permitted to drink on board *Ville de Québec* or any other NATO ship. These are the officers who came forward and admitted having more than two drinks. Danielle will conduct an investigation of the rest of us. The officers who were openly drunk will be charged and given a summary trial.

Vessels held by Somali pirates: *Yenegoa Ocean, Stolt Valor, Centauri, Great Creation, Capt Stefanos, Faina, Genius, Wael H, Action, African Sanderling*

CHAPTER 23

A LIFE AT SEA

The *Yasa Neslihan* crisis raised the number of attacks on ships in the African waters this year to 77. Thirty-one ships have been hijacked, and 10 remain in the hands of pirates along with nearly 200 crew members, Choong said.[1]

— CBC, October 30, 2008

Our frigate has glided in seamless transition from the warm air of the Red Sea into the still heat of the Suez Canal, the benchmark that separates one mission area from the next, and then into the cooler climes of the Mediterranean. The waters beyond Port Said at the canal's exit lap at our hull. The density of marine traffic — tankers, fishing boats, cargo ships — is overwhelming after the emptiness of the Indian Ocean. As we resume patrols in the central Med as part of the original counter-terrorism mission, the crew settles again into daily routine.

In the darkened captain's flats outside of the communications control room, Kate beckons me over to where she is pedalling on the exercise bike. Her legs stop at my approach.

"Jen, I want to ask you a favour," she says, speaking quietly, her low tone and defensive body language revealing her discomfort. "I know you're really busy, and you should feel free to say no if you don't want to do it. I was wondering if you'd consider being my assisting officer. I'm facing a charge under the National Defence Act."

"Oh!"

So surprising is the idea of Kate being charged that at first I think I've misheard her. Surely she's asking me to assist one of her subordinates. It takes a moment to register that she is asking me to be *her* assisting officer. Only then do I recall the rumours about her blog. She had apparently written journal entries critiquing aspects of the mission and had published them on the Internet, in contravention of military regulations. A public affairs unit in Ottawa responsible for monitoring media for mention of the defence department had found it and forwarded it on to the ship. Months have passed since I've thought of the blog, or of potential ramifications.

I recover quickly from my surprise, "Of course I'll do it, Kate. I don't have experience in acting as assisting officer, but I've at least attended a summary trial so I have some idea of how they run."

"Great, thank you," she says from her perch. Relief is apparent in her voice, her dark eyes hidden in the gloom of the flats. Still, it's clear that she's not used to asking for favours. "I'll get together some materials for you."

~

I'm grateful that the battle rhythm has relaxed into a more manageable routine since we entered more benign waters. Becoming involved in shipboard life in a different way will be a welcome change of pace. Getting to know Kate, a complex and interesting figure, will assuage some of my regret at not having done so before now. In the wardroom the next day, she sits beside me on the settee.

"Here's some background reading on summary trials and the duties of an assisting officer, as well as the details of the charge," she says, her gaze meeting mine for the first time. "I think Danielle wants to meet with us tomorrow."

"Thanks. I'll take a good read-through and figure out what I need to counsel you on," I say, with what I hope is an ironic smile. "It seems that you're way ahead of me on this already."

I scan the paperwork. As assisting officer, I'm responsible for ensuring that Kate is fully aware of the charges — transgressing Queen's Regulations & Orders 19.36, Disclosure of Information or Opinion, for publishing without permission the member's views on any military subject to unauthorized persons — and the evidence against her. She regularly uses her blog, intended for the consumption of family and close friends, to express her thoughts and opinions on any number of subjects. Her options now include electing a summary trial, which would take place on board the ship and be presided over by the captain, or a court martial by an external military court that can draw out the process to painful length.

I read an excerpt from her blog transcript that is cited as evidence in the charge against her. Kate's blog entry critiques the utility of the mission, based partly on the belief that some of the food is being looted once it's ashore in Somalia. Her antagonistic words are almost poetic in their expression.

I glance up from the paper at Kate. "Well, I do have to admire your way with words," I say with sincerity, laughing a little as something inside me takes breath. Her comments about the food looting ashore represent only a partial truth; much of the food is getting through to people who need it. But I know the mission's true bottom line now — and I think she knows it too — so I find no threat in her published remarks. "You're pretty gutsy to lay down such a strong opinion. And I certainly under-stand the drive to express it." I smile, now irrevocably committed to her, and she smiles back.

"Gutsy or stupid, I guess I should have made that one a private blog."

The next day we meet with Danielle in her cabin. "Come on in, ladies," she says in her soft-serious voice. Once we are seated on the settee beside her tidy desk, she hands each of us copies of the charges and evidence against Kate. None of it is a surprise.

"You have twenty-four hours to elect between a summary trial or court martial," begins Danielle in a low voice.

"I've already decided on a summary trial," interrupts Kate, impatient to finish with the questioning.

"Still, I can't accept your choice for twenty-four hours, now that you have been officially advised."

Reading through the paperwork, the case is clear cut. Kate admits her guilt — there is no denying that she posted the blog to the Internet, criticizing the mission. The trial, once it's set, should be straightforward. The outcome is less predictable.

~

Her coffee eyes show no expression, but it's clear that Kate is tense on her day of judgment. She stands with her back pressed against the bulkhead. Her usual flight suit has been replaced with a smartly pressed air force tunic and wool pants. A neat bun beneath her wedge cap takes the place of her regular braid.

We wait in the flats to be called into the captain's cabin. Kate stares ahead, saying nothing.

"Are you doing okay?" I ask. The formality of these trials, with the commanding officer sitting in judgment, is enough to instill fear in the most stoic of sailors.

"Yeah, I'm fine," Kate says in a neutral tone. But she keeps her eyes averted. "I'd just like to get this over with."

On cue, the door swings opens and the coxswain, Chief Richards, pokes his head out.

"March yourselves in."

Inside, we halt in front of a wooden podium, behind which the grim-faced captain stands as Presiding Officer. Kate salutes him smartly. We remain at attention, arms thrust down at our sides. To our left stands the coxswain, who will assist the captain in running the trial. Behind him, the chief clerk, PO Adams, will take notes throughout the proceedings. TiFou, Kate's divisional officer, stands to our rear.

"I bring this trial to order," says the captain. He bangs his wooden gavel on the podium and firmly adds, "I solemnly affirm that I will duly administer justice according to law, without partiality, favour, or affection."

"Stand at ease," says the coxswain.

We step out our left legs to broaden our stance and simultaneously link our our left hands with our right behind our backs.

"Remove headdress."

Kate reaches up and removes her wedge cap.

"Attention!" orders the coxswain. Our heels click together, arms thrust to our sides.

"Coxswain, read the charges," orders the CO.

"Captain Kate Mason," reads the coxswain from a paper in his hand. "is charged with transgressing Queen's Regulations and Orders 19.36,

244

Disclosure of Information or Opinion, that is, publishing, without permission, in any form whatever any military information or the member's views on any military subject to unauthorized persons."

He addresses the next question to Kate and me. "Have you had enough time to fully review your case?"

"Yes, sir, we have," I reply.

"Do you wish to admit any of the particulars of the charge?"

I look at Kate. She takes a deep breath, composing herself before she speaks.

"Yes, sir, I wish to admit to all of the particulars of the charge against me," she manages. And why not? Her guilt in this matter would be difficult to deny. Her admission eliminates the need for the captain to bring forth evidence or witnesses.

"Very well. I'll now review the particulars of the charge," says the CO. "Captain Mason's blog, posted to the Internet without authorization, publicly criticized HMCS *Ville de Québec*'s escort mission in contravention of Queen's Regulations and Orders 19.36."

As he quotes excerpts from her blog, his face becomes pained. That one of his trusted officers should call the integrity of the mission into question appears to genuinely distress him.

Now he looks up and directly at Kate.

"I find Captain Kate Mason guilty of transgressing Queen's Regulation and Orders 19.36, Disclosure of Information or Opinion."

Kate struggles to hold back tears, so heavy is the cloak of guilt laid upon her.

"I'll now receive any evidence concerning the appropriate sentence to be imposed."

TiFou steps forward in his flight suit. "Sir," he says, "I'd like to speak on behalf of Captain Mason as her divisional officer," he says. "I believe there are some mitigating factors that should be considered before sentencing. Captain Mason has demonstrated a very strong work ethic and dedication to the air crew, and has never presented any disciplinary problems." Then he steps back.

"Those factors will be considered," says the captain. "Lieutenant Savidge, do you have anything to tell us as Captain Mason's assisting officer?"

"Yes, sir, I do," I say. "I would like to speak to Captain Mason's character. I have witnessed on a number of occasions throughout this deployment Captain Mason's commitment to her job and to this mission. I've seen her put in extra hours working with the maintenance crew on the helicopter, and willingly take on additional tasks to help the air crew perform successfully. She puts more of herself into her job, which she loves, and into this mission than nearly anyone I have come across on board." I mean every word I say.

"Captain Mason has expressed to me her remorse for the negative comments she made about the ship and the mission in a public forum," I continue. "While she was expressing what she felt at the time, on impulse, she is a firm supporter of the mission."

The captain shifts his eyes from me to Kate.

"Is this true?" he asks her.

Kate hesitates, pausing to control her emotions before she speaks. I glance at her, suddenly nervous. "Yes it is, sir," she says.

His eyes soften in response.

"Very well," he says. "We will adjourn while I decide upon sentencing. You can wait in the flats."

As if emerging from desert dunes toward an oasis, Kate and I escape the cabin's oppressive air. Lined up in the flats are a half-dozen solemn-looking officers. Some are awaiting their own summary trials for drunkeness the fateful night of the Red Sea rig dinner. Others wait to be called as witnesses. They eye us, wondering at our verdict, dreading their own turns at trial. Or perhaps, like Kate, they are eager to have their day of judgment over and done with. We give nothing away.

After five minutes the coxswain invites us into the cabin. The captain is standing at his podium and looks directly at Kate once she has taken up her position.

"Captain Mason, I hereby fine you three hundred dollars. Do you have any questions?"

Kate knows she has gotten off lightly. "No, sir, I don't."

"Very well. This court is adjourned."

With a bang of his gavel he exits the room.

~

After a day alongside in Toulon, France, the CO, Jeff, and I depart for what I have dubbed our NATO World Speaking Tour. It consists of travelling to NATO facilities in just two countries, the United Kingdom and Belgium, but after the confinement of the ship it has an equivalent grandeur.

The captain speaks with passion of the mission, to large audiences of important, greying men. Jeff and I are there to answer any questions that come our way. After the speaking fiasco on the Italian ship, I'm happy enough to stay silent.

We share a three-bedroom apartment on the NATO base in Mons, its bland colours and generic furniture immediately identifying it as military accommodation, reminiscent of that at home. On the second evening I emerge from my room and enter the living room to await our departure for dinner downtown.

The captain sits on the cheap couch, his BlackBerry dangling in his hand between his knees. He stares blankly ahead. A leaden air envelops him.

"Hi, sir. How are you?" I ask, concerned.

He looks up slowly, weary eyes barely seeming to register my presence.

"My wife and I are getting a divorce," he says. In his voice I hear pure disillusionment, the understanding that there is no going back now.

Silence fills the room. Though he has made his admission out loud, the revelation seems more directed at himself than at me. Still, I need to say something, however trite it will sound.

"Sir, I'm so sorry."

And I am. I think of his two children, of his wife. Of his decades at sea. Of his love for what he does. And I think of Amanda, still captive in Mogadishu, and of her great loss. Of our crew's casualties, small by comparison but so significant — compromised relationships, broken marriages, eroding families, missed experiences, idealism lost. Of my own relationship, and the tradeoffs we've accepted. *Is it worth it?* I wonder. The risk we all take in trying to strike that fragile balance between our private and public lives, between personal needs and the search for that elusive sense of purpose that comes from serving something larger than ourselves? Trying to understand motivations that are opaque even to us? I don't know the answer. Probably I never will. I wonder if Amanda will when — if — she returns home, surely a different person than when she left. Maybe the only thing to do is appreciate the moments we live without losing focus on the future. A life at sea. How to achieve a balance — that is anyone's guess.

August 2007

From the front of his skiff, Abdi watches the cargo ship from a distance. The vessel, its paint faded into a nondescript muddy colour, sits low in the water, weighted down by full holds. It sails at a moderate pace from the direction of Mombasa to the south. Abdi, the leader of this operation, knows the vessel's destination is the capital, lying only a few dozen kilometres northeast. Through word of mouth passed from Mombasa all the way to his village, he has known that a ship transporting food aid to Mogadishu — an easy target — would be moving this way.

"Let's go!" he directs his crew in a confident, aggressive tone, gesturing at his prey. Rifles and the thick shape of a single rocket-propelled grenade launcher line the bottom of their skiff alongside bunches of fresh khat and cans of fuel and water. They have already spat substantial quantities of the chewed narcotic leaf overboard. The driver guns the two outboards and they surge forward. The second skiff, with another five of his crew, does the same.

At their approach, the cargo vessel tries unsuccessfully to evade them, zigzagging this way and that as the men in the skiff fire shots at the ship. Omar, a more junior member of the group, climbs quickly aboard and continues to fire at the bridge windows. Then Abdi and the rest are aboard. To intimidate the crew into stopping the ship, Abdi fires his rifle in the general direction of the bridge, then glances around.

Rows of covered holds line the deck. Beside them, shovels peek out from tarpaulin-covered mounds. Then he sees them. A neat pile of white canvas bags, stuffed to overflowing, words he can't quite make out stencilled on the sides. He doesn't know what's inside. But suddenly, irrationally, he is convinced that they must hold beans, rice. He is mesmerized.

In his mind he sees himself running in his sandals to where soldiers unload sack after sack of food from a white truck. He remembers the soldier, who fixed him with his green eyes and carried food to the door of his hut, slitting it from end to end so that nobody could steal it from them. He can't dispel the vision of his mother upon seeing the food, her sad, gaunt face transformed with relief. A flash of understanding rips through him, through his narcotic haze. He is paralyzed to the spot.

When he finally looks up toward the bridge he sees a flash of movement. Somebody, a security guard, leans out the open bridge door, aims a rifle in his direction. Abdi takes this all in but does nothing. His arms leaden, he is incapable now of training his weapon. His crew stand slightly ahead of him on the deck and lift their own weapons in response. But it's too late. His father's rifle remains cradled in his arms as his body hits the deck.

Vessels held by Somali pirates: *Yenegoa Ocean, Stolt Valor, Centauri, Great Creation, Capt Stefanos, Faina, Genius, Wael H, Action, Africa Sanderling, Yasa Yeslihan, CEC Future, Stolt Strength, Karagol, Tianyu No. 8, Chemstar Venus, Delight, Ekawatnava 5, Biscaglia*

Suspected pirates with hands in the air, as directed by US Vella Gulf, *as the ship prepares to board them as part of counter-piracy operations, February 11, 2009.*

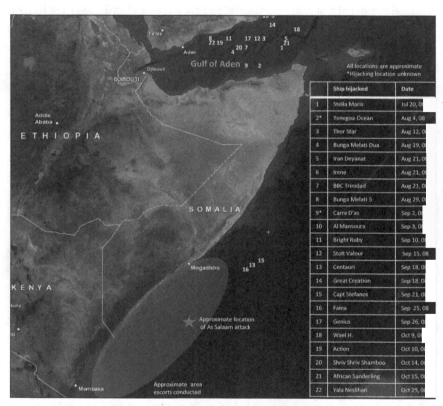

Map 2: Hijackings by Somali pirates, July–October 2008. Positions derived from open-source reporting. Screenshot used by permission. Copyright © 2013 Esri. All rights reserved.

AFTERWORD

Pirates eventually released all of the crew and vessels hijacked off the coast of Somalia from July to December 2008, most after ransoms of undisclosed amounts were paid by ship owners, except in the tragic case of fishing vessel *Ekawatnava 5* (see below). Two crewmembers also died aboard MV *Faina* and *Bunga Melati Dua*.

The German sailing yacht *Rockall*, hijacked on June 23, 2008, in the Gulf of Aden, was released on August 14, 2008.

The Japanese bulk carrier MV *Stella Maris*, hijacked in the Gulf of Aden on July 20, 2008, was released on September 27, 2008.

The Nigerian tugboat MT *Yenegoa Ocean*, hijacked on August 5, 2008, was released on June 6, 2009.

The Thai cargo ship MV *Thor Star*, hijacked on August 12, 2008, in the Gulf of Aden, was released on October 13, 2008.

The Malaysian chemical tanker MT *Bunga Melati Dua*, hijacked on August 19, 2008, in the Gulf of Aden, was released on September 29, 2008. A Filipino crewman was killed by a stray bullet during the hostage-taking.

The Iranian bulk carrier MV *Iran Deyanat*, hijacked on August 21, 2008, in the Gulf of Aden, was released on October 10, 2008.

The Panamanian-flagged chemical tanker MT *Irene*, hijacked on August 21, 2008, in the Gulf of Aden, was released on approximately October 8, 2008.

The Antigua and Barbuda–flagged general cargo ship MV *BBC Trinidad*, hijacked on August 21, 2008, in the Gulf of Aden, was released on September 11, 2008.

The Malaysian chemical tanker MT *Bunga Melati 5*, hijacked on August 29, 2008, in the Gulf of Aden, was released on September 27, 2008.

The Panamanian-flagged general cargo ship MV *Al Mansoura*, hijacked on September 3, 2008, in the Gulf of Aden, was released on September 27, 2008.

The South Korean bulk carrier MV *Bright Ruby*, hijacked on September 10, 2008, in the Gulf of Aden, was released on October 15, 2008.

The Hong Kong–flagged chemical tanker MT *Stolt Valor*, hijacked on September 15, 2008, in the Gulf of Aden, was released on November 16, 2008.

The Malta-flagged bulk carrier MV *Centauri*, hijacked on September 18, 2008, in the Indian Ocean, was released on November 27, 2008.

The Hong Kong–flagged bulk carrier MV *Great Creation*, hijacked September 18, 2008, in the Gulf of Aden, was released on November 19, 2008.

The bulk carrier MV *Capt Stefanos*, hijacked on September 21, 2008, in the Indian Ocean, was released on December 7, 2008.

The Belize-flagged ro-ro ship MV *Faina*, hijacked on September 25, 2008, in the Indian Ocean, was released on February 5, 2009. The master died of a heart attack while the ship was held captive.

The Liberian-flagged chemical tanker MT *Genius*, hijacked September 26, 2008, in the Gulf of Aden, was released on November 22, 2008.

The Panamanian-flagged general cargo ship MV *Wael H*, hijacked on October 9, 2008, in the Gulf of Aden, was rescued by Somali Puntland soldiers on October 14, 2008.

The Panamanian-flagged chemical tanker MT *Action*, hijacked on October 10, 2008, in the Gulf of Aden, was released on December 12, 2008.

The Indian dhow *Shri Shiv Shamboo*, hijacked on October 14, 2008, in the Gulf of Aden, was released on October 23, 2008.

The Panamian-flagged bulk carrier MV *Africa Sanderling*, hijacked on October 15, 2008, in the Gulf of Aden, was released on January 12, 2009.

The Marshall Islands–flagged bulk carrier MV *Yasa Yeslihan*, hijacked on October 29, 2008, in the Gulf of Aden, was released on January 7, 2009.

The Bahamas general cargo ship MV *CEC Future*, hijacked on November 7, 2008, in the Gulf of Aden, was released on January 16, 2008.

The Philippines-flagged chemical tanker MT *Stolt Strength*, hijacked on November 10, 2008, in the Gulf of Aden, was released on April 21, 2009.

The Turkish-flagged chemical tanker MT *Karagol*, hijacked on November 12, 2008, in the Gulf of Aden, was released on January 13, 2009.

The Chinese fishing vessel *Tianyu No. 8*, hijacked November 14, 2008, in the Indian Ocean, was released on February 8, 2009.

The Panamanian-flagged chemical tanker MT *Chemstar Venus*, hijacked on November 15, 2008, in the Gulf of Aden, was released on February 12, 2009.

The Hong Kong bulk carrier MV *Delight*, hijacked on November 18, 2008, in the Gulf of Aden, was released on January 10, 2009.

The Kiribati-flagged fishing vessel *Ekawatnava 5*, hijacked on November 18, 2008, in the Gulf of Aden, was sunk in an exchange of fire after pirates shot at an approaching warship. One crewmember was rescued, one confirmed dead, and fourteen are missing and feared dead.[1]

The Liberian-flagged chemical tanker MT *Biscaglia*, hijacked November 28, 2008, in the Gulf of Aden, was released on January 22, 2009.

Once their families had paid a ransom, journalist Amanda Lindhout and photojournalist Nigel Brennan were released on November 25, 2009, by the Islamic fundamentalist teenage boys who held them. They were in captivity for 460 days.[2] Two drivers and their Somali translator, Abdifatah Mohammed Elmi, who were abducted alongside them, were released on January 15, 2009.[3]

NOTES

Overviews of the piracy attacks and hijacking, many of which were widely reported, were taken from a range of online news articles and from memory. In cases where specific quotes or details were uniquely reported, the sources are provided below.

Chapter 2: Mission Change

1. Emily Macdonald, "Pirates Hijack Ship for Ransom after Leaving Townsville Port," *Townsville Bulletin*, July 25, 2008: *www.townsville bulletin.com.au/article/2008/07/25/14912_hpnews.html.*
2. "English Jokes," May 4, 2011: *http://englishjokes.blog.interia.pl.*

Chapter 3: New Horizons

1. Chris Lambie, "Combating Piracy; *Ville de Québec* Expected to Patrol Waters Off Somalia," *The Chronicle Herald*, August 6, 2008: A1.

Chapter 4: Life at Sea

1. *CBC News*, "Patrol Frigate to Escort Aid Ships in Somalia," *CBC News Online*, August 6, 2008: *www.cbc.ca/news/canada/nova-scotia/story/2008/08/06/frigate-somalia.html.*
2. OCHA Somalia. *Somalia Humanitarian Overview*, Vol. 1, Issue 8 (August 2008): 1.
3. *Ibid.*
4. Department of National Defence. "Executive Summary," *Report of Somalia Commission of Inquiry* (July 1997): *www.forces.gc.ca/somalia/somaliae.htm.* Accessed July 16, 2013.

5. "Ships Re-route to Avoid Pirate-Infested Waters," *Al Arabiya News*, November 21, 2008: *www.alarabiya.net/articles/2008/11/21/60544.html*.

Chapter 5: Ashore

1. Christian Okpara, "Nigerian Ship Hijacked in Somalia," *Nigerian Daily News*, August 10, 2008: *http://ndn.nigeriadailynews.com/templates/?a=11384*.

Chapter 6: Suez

1. "Somali Pirates Can Divert Maritime Routes Away from Suez Canal," Manar Ammar, *Daily News Egypt*, October 17, 2008: *www.masress.com/en/dailynews/104541*.
2. Patrick Lennox, *Contemporary Piracy off the Horn of Africa*, Canadian Defence and Foreign Affairs Institute (December 2008), 8–9: *www.cdfai.org/PDF/Contemporary%20Piracy%20off%20the%20Horn%20of%20Africa.pdf*.

Chapter 7: The Gulf of Aden

1. CNN, "Pirates Hijack Thai Ship Off Somalia," *CNN.com International*, August 14, 2010: *http://edition.cnn.com/2008/WORLD/americas/08/14/somalia.piracy.thai.cargo/index.html*.
2. ICC International Maritime Bureau, *Piracy and Armed Robbery Against Ships, Annual Report, 1 January–31 December 2008*: 31.
3. Alejandra Roman, "Bab el-Mandeb," *Encyclopedia of Earth*, September 12, 2008: *www.eoearth.org/article/Bab_el-Mandeb*.
4. "Final Preps Before Mission Start," Canadian Navy: *HMCS Ville de Quebec News & Events*, August 2008: *www.navy.forces.gc.ca/villedequebec/2/2-s_eng.asp?category=273&title=1949*. Retrieved April 9, 2009.
5. *Ibid.*

Chapter 8: Rough Seas

1. "Kidnapped German Sailors Reach Malaysia in Reclaimed Yacht," *Sail-World Cruising*, October 19, 2009: *www.sail-world.com/Cruising/Kidnapped-German-sailors-reach-Malaysia-in-reclaimed-yacht/62402*.

2. UKMTO, "UKMTO Dubai Press Report on *Stella Maris*," *Stella Maris — Inchcape Shipping Services News and Media*, July 20, 2008: *www. iss-shipping.com/NewsDetails.aspx?newsid=2334.*

3. Timothy Paris, "Marine, Navy Team Thwarts Pirates," *15th Marine Expeditionary Unit*, August 8, 2008: *www.15thmeu.marines.mil/News/ NewsArticleDisplay/tabid/8671/Article/82521/marine-navy-team-thwarts-pirates.aspx.*

Chapter 9: The Indian Ocean

1. Chris Lambie, "Frigate Spots Pirate Victims on Radar; HMCS *Ville de Québec* Under Orders Not to Stop out of Concern for Hostages," *The Chronicle-Herald*, August 20, 2008: B1.

2. Department of Public Information, "Security Council SC/9344," United Nations Meetings Coverage and Press Releases, June 2, 2008: *www.un.org/News/Press/docs/2008/sc9344.doc.htm.*

3. William Pentland Forbes, "Sea Piracy's Bloody Growth," *CBC News*, June 20, 2008: *www.cbc.ca/money/story/2008/06/19/f-forbes-seapiracy.html.*

Chapter 10: Mombasa

1. "Another Pirate Attack off Somalia," *Sky News*, August 20, 2008: *http:// news.sky.com/skynews/Home/World-News/Somalia-Pirates-Hijack-Malaysian-Ship-In-Gulf-Of-Aden/Article/200808315082796.*

Chapter 11: Escort

1. "Seized Ship's Cargo Deadly," *Vancouver Sun*, October 27, 2008: *www. canada.com/vancouversun/news/business/story.html?id=ca1a1c5b-24e2-47d0-bb6c-066db4031957.*

2. "VDQ Overall Deployment Brief" [PowerPoint slides], HMCS *Ville de Québec*, November 2008.

3. World Food Programme, "New Pirate Attack on Aid Ship; World Food Programme Urges High-Level International Action Against Somali Piracy," *World Food Programme News*, May 21, 2007: *www.World Food Programme.org/node/369.*

4. Jeevan Vasagar, "Pirates Threaten Lives of Somalia's Poor," *The Hindu*, January 20, 2006: *www.hindu.com/2006/01/20/stories/2006 012003241100.htm.*

5. *Ibid.*
6. Daniel Sekulich, *Terror on the Seas: True Tales of Modern-Day Pirates*, 4.
7. Jeevan Vasagar, "Pirates Threaten Lives of Somalia's Poor," *The Hindu*, January 20, 2006: *www.hindu.com/2006/01/20/stories/2006012003 241100.htm.*
8. Chris Lambie, "MacKay: African Mission Crucial; Navy to Escort Food Aid Shipments to Somalia," *Chronicle-Herald*, August 7, 2008: B1.

Chapter 12: Mogadishu

1. Ivan Watson, "Authorities Struggle to Thwart Pirates' Plundering," September 29, 2008: *www.npr.org/templates/story/story.php?storyId= 95174640.*
2. "Somali Pirates Release German, Japanese Ships: Maritime Group," AFP Google, September 11, 2008: *http://afp.google.com/article/ALeq M5jVT4IZcmwMTPVm1yw2hKbb7Aqm-g.*
3. Shaju Philip, "At Gunpoint, We Survived on Bread and Two Cups of Water," The *Indian Express*, October 18, 2008: *www.indianexpress. com/news/at-gunpoint-we-survived-on-bread-and-two-cups-of-water/374895/1.*
4. Sebastian Rosener, "Hijacked — How the 'BBC Trinidad' Was Freed," Bild.de, April 27, 2009: *www.bild.de/BILD/news/bild-english/world-news/2008/09/15/head-of-german-beluga-shipping-company-reveals/pirate-negotiations-that-freed-hijacked-freighter-bbc-trinidad.html.*
5. "OPRF MARINT Monthly Report," Ocean Policy Research Foundation, August 2008: 1. *www.sof.or.jp/en/monthly/pdf/200808.pdf.*
6. ICC International Maritime Bureau, *Piracy and Armed Robbery Against Ships, Annual Report, 1 January–31 December 2008*: 30.
7. Robert Draper, "Shattered Somalia," *National Geographic*, June 2009: 88.
8. *Ibid.*
9. "Crowds Loot Food from UN Trucks in Somalia: Official," Agence France-Presse, September 25, 2008: *http://reliefweb.int/report/somalia/crowds-loot-food-un-trucks-somalia-official.*
10. "Fourth WFP-contracted Driver Killed in Somalia This Year," World Food Programme, September 7, 2008: *www.wfp.org/content/fourth-wfp-contracted-driver-killed-somalia-year.*

11. "Mogadishu Port Rehabilitation Project," Mogadishu Port Authority: *www.mogadishoport.com/pages/r_project.htm*.

12. "11 Belarussians Killed in Somalia Plane Crash After Missile Attack," Rianovosti, March 24, 2007: *http://en.rian.ru/world/20070324/62560995.html*.

13. "Annual Report — 2008," Mogadishu Port Authority: *www.mogadishoport.com/pages/y_report.htm*. Accessed July 16, 2013.

14. "*Ville De Québec* and the *Abdul Rahman*," Royal Canadian Navy, HMCS *Ville de Québec* News and Events: *www.navy.forces.gc.ca/villedequebec/2/2-s_eng.asp?category=273&title=1954*. Retrieved April 9, 2009.

Chapter 13: Zang Za

1. Daniel Wallis, "Somali Pirates Hijack Another Malaysian Vessel," Reuters, August 30, 2008: *www.reuters.com/article/2008/08/30/somalia-piracy-idUSLU72369520080830*.

2. "Freed Malaysian Crew Tell of Somali Hijacking Drama," Reuters, October 4, 2008: *www.reuters.com/article/worldNews/idUSTRE4931M920081004?feedType=RSS&feedName=worldNews*.

3. *Ibid.*

4. *Ibid.*

5. "Malaysian Shipping Firm Issues Gulf of Aden Ban," Hiiraan Online, September 7, 2008: *www.hiiraan.com/news4/2008/Sept/7806/malaysian_shipping_firm_issues_gulf_of_aden_ban.aspx*.

6. "Somalia Pirates — French Hostages Phone Home," *Yacht Pals*, September 6, 2008: *http://yachtpals.com/french-hostages-somalia-pirates-3050*.

7. Edward Cody, "France Rescues Two Hostages," *Washington Post*, September 17, 2008: *www.washingtonpost.com/wp-dyn/content/article/2008/09/16/AR2008091603005.html*.

8. "VDQ Overall Deployment Brief" [PowerPoint slides], HMCS *Ville de Québec*, November, 2008.

9. "Mogadishu Port Rehabilitation Project," Mogadishu Port Authority: *www.mogadishoport.com/pages/r_project.htm*.

Chapter 14: Shore Leave

1. Edward Cody, "France Rescues Two Hostages," *Washington Post*, September 17, 2008: *http://articles.washingtonpost.com/2008-09-17/*

world/36825808_1_french-hostages-french-soldiers-jean-louis-georgelin.

2. "2008 Country Profile: Kenya," *The President's Emergency Plan for AIDS Relief*, 2008: *http://2006-2009.pepfar.gov/press/81596.htm*.

Chapter 15: Farewell

1. Manar Ammar, "Somali Pirates Can Divert Maritime Routes Away from Suez Canal," *Daily News Egypt*, October 18–19, 2008: 1.

2. "VDQ Overall Deployment Brief" [PowerPoint slides], HMCS *Ville de Québec*, November 2008.

3. The Crossing the Line ceremony was eventually completed, when a break in the escort schedule and weather finally permitted.

Chapter 16: Ashore Again

1. "Somali Pirates Hijack South Korean Cargo Ship," China Economic Net, September 11, 2008: *http://en.ce.cn/World/Africa/200809/11/t20080911_16776804.shtml*.

2. *Ibid.*

3. *Ibid.*

4. "Pirates Free *BBC Trinidad* and MT *Irene*," Maritime Information Centre, September 12, 2008: *www.micportal.com/index.php?option=com_content&view=article&id=953:pirates-free-bbc-trinidad-and-mt-irene&catid=25:security-measures&Itemid=38*.

5. Udo Ludwig and Holger Stark, "German Shipowner Paid Ransom to Somali Pirates," Spiegel Online International, September 16, 2008: *www.spiegel.de/international/world/0,1518,578495,00.html*.

6. "M/T *Stolt Valor* — Know the Facts: A Message from the Company," Ebony Ship Management Pvt. Ltd. & Fleet Management Ltd.: *www.fleetship.com/fleetnews/Stolt_Valor_Incident.pdf*, 1.

Chapter 17: Media

1. "Hong Kong Ship Hijacked, 18 Indians in Trouble," *IBN Live*, September 17, 2008: *http://ibnlive.in.com/news/hong-kong-ship-hijacked-18-indians-in-the-crew/73748-2.html*.

2. Nick Grace, "Shabaab Vows to Close Mogadishu's Airport," *The Long War Journal*, September 15, 2008: *www.longwarjournal.org/*

archives/2008/09/shabaab_vows_to_clos_1.php.

3. *Ibid.*

4. "French Commandos Storm Yacht to Free Couple Held Hostage by Somali Pirates," *The Times Online*, September 17, 2008: *www.timeson line.co.uk/tol/news/world/europe/article4765041.ece.*

5. *Ibid.*

6. Katharine Houreld, "Freed Hostages Describe Hijacking," *Seattlepi*, December 4, 2008: *www.seattlepi.com/national/article/Freed-hostages-describe-hijacking-1293732.php.*

7. "Somalia: Al Shabaab Defends Attack on Mogadishu's Airport," *Garowe Online*, September 23, 2008: *www.garoweonline.com/art man2/publish/Somalia_27/Somalia_al_Shabaab_defend_attacks_on_ Mogadishu_s_airport.shtml.*

8. "VDQ Overall Deployment Brief" [PowerPoint slides], HMCS *Ville de Québec*, November 2008.

Chapter 18: As Salaam

1. "Ships Hijacked off Somalia Coast," *Al Jazeera*, September 18, 2008: *www.aljazeera.com/news/europe/2008/09/200891815175330873. html.*

2. Xan Rice, "Somali Pirates Capture Ukrainian Cargo Ship Loaded with Military Hardware," *The Guardian*, September 27, 2008: *www.guardian. co.uk/world/2008/sep/27/3.*

3. "USS *Howard* Monitoring MV *Faina*," U.S. Naval Forces Central Command/5th Fleet Public Affairs, September 28, 2008: *www.navy. mil/submit/display.asp?story_id=40045.*

4. Robyn Hunter, "Somali Pirates Living the High Life," *BBC News*, October 28, 2008: *http://news.bbc.co.uk/2/hi/7650415.stm.*

Chapter 19: Breakdown

1. "*Faina* Hijackers Issue Ultimatum," *Taipei Times*, October 12, 2008: *www.taipeitimes.com/News/world/archives/2008/10/12/2003425701.*

2. World Food Programme, "New Pirate Attack on Aid Ship; World Food Programme Urges High-Level International Action Against Somali Piracy," *World Food Programme News*, May 21, 2007: *www.World Food Programme.org/node/369.*

3. Old Sailor, "MV *Victoria*: Not Always Lucky to Escape Somalia Piracy Attack": *MarineBuzz.com*, May 20, 2008, *www.marinebuzz. com/2008/05/20/mv-victoria-not-always-lucky-to-escape-somalia-piracy-attack*.
4. "Six Killed in Clashes Between Somali Pirates and Islamists," *AFP Google*, May 24, 2008: *http://afp.google.com/article/ALeqM5huZX1j35 evP_2f7juvNifVKrMboQ*.
5. Daniel Sekulich, *Terror on the Seas: True Tales of Modern-Day Pirates*, 5.

Chapter 20: Thwarted

1. "Second MISC Ship Freed," *Bernama Maritime News Update*, September 30, 2008: *http://maritime.bernama.com/news.php?id=362012&lang=en*.

Chapter 21: Dar

1. "Somali Forces Free Pirate Hostages," CNN, October 14, 2008: *www.cnn. com/2008/WORLD/africa/10/14/pirates/index.html?_s=PM:WORLD*.

Chapter 22: The Red Sea

1. "DFA: Ship Hijacked, 21 Pinoy Seamen Hostaged in Somalia," *Pinoy Abroad*, October 16, 2008: *www.gmanetwork.com/news/story/127439/ pinoyabroad/dfa-ship-hijacked-21-pinoy-seamen-hostaged-in-somalia*.
2. "Red Sea Rig" ReadyAyeReady.com: *www.readyayeready.com/jack-speak/termview.php?id=293*. Accessed July 16, 2013.

Chapter 23: A Life at Sea

1. "Pirates Hijack Turkish Ship off Somalia Coast," *CBC News*, October 30, 2008: *www.cbc.ca/news/world/story/2008/10/30/somalia-pirates.html*.

Afterword

1. *Piracy and Armed Robbery Against Ships, Annual Report, 1 January–31 December 2008*, ICC International Maritime Bureau, 33.
2. Isabel Teotonio, "Nightmares Haunt Former Hostage Amanda Lindhout," *Toronto Star*, November 22, 2010: *www.thestar.com/news/gta/ 2010/11/22/nightmares_haunt_former_hostage_amanda_lindhout. html*.

3. "Captors Free Somali Journalist but No Word on Canadian Colleague,"
    January 16, 2009: *www.cbc.ca/news/world/story/2009/01/16/somali-journalist.html*.

NAUTICAL GLOSSARY

Definitions and acronyms for nautical and naval terms as they are used in *Hostile Seas*.

abeam: Beside or to the side of a vessel.

aft: At the back or toward the rear of a vessel, or behind.

air det: Air detachment; the air force personnel on board for the duration of the mission to crew and maintain the helicopter.

astern: Behind or toward the rear of a vessel; going astern means travelling backward.

AWOL: Absent without leave, a chargeable offence.

banyan: Outdoor barbecue on board ship.

berth: A designated spot on a jetty, pier or seawall for securing a vessel alongside.

boat coxswain: The individual in charge of the ship's boat and often responsible for driving.

bow: The front of a vessel.

bridge: Area from which a ship is controlled, conned and steered.

bulkhead: Wall within a ship; generally watertight.

CCR: Communications control room, from which most external communications are controlled.

chart: A map-like guide to navigation for vessels.

CO (commanding officer): The CO also holds the position of captain or master of the vessel although they are distinctly different. CO refers to a command position granted by the Canadian Forces that constitutes certain responsibilities. Captain of a ship is a different set of responsibilities covering the naval and maritime aspects.

combats: Naval combats, the shipboard naval uniform.

coxswain: The senior non-commissioned member on board a naval vessel; responsible for discipline and personnel matters of non-commissioned members.

deck: The indoor or outdoor floor on a vessel.

duff: Dessert.

"D'ya hear there": Naval introduction to an announcement over a loudspeaker, to gain the attention of the crew.

embark: Board a vessel.

flats: Hallways or passageways on a vessel.

flight deck: Deck on a ship where a helicopter can take off and land.

fo'c's'le: Forecastle; the forward deck on a vessel.

forward: Toward the front of a vessel.

FV: fishing vessel.

freeboard: The distance between the waterline and the weather deck.

galley: Kitchen on board a vessel, where food is prepared.

gangway/gangplank/brow: Temporary mobile bridgeway or ramp connecting a vessel with a jetty.

hangar: Housing and maintenance area for aircraft.

hatch: Watertight door in the floor or ceiling of a vessel.

head: Bathroom aboard a vessel.

helm: Position from which a vessel can be controlled or steered.

hull: The frame or body of a ship.

jetty: A long flat structure extending from land into a body of water, where vessels can tie up.

junior rank: Non-commissioned member below the rank of petty officer, 2nd class.

junior ranks mess: Cafeteria and bar where the junior ranks eat, drink, and socialize.

ladder: Steep staircase or ladder on board a vessel.

leave: Vacation or time off.

lookout: Person designated to scan the water around a vessel and report contacts to the officer of the watch or captain, usually equipped with binoculars.

master: Captain of a seagoing vessel.

mess: Sleeping quarters or eating quarters on board ship.

mess deck: Sleeping quarters on board ship.

mettech: Meteorological technician, responsible for interpreting and reporting weather conditions.

"morning prayers": Morning meeting on board ship.

MV: Merchant vessel.

nautical mile: 1 nautical mile is equivalent to 1.15 miles, or 1.85 kilometres.

NAST: Naval Armed Security Team.

NATO: North Atlantic Treaty Organization.

pilot (sea): A trained mariner who guides a vessel through difficult waterways.

pipe: Announcement.

PO (petty officer): there are two petty officer ranks in the Royal Canadian Navy. Petty officer, 2nd class (PO2) is equivalent to a sergeant, 1st class (PO1) is equivalent to a warrant officer.

port: The left side of a vessel orientated forward.

"pusser shower": Short shipboard shower, no more than two minutes in order to conserve fresh water.

quartermaster: Sailor manning the ship's brow or gangway, who controls the comings and goings of personnel while alongside.

rack: Bed on board ship.

RV: Rendezvous; meet-up point.

ship's company: Crew of a ship.

sick bay: Medical area on board ship.

sitrep: Situation report.

starboard: The right side of a vessel orientated forward.

stern: Rear of a vessel.

superstructure: Structures extending above the ship's main deck.

swells: The undulation of the sea caused by a disruption elsewhere.

upper decks: Outdoor decks of a vessel.

wardroom: Officers' eating, relaxing, and gathering area.

watch: Duration of duty on board a ship.

World Food Programme (WFP): United Nations agency addressing world hunger.

XO (executive officer): second in command of a navy ship.

BIBLIOGRAPHY

Bahadur, Jay. *The Pirates of Somalia: Inside Their Hidden World*. Toronto: HarperCollins Publisher Ltd., 2011.

Bélanger, Stéphanie A.H., and Karen D. Davis, eds. *Transforming Traditions: Women, Leadership and the Canadian Navy, 1942–2010*. Kingston: Canadian Defence Academy Press, 2010.

Eichstaedt, Peter. *Pirate State: Inside Somalia's Terrorism at Sea*. Chicago: Lawrence Hill Press, 2010.

Freeman, Colin. *Kidnapped: Life as a Somali Pirate Hostage*. Wolvey, UK: Monday Books, 2011.

Hansen, Stig Jarle. *Piracy in the Greater Gulf of Aden: Myths, Misconceptions, and Remedies*. Oslo: Norwegian Institute for Urban and Regional Research, 2009. Retrieved February 18, 2013: *http://estaticos.elmundo.es/documentos/2009/11/12/piratas.pdf*.

Harper, Mary. *Getting Somalia Wrong? Faith, War, and Hope in a Shattered State*. New York: Zed Books, 2012.

ICC International Maritime Bureau. *Piracy and Armed Robbery Against Ships, Annual Report, 1 January–31 December 2008*. London: ICC International Maritime Bureau, 2009.

Mohamed, Mohamed Mohamud, and Mahamud Hirad Herzi. "Feasibility Report on the Fisheries Sector in Puntland." *Poverty Reduction and Economic Recovery*. Bossasso: Ocean Training and Promotion/UNDP Somalia, 2005: *http://mirror.undp.org/somalia/publications.htm*.

Phillips, Serge, and Stephan Talty. *A Captain's Duty: Somali Pirates, Navy Seals, and Dangerous Days at Sea*. New York: Hyperion, 2011.

Pupetz, Neil, ed. *In the Line of Duty: Canadian Joint Forces Somalia, 1992–1993*. National Defence, 1994.

Sekulich, Daniel. *Terror on the Seas: True Tales of Modern-Day Pirates.* New York: St. Martin's Press, 2009.

UKMTO. *BMP: Best Management Practices to Deter Piracy off the Coast of Somalia and in the Arabian Sea Area* (Version 3, June 2010). Edinburgh: Witherby Seamanship International Ltd., 2010.